AF600534

# DILEMMAS IN MODERN JEWISH THOUGHT

# DILEMMAS IN MODERN JEWISH THOUGHT

## The Dialectics of Revelation and History

Michael L. Morgan

*Indiana University Press*
BLOOMINGTON & INDIANAPOLIS

The paper used in this publication meets the minimum requirements of American National Standard for Information Sciences—Permanence of Paper for Printed Library Materials, ANSI Z39.48–1984.

∞™

Manufactured in the United States of America

**Library of Congress Cataloging-in-Publication Data**

Morgan, Michael L., date
Dilemmas in modern Jewish thought : the dialectics of revelation and history / Michael L. Morgan.
p. cm.
Includes bibliographical references and index.
ISBN 0-253-33878-6 (cloth)
1. Judaism—History—Philosophy. 2. Judaism—Historiography. 3. Jews—History—Philosophy. 4. Judaism—20th century. 5. Revelation (Jewish theology)—History of doctrines. I. Title.
BM160.M67 1992
296.3'11—dc20 92-7724

1 2 3 4 5 96 95 94 93 92

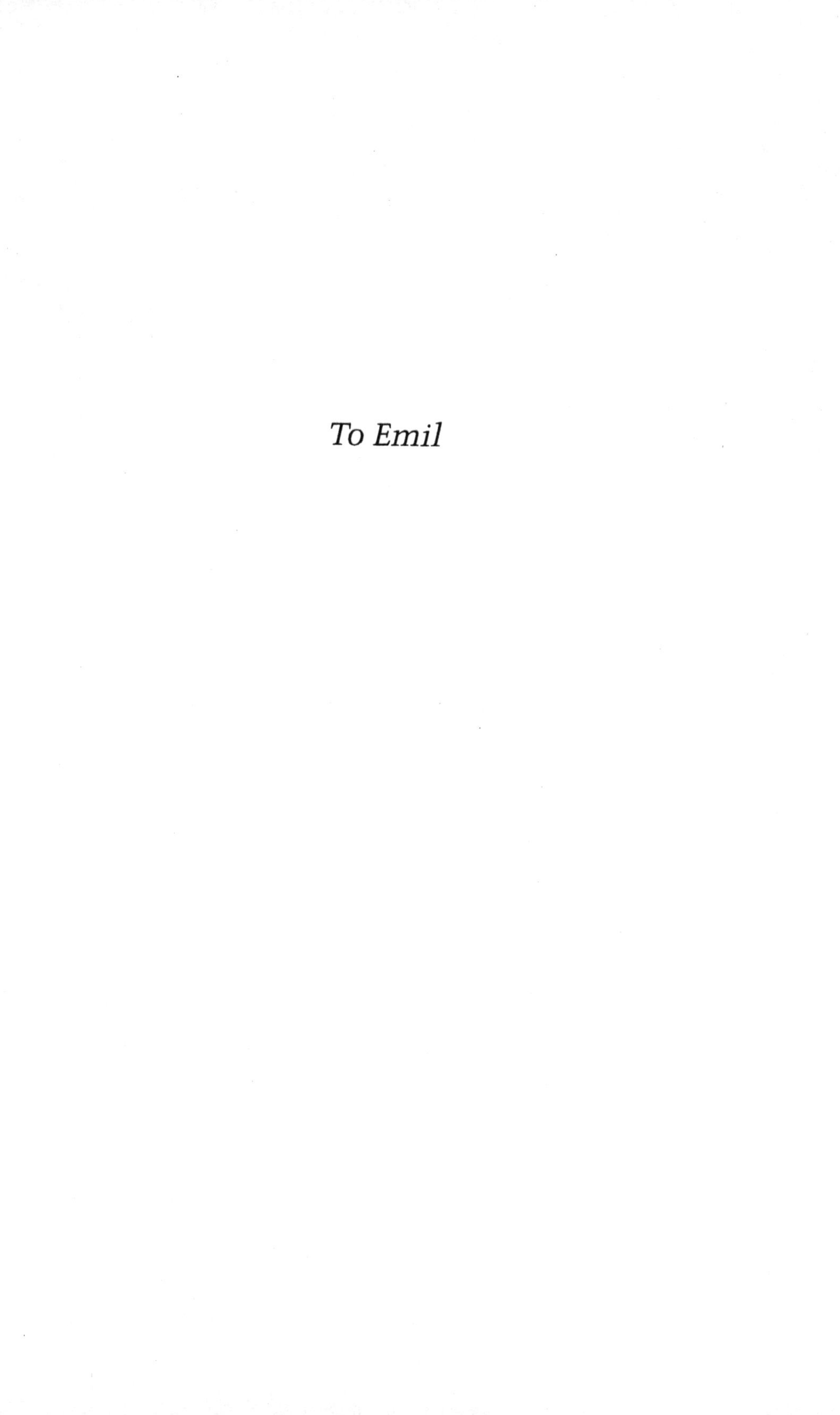

*To Emil*

# CONTENTS

# *Acknowledgments*

This book has come into being over a number of years. During that time many friends and colleagues have provided encouragement, read chapters, and given valuable advice. I would like to express to them my thanks: Howard Eilberg-Schwartz, Arnold Eisen, David Ellenson, Michael Fishbane, Warren Harvey, Jon Levenson, Jonathan Malino, Paul Mendes-Flohr, Michael Meyer, David Myers, Aron Rodrigue, Tamar Rudavsky, David Ruderman, Kenneth Seeskin, Josef Stern, Rabbi Michael Stroh, and Rabbi Sheldon Zimmerman. I thank too Pete Steeves for preparing the index.

For sixteen years my classes in Jewish thought and philosophy at Indiana University have been a delight to teach; the hundreds of students whom I have come to know have taught me as much as I have taught them. I hope that this book, in some small way, testifies to their passion, their energy, and their commitment.

The book is dedicated to Emil Fackenheim. For more than two decades Emil has been my teacher, my guide, and more; our friendship is one of the real treasures of my life. Audrey, Debbie, and Sara are the other treasures. With good humor and tolerance, they reminded me, when I was prone to forget, that the richest rewards and the greatest joys of Jewish thought really only come in Jewish life.

# *Introduction*

The Jewish people is a historical people—a people with a past, a long and complex history of large and small events, of influential and relatively insignificant figures, of customs, laws, and practices, of texts and commentaries, and of much more. In this sense, the Jewish people is like other religious, ethnic, and national groups that emerge on the historical stage, play their various parts, and continue or cease to continue. All peoples share these features, although their historical and contextual character has not always been of great interest either to scholars examining them or to the groups themselves.

But if it is obvious that the Jewish people is historical, it is also controversial whether Judaism itself is historical. In this regard Judaism, as a conglomerate of religious beliefs and practices, is not unlike other Western religions, or philosophy, or science. Clearly the Catholic church or Western philosophy or the natural sciences have histories; each has a past or many pasts that can be studied, recounted, and reconstructed. But is Catholicism or philosophy or science historical? Is their content general, universal, and timelessly true or rather historical, conditional, changing, and limited? It is a controversial and troubling question whether Judaism should be viewed as historical. This book is an attempt to explore this problem of Judaism and history and to show how, since the seventeenth century, the historical character of Judaism has become increasingly central to reflection on Judaism and its nature in the modern world.

One dimension of this problem about the historical character of Judaism concerns the historicity of Jewish beliefs and practices. Do Jewish beliefs, for example, have the very same meanings in all times and in all places, and are they timelessly true by virtue of those meanings and their verification in texts, or through revelation, or rational argument, or experience? If indeed the meanings and truth of central Jewish principles and affirmations change when the historical context changes, then we might say that Judaism is essentially historical or, alternatively, that there is no Jewish essence at all but only a vast array of episodes or historical manifestations of a phenomenon that undergoes constant alteration, revision, and ramification.

There is another way in which the problem of the historical character of Judaism expresses itself. We might call this the problem of the remoteness of the past. In the sixteenth and seventeenth centuries a new sense of history and historiography arose. Prior to this period and especially in the Renaissance, historical accounts, on the model of Roman historians such as Tacitus, were considered moral treatises, portraits of exemplary individuals and exemplary conduct. In a sense history was studied in order to locate models of moral conduct and character. It was viewed as continuous with the present, indeed without any special attention to its temporality or temporal distance. But with the rise of the new historiography, the critical examination of evidence and texts, history came to be viewed as a distant and remote domain. The accuracy of historical accounts was measured by the degree to which they precisely situated events, people, and texts in the very particular context or world in which they occurred. Hence, history came to be viewed as discontinuous with the present, as a distant and remote world, almost like a foreign country with its strange and discrete practices and culture.

If we apply this new understanding of history to Judaism, the result is that Judaism in the present may very well be viewed as radically detached from Judaism in the past. Each historical manifestation of Jewish beliefs and practices is severed from every other such manifestation, or at least partially severed. The more accurate our understanding of Judaism in the second century, after the destruction of the Temple in ancient Palestine, the more remote that Judaism is from our own contemporary Judaism, situated in modern, industrial society, after the Enlightenment, the Holocaust, the rise of Zionism, the establishment of the Third Jewish State, and so on. What do we learn about ourselves when we study the meaning of Torah, of Midrash, of God, and of covenant in that remote, second-century world? If Judaism, and not just the Jewish people, is historical, then where is the continuity in this discontinuity? How indeed can memory overcome the remoteness of the historical past?

On the one hand, reflections on the character of Judaism in the modern world have incorporated worries about the possibility that Judaism is a temporal, conditional, and changing entity and not a set of universal, timeless, and permanent truths about God, the world, the Jews, Jewish destiny, and humankind. On the other hand, such reflections have become increasingly historiographical, giving rise to the worry that historical accuracy may make the past not a rich resource for contemporary identification but rather a remote and irrelevant set of accounts, reconstructions of distant and foreign practices, beliefs, and commitments that exhibit at best our origins or earlier stages in our growth and development but that are not accessible in any way as models or paradigms for our own lives. Both of these dimensions of the problem of history have become prominent features of modern Jewish thought, but they do not exhaust that problematic, for neither arises peculiarly out of the Jewish religious situation, that is, out of the ways in which the relation between the Divine and the human have entered into Judaism and Jewish experience.

Even in the Midrashic literature the understanding of God raises the problem of history in a way that is not present in the Bible. The biblical Jew interacted with God as a divine person, listening to Him, challenging Him, and traveling with Him. But by the Hellenistic and Rabbinic periods, after the encounter with Greek culture and thought, Judaism came to recognize the transcendence of the Divine and sought ways to acknowledge that transcendence and at the same time to overcome it. That is, once the Divine was associated with eternity, omnipotence, and a timeless, objective perspective on human affairs and history, the Midrash emerged as a literary context in which the interaction between that timeless and unconditional divine nature and the domain of human experience was portrayed. Torah as revelation became one manifestation of this encounter between the human and the Divine; miracles were another, both as signs and as saving acts. And the timeless purity of the Divine came to be expressed in terms of permanent patterns of divine conduct, mercy and justice, and hence as principles akin to laws of nature. Eventually, with the cultivation of the centrality of reason and rational knowledge in Graeco-Roman philosophy and then in the Middle Ages, some thinkers associated revelation not only with the content of Divine Torah but also with the attainments of rational thought. In this way, the vehicle for human aspiration to objectivity and universality, reason itself, came to be identified with the eternal and ahistorical perspective of the theocentric point of view. Slowly but surely, in antiquity and the Middle Ages, the relativity and conditionality of the historical were superseded.

Against this background, the problem of history for Jewish self-understanding arose in this sphere of the divine-human encounter. The problem first expressed itself when in the seventeenth century the biblical text, the primary manifestation of Torah as divine revelation, began to be treated as a historical document, as evidence, like any other, for access to and reconstruction of the historical past. Spinoza held that the Bible should be treated like any other natural object, investigated in the same way and subjected to the same kind of causal and explanatory investigation. But the problem of history manifested itself in another way in the late eighteenth century and then, dramatically, in the nineteenth century, when the connection between faith and the divine-human relationship, on the one hand, and reason, on the other, was denied. Lessing was a central figure in this tradition, as was Kierkegaard; in the twentieth century the most important Jewish thinkers were of course Buber and Rosenzweig and all those post–Second World War American theologians who followed them in acknowledging the centrality of faith and the event of revelation as independent of our everyday moral, scientific, and other modes of experience and discourse.

No longer was revelation treated as a discursive, literal content; rather, it was viewed as an event, an encounter between the Infinite and the finite, between the Unconditional and the human in the context of the world, of history, of what is thoroughly conditioned, changing, and contingent. Here, then, the problem of history arose again but this time as a difficulty about how to comprehend the historical dimensions of the encounter of the Divine and the human, while acknowledging at the same time their true character. In the shadow of the Kantian dichotomy of the autonomous and the heteronomous, many viewed this problem as the need to reconcile Divine Power and human freedom. But in fact the parameters of the issue are wider than this; it concerns the human aspiration to objectivity and universality, the encounter with God as the locus of both, and the character of the human, historical life in which that encounter occurs. Could it be, one must ask, that only the event of the divine-human encounter itself is what remains of transcendence *within* human experience and history and that all the rest, the openness to revelation and the response to it, is necessarily historical? Or can there be modes of human experience, of Jewish experience, that themselves reach toward eternality and the Divine, thereby transcending the grip of the historical? Rosenzweig and Buber, each in his own way, grappled with these questions, as have other thinkers after them. All have seen that the central issue concerning revelation and modern Jewish experience is the problem of history.

These issues and others concerning history and modern Jewish self-understanding have arisen in the modern world, as Jewish thinkers have attempted to articulate what Judaism means in terms of the compelling features of their situations. These features include the rise of the new science in the seventeenth century, the Enlightenment in the eighteenth, the emergence of Romanticism and Idealism and the reactions to them in the nineteenth, the rise of Zionism, the rise of modernism and modernist culture, World War I, the rise of Nazism, the Holocaust, the establishment of the Jewish state, and much else. Just as Jewish thinkers internalized the problem of history, they internalized modern thought and interpretations of the events, ideas, and movements of these centuries. Often thinkers were forced to tread a narrow and perilous ridge in order to achieve their goals, and often too their goals were not the same as ours are today. Some sought a rational, moral conception of religion and faith that eschewed religious particularity; others labored to remain distinctly Jewish at the same time that they acknowledged the compelling nature of modern thinking and recent events. Some speak about Judaism from a vantage point outside the normative Jewish worlds of their day; others speak from within those worlds. But all of those whom I discuss in this book and many others speak importantly to us as Jews, precisely because they recognized the complex problem of history for modern Jewish self-understanding.

The essays that follow might also be viewed as advancing a new way of understanding the dilemma of liberal Judaism. By this latter expression I do not mean any single Jewish denomination or institutional organization. Rather, I mean that type of modern Judaism that aspires to a form of Jewish life that is genuinely Jewish and also liberal, where that includes a respect for the individual, for individual self-determination, and for individual rights, among other widely shared values of modern democratic societies. In the writings of the 1950s and 1960s the dilemma of liberal Judaism was generally portrayed in terms of the tension between authority and freedom or autonomy. The lineage of this type of formulation is decidedly Kantian, and one finds the formulation in Jewish thinkers of all persuasions. The dilemma can be characterized this way: how can a modern, liberal Jew recognize the authority of the past, of tradition, of Halachah and rabbinic law, and of the community and, at the same time, adhere to the priority of personal self-determination, autonomy, and free decision, and hence of the present, of the individual, and ultimately of the human over the Divine? Again and again, as one reads the theologians of these post–Second World War decades, the problem for the modern Jew is formulated this way. One even finds it cast in these terms by Martin Buber in a famous passage in *I and Thou*, where he cites the Kantian antinomy of freedom and causality as the appropriate background for understanding the existential paradox of the modern Jew. And one finds it, too, in modern Orthodox thinkers who try to negotiate the ridge between allegiance to the Halachic tradition and commitment to liberal principles dissonant with that tradition.

This tension between traditional authority that is ultimately grounded in Divine Will and individual self-determination and freedom is the old dilemma of liberal Judaism. The new dilemma begins once we recognize and set aside the assumptions on which the old dilemma is based. One of these assumptions is the priority of the individual, the belief that what we do and believe arises out of us as discrete, isolated individuals and is grounded in our choices and our reasons for making them. In place of this commitment to the primacy of the distinct individual as the locus of choice and conduct, we have come to appreciate the primacy of the communities of which we are a part and the complex ways in which we are related to those communities. In one sense this is an old Greek insight modernized by such thinkers as Hegel and Marx; in another it is a deeply Jewish insight about the primacy of peoplehood and covenant in articulating and understanding who we are as Jews. In any case, the important point is that the old dilemma of liberal Judaism depended on treating the individual as Hobbes, Locke, Kant, and others did, without sufficient attention to the ways in which the values and character of community subtly influence our beliefs, choices, and actions.

The second assumption that must be rethought concerns the notion of agency and selfhood incorporated in the old dilemma. In terms that I will use later to explore features of Mendelssohn's thought, the old dilemma rests on a conception of the universal self, whereas our real identities are deeply embedded in the particular, historical soil of past and future. We simply cannot be who we are once we are divorced from our particular families, locale, customs, language, friends, resources, hopes, skills, and so on. This complex network of connections, influences, and relationships constitutes our world and ourselves, and our decisions and conduct are carried out within this context and within the particular situation that locates us in history. The old dilemma functioned, then, at an abstract level and asked how we as free agents, choosing what to do and believe, could act spontaneously and simultaneously acknowledge the force of authority, be it divine or delegated. Hence it seemed rationally unresolvable, insofar as it required us to be totally active and totally passive simultaneously and precisely. But conceived this way, the dilemma divorces us from the particularity of our situation or any situation. It is a dilemma about agency and selfhood themselves and not about any particular kind of agency or selfhood, certainly not about any historically determined cases of agency or selfhood.

The new dilemma of liberal Judaism has a different tone from the old. The old was really about how, given the attractions of the modern world and of liberal values, one could still be Jewish. The new dilemma is about how, given the historical fact of our Jewishness and indeed the diversity of our Jewishnesses, one can still be liberal. Once, that is, we acknowledge that we are all situated in communities, in history, and hence in a complex network of frameworks for interpreting and shaping the world, how can we nonetheless identify values and principles that have an uncompromising weight for us? How can we accept certain goals and values as unconditionally important and reject certain types of conduct as unconditionally evil? Once we appreciate that there is no absolute freedom and no absolute authority, that all we do involves an interaction between ourselves and our world, with its groups, its institutions, and its past, how can we find, indeed *can* we find values, principles, and goals that carry conviction and brook no compromise?

This is a major problem for all those committed to, or at least all those who admit, the force of some form of postmodernism or idealism. It is also, I think, a major problem for all those thinkers, religious and philosophical, who recognize in the Holocaust an unprecedented explosion of evil that threatens to alter all our principles, concepts, and beliefs, and yet seems to require an uncompromising opposition to all that made that evil possible and indeed actual. One may not know why such opposition is necessary or even how it is possible, but one must still know *that* one must oppose the demons of Auschwitz and that one can succeed in such opposition. The new dilemma of liberal Judaism is to articulate the lineaments of such opposition even with the recognition that all commitments, decisions, and policies are essentially historical and that Auschwitz threatens to overwhelm them all. To live in a post-Holocaust world is not to be fixated on that event; it is to be intensely moved by it to take Auschwitz seriously as a rupture in history itself. It is to admit that all we believe has been potentially destroyed or eroded and yet to hope that there are some things that must survive and be true.

The new dilemma of liberal Judaism, then, is about history and principle, about contingency and necessity, time and eternity. But it is about these things in a new way. Moreover, it is a dilemma that might seem to be solved in theory but not in fact. Some contemporary philosophers have addressed this very problem. Richard Rorty, for example, asks how an ironist, who is convinced that our understanding of the world and ourselves is interpretation through and through, can still be a liberal, committed to treating some acts, such as torture, as absolutely and unconditionally wrong. Hilary Putnam and, I think, Charles Taylor claim that as agents we are intrinsically situated and hence always engaged in conduct from a particular point of view and within a particular context. Nonetheless, some things are important to us unconditionally and fundamentally; we have standards of value, models of purpose, and guidelines to truth and virtue. Moreover, that we do have such standards and models is part of our selfhood and part of what it means for us to be human agents. Indeed, to believe otherwise, to doubt that any beliefs or conduct could be unconditionally true or right, is artificial. It is to believe that we could attain a timeless, ahistorical, detached, disengaged perspective on all agents, all frameworks or conceptual schemes, and judge them all equally true or deny any of them the status of perfect truth or perfect right. But this perspective is beyond us. We cannot attain it, no matter how we might seem to do so or hope to do so. Hence, the dilemma of history and principle seems to be solved by theoretically disposing of its opponents; neither skepticism nor idealism can be true, for both presuppose a transcendent and detached perspective that is beyond the human condition.[1]

But this same dilemma, which seems to find a theoretical resolution in what Putnam calls internal realism, recurs at the existential level, when, in historically particular situations, we seek firm principles and unconditional guidelines. With our appreciation of the historical character of our lives comes a conviction in the temporary, contingent, and conditional nature of all we believe and do. We cannot simply deny these feelings of temporality, this sense that even our deepest commitments and principles may not always be appropriate, compelling, and elevating. Our task cannot end with a moment of satisfaction, for we do not know what the future will bring. Rather, we must use the resources of the past, memories guided by text, ritual, and study, in order to articulate principles that then become our guides for shaping the world. What firmness we gain will be in part the outcome of deliberation and dialogue, in part the result of a concerted effort to realize principle and value in conduct and hence in the world itself. There are no absolute authorities, and there is no absolute confirmation, but there are firm principles of conduct, wrestled from the past by a process of study and cooperative, rational dialogue, and secure achievements in the future. Both make our beliefs and our practices as unconditional and solid as they can be.

Such themes have guided my examination of figures and issues in modern Jewish thought as they relate to the problem of history. At times I focus on the relation between past and present, at times on the relation between revelation and history, and often on the historicity of Judaism itself. I view these issues as central to the enterprise of modern Jewish self-understanding. By examining this thematic core, we identify a continuity that unites deep strains of modern Jewish thought.

In the first of these essays I discuss Yosef Yerushalmi's influential reflection on history and memory, *Zakhor*, and show that historiography in fact impedes rather than facilitates the continuity between the Jewish past and Jewish identity. I suggest, moreover, that Moses Mendelssohn, in his response to Spinoza's historical and political disposal of the ceremonial law, already appreciated this feature of modern, scientific historiography. In the second essay I elaborate on this confrontation between Spinoza and Mendelssohn concerning the obligatory character of the ceremonial or ritual law. What Mendelssohn seeks to achieve, I believe, is an ahistorical, indeed rational ground for Jewish distinctiveness. In this way he shows a recognition of both the attractions and the risks of historicity.

This tension in Mendelssohn's thought can be uncovered in another way. The third chapter focuses on Mendelssohn's liberalism, his commitment to the liberal state, to tolerance, and to the type of selfhood that underlies such an Enlightenment conception. That type of selfhood is universal, a collection of interests, abilities, desires, rights, and obligations shared by all. But, at the same time, Mendelssohn recognizes the importance of the particular, historically situated self, the Jewish person whose distinctiveness is ultimately grounded in Divine Providence and history. Mendelssohn never really resolved this tension or overcame it; in a sense, it remained a mystery to him, one that he could only acknowledge and suffer.

As a paradigmatic Enlightenment thinker, Mendelssohn exhibited a loyalty to reason and a commitment to universality and detachment from history that were uncompromising, if nonetheless complex. Leo Strauss, responding to the failures of Weimar and the rise of Nazism, develops his thinking about Judaism, politics, philosophy, and religion with a renewed commitment to objectivity and transcendence in an environment rife with relativism and the abuse of power. Two chapters deal with Strauss as a Jewish thinker. One traces the core of Strauss's biographical reflections in his Preface to the English edition of his book on Spinoza where Strauss argues for Jewish orthodoxy but exhibits simultaneously a complicated relationship with history. Chapter five develops an account of Strauss's political philosophy and his critique of modernity and shows how for Strauss philosophy and religion, Athens and Jerusalem, incorporate exclusive conceptions of the good life and hence must forever remain incommensurable. Strauss's argument, then, concludes that a genuine Jewish philosophy is impossible, for both the method of thought and the conceptions of human existence of philosophy and religion are dissonant and indeed incompatible.

For Strauss one expression of history in the modern world is the primacy of instrumental reasoning, of the social sciences, of Hobbesian individualism, and the threat of relativism. To confront this constellation one must acknowledge the primacy of objectivity and universality, liberal values and rational principles, and one strategy to achieve these goals would be to return to the past, to a time prior to the assault of modernity. But modernity brings other problems, among them an occlusion of the Divine and the complications of materialist mentality and the denial of spirituality. In the early part of this century Martin Buber and Franz Rosenzweig sought to challenge these trends in modernity; in the 1950s and 1960s a number of Jewish theologians in North America appropriated Buber and Rosenzweig in order to mount their own attack on secularism and its associated vices. But this attack brought with it risks, not the least of which was the possibility of excess, of responding to a thoroughly historical perspective with a decidedly other-worldly one. Chapter Six discusses how Peter Berger, a prominent sociologist of religion and Lutheran theologian, succumbs to just this threat. Berger seeks relief from modernity in signals of transcendence, an openness to religious experience that never authentically confronts the realities of contemporary religious and political life.

Chapters seven, eight, and nine, in one way or another, deal with Jewish thought that attempts to interpret Judaism in terms of a genuine confrontation with the Holocaust. I begin with moral questions. How can one honestly confront Auschwitz and yet recover moral principles for a post-Holocaust world? In chapter seven, developing a line of thinking from Emil Fackenheim's work, I sketch an account of how Jewish ethics might do just this. Chapter eight discusses how three of the most prominent post-Holocaust Jewish thinkers, Emil Fackenheim, Eliezer Berkovits, and Irving Greenberg, have themselves recognized the relationship between history and moral thinking in a post-Holocaust situation.

Chapter nine deals with philosophy and Jewish thought in Emil Fackenheim's work. I trace the tension between historicity and transcendence in Fackenheim's thinking from his early monograph *Metaphysics and Historicity* to *To Mend the World*. I argue that Fackenheim's way of confronting Auschwitz and responding to it is grounded in his own Jewish and philosophical life, a constellation of Jewish experience, immersion in Jewish life and learning, and philosophical sophistication. Because that life, however, issues in an interpretive account of what the evil of Auschwitz was and how Jews and others should respond to it, an account that is the result of careful reflection and rational argumentation, that account is not merely a collection of Fackenheim's own arbitrary proposals; rather, it presents itself as a compelling attempt to understand the *demands* of history and Jewish life—perhaps even the divine demands—for us all.

Fackenheim's existential thinking raises the question whether personal experience and interpretation can be objectively true or universally compelling. Chapter ten examines Franz Rosenzweig's solution to this problem in *The Star of Redemption*. The general problem is whether religious and philosophical thought can transcend its historical situation.

Chapter eleven provides a perspective on the way in which historical self-consciousness, the awareness of the problem of history as I have described it, has been a central feature of modern Jewish thinking from Spinoza and Mendelssohn to our own day. In this respect post-Holocaust Jewish thought, which is deeply immersed in reflections about Judaism and history, is profoundly continuous with modern Jewish thought. The themes of temporality, conditionality, and remoteness are constant features of modern Jewish thought. This essay shows that the post-Holocaust thinkers appreciate these themes better than did any of their predecessors. In addressing and encountering Auschwitz, they form the most recent stage in the tradition of modern Jewish thought.

Chapter twelve turns to the themes of the 1950s and 1960s, which centered on the possibility of faith and revelation in contemporary life and which included as well the role of freedom and authority in contemporary Jewish life and the implications for moral experience in Judaism. It concludes by identifying briefly some of the features of recent Jewish thought and by anticipating the next stage of serious reflection on Judaism and the Jewish experience.

Before we forge ahead, however, we must turn to the past, and the first task of that reflective return must be to try to understand fully the meaning of the work of Emil Fackenheim, Irving Greenberg, Eliezer Berkovits, Richard Rubenstein, and Arthur Cohen, and that mode of Jewish thought that we call post-Holocaust. Such an inquiry will require us to understand a good deal: for example, the context for their work, the political and cultural world of America in the decades since the Second World War, the emergence and the character of postmodernism and interpretive idealism, the post-Holocaust and Israel-oriented thinking of a variety of Christian theologians, and the struggles with history and memory by neoconservatives in America and in Germany. But such demands are not surprising; there is no easy way to historical reflection, nor can such recovery of the past be avoided. Jewish self-understanding must always return to the Jewish past, to the texts, the teachings, the events, the personalities, all that constitutes a rich and variegated tradition that stretches from us back to Sinai and beyond. Our relation to this past, however, will always be complex and dialectically subtle. But at some point, before we seek special guidance from Torah or Midrash or Responsa or much else, we must come to grips with the configuration of events and reflection that defines our immediate situation. Among the elements of that configuration, the Holocaust, Israel, and the Jewish thought responsive to them are central. As it happens, moreover, the themes that are intensely addressed by this configuration concern the problem of history and its many dimensions. This book explores some of those dimensions, and especially the historical character of Judaism as a preface, as it were, to the study of their emergence in recent years, all in the service of a more distant and yet, at the same time, more immediate and urgent goal, an understanding of Judaism and Jewish life for the decades to come.

# DILEMMAS IN MODERN JEWISH THOUGHT

ONE

# Overcoming the Remoteness of the Past

## Memory and Historiography in Modern Jewish Thought

The past is both near and far, both inescapable and unreachable. What access we have to it comes through memory and historiography,[1] two vehicles, some think, to a common destination. But the truth about this pair and their relations to past and present is more complex than this simple metaphor conveys. And the complexity comes in part from the fact that while both memory and historiography begin in the present, they nonetheless point to a past that is both unavoidably proximate and yet utterly beyond our grasp.

Historians may worry about this complexity, in the course of trying to understand themselves and what they are doing. Yosef Yerushalmi writes, in *Zakhor: Jewish History and Jewish Memory*, of his "effort to understand [himself] as a Jewish historian, not within the objective context of the global scholarly enterprise, but within the inner framework of Jewish history itself."[2] His task, in other words, is to try to understand the role that Jewish historians and historiography have played within Jewish life and Jewish self-understanding. Jewish experience involves memory, he claims, but rarely has the Jewish historian been its "primary custodian" *(Zakhor*, xiv). Ritual, social structure, texts—all these and more have been the Jewish vehicles to the past; not the historian and his narrative accounts of people, places, and events. Yerushalmi admits to having begun by thinking this a paradox; he ended by realizing why, at least for him and post-nineteenth-century Jewish historians, it is not paradoxical at all but rather manifest and understandable. The Jewish past viewed from the subjective perspective of the committed Jew is not the same as that same past viewed—indeed reconstructed—from the objective standpoint of the scholarly historian.

How indeed can Jewish memory *survive* modern historiography? How can Jewish collective memory and traditionalism, the communal recovery of the past, survive the success of Jewish historiography after the nineteenth century? For the historian studies and indeed shapes a past that is remote, distant, and isolated, while the faithful devotee recalls a past that is powerfully immediate, assimilated to the world of memory, imaginatively current. The historian produces a past that is very past, while memory finds a past that is very present. The historian returns, so far as he or she is able, to another time; the rememberer welcomes another time into his or her own. To one the past is treated *as past*, to the other *as present*.

I propose the following four theses about memory and historiography in order to clarify this problem. They embody not a program for how these activities might be conducted but rather a partial descriptive and analytical account of what goes on when they are performed.[3]

(1) *Literal memory is subjective*. It is a first-person activity whereby an agent who has once apprehended or experienced a person, place, event, belief, emotion, etc., but since forgotten it, once again becomes aware of it, usually aided by a current experience that facilitates the new awareness. But it is a first-person experience in two ways. First, remembering is first and foremost a kind of internal mental activity or experience which individuals report themselves as performing or experiencing, as having performed or having experienced.

More important, literal memory involves the returning to consciousness of images, events, actions, beliefs, emotions, etc. not, as it were, in and of themselves, but rather as the rememberer had experienced them or as they had been experienced by the rememberer. That is, we do not remember objectively, from no standpoint at all; rather, we remember subjectively, from a particular point of view. We remember a tree, thereby having an image of a tree viewed from a certain perspective, or we recall a melody, mentally hearing it in a certain way.[4]

Hence, memory depends upon and valuably reinforces the identity of the rememberer. Only if we have a sense of ourselves as agents could we remember, and only if we had a sense of ourselves as enduring subjects of experience. There is no impersonal recollection. By remembering we acknowledge that we are continuing subjects and we add content to who that subject is.[5]

(2) *"Metaphorical" memory is imaginatively subjective*. When encouraged or invited to recall a past event we never experienced or never could have experienced, and perhaps to do so together with others, we are asked to project ourselves imaginatively into the position of experiencing that event as described in a certain way, and hence we are invited to attend to the content as experienced from a particular point of view, the one defined by the way the event is described.[6] Let us call this type of activity "metaphorical memory." It is frequently associated with reenactment, an activity that emphasizes the imaginative identification with a particular, other agent. For this reason, such invitations to engage in a memory-like experience add to our sense of ourselves as subjects and encourage our sense of "identification" with other selves as cooperative

subjects. That is, we come to identify with others who both "recall" the same events as we do and "recall" them as experienced in the same way, from the same point of view. The group of those who "remember" the same event in this way gains a kind of unity through the common point of view that is the standpoint for the act of awareness.

(3) *Historiography is objective.* That is, the historian considers, describes, explains, and understands a past event or action in its own context and in a way or in ways that frequently are inaccessible to any agent who actually experienced the event. The historian, in other words, attends to a remote event, emphasizing its remoteness and its particular historical context, attempts to understand it comprehensively, and does so from a variety of perspectives or from no particular point of view at all. At one level, he or she seeks to accumulate points of view, fully developed, of both agents and later subjects; at another, the historian seeks to transcend all particular points of view in favor of an absolute or unconditioned standpoint from which the event can be viewed as no participating individual or individuals could view it. The historiographical result is a grasp of an event from no particular point of view or, if for narrative purposes, from the point of view of a random, ideally informed spectator or of a particular participant—but *not* the historian's or the reader's particular points of view.[7]

(4) *Hence, while memory brings a past event into a subject's present experience, historiography distances and isolates an event from the present and from the particular experiencing subject.* Memory unites while historiography separates the past and the present self. Memory makes the past present; historiography makes the past past. To be sure, the historian thinks about the past, and therefore it or an account of it is the object of his or her *present experience*. But there is no effort to incorporate the past as subjectively given to the thinker. The past is separated, distanced, and insulated from experience in this sense. It is experienced in the present, but it is *not made present* thereby. The historian's thinking is present, but the object of his thinking is "pushed" into the past, whereas the rememberer's action and object, both the recalling and the recalled, are "drawn" into the present.

Doubtless some will object that history, like memory, is interpretive and therefore shaped by the attitudes, concepts, beliefs, and understanding of the historian. Therefore, historiography no more than memory really reaches the past itself. Texts and artifacts are interpreted in such a way that an account of a past event or a narrative of a series of events is constructed. But the result, no less than the results of recall, is both present here and now and defined by the resources of the present.[8]

This form of antirealism may be theoretically right. But even if it is, and even if the historian accepts it, the problem of memory and historiography does not dissolve. The antirealist wants to blur or even deny the distinction I have described between memory and historiography. In defense, we can say three things. First, even within the context of an overall commitment to pragmatism or antifoundationalism, one can and should still make a distinction between constructing an objective account of a past that is distant and remote from the historical present and appropriating subjectively a past event or experience into one's own world as remembered, as an object of recognition, delight, anxiety, attraction, and so forth.[9] Some distinction like this has a role to play for us as agents; it would be a deficiency of antirealism if it did not allow us to acknowledge a difference that is so present in our experience and is so vividly distinct. Second, the issue between memory and historiography is *not settled* by claiming that there is no real, independent past given to us. For we admit that both memory and historiography are experiences shaped by the subject's attitudes, concepts, etc. The point is that even if they are relative to the subject, we should be able to distinguish awareness of an event as experienced from a particular point of view and awareness of an event but not as experienced from some particular standpoint. Finally, even if *we* doubt this distinction, Jewish thinkers of the eighteenth, nineteenth, and early twentieth centuries would surely have accepted it, and this is sufficient for our purposes.[10]

With these four theses in hand, we can deepen our understanding of Yerushalmi's discussion. In the end, for Yerushalmi, modern Jewish historiography is *not* a mode of Jewish memory at all. Yerushalmi only obliquely denies that premodern Jewish historical writing, say that of the sixteenth century, ever was such a mode of remembering (*Zakhor,* 73–74). But when he comes, in his last chapter, to the historiography of the nineteenth and twentieth centuries, he is unambiguous. To be sure, to a certain degree when faith and texts no longer validate Jewish self-definition, history may be appealed to, the secularized arbiter of naturalized Jewish commitment. Indeed, such historiography may exist as the "faith of fallen Jews" (86). But, more prominently, "only in the modern era do we really find, for the first time, a Jewish historiography divorced from Jewish collective memory and, in crucial respects, thoroughly at odds with it" (93). Yerushalmi, I must admit, is not as helpful about why this is so. He points to the selectivity of memory but never really shows why historiography, as the objective reconstruction of remote events etc. in their own time, place, and overall context, is at odds with an appropriative memory that incorporates aspects of the past for present response and impact. This clarification is the purpose of our four theses, for they show exactly why historical analysis and historiography are in tension with memory. This tension is the primary reason why historiography cannot replace an eroded faithfulness that once was the impulse behind collective remembering.[11]

In the end, then, the past has multiple ways of being present, and the rise of a modern form of historiographical research makes that past remote and isolated. The really *paradoxical* result of Yerushalmi's discussion concerns the outcome of historiographical research, that in recognizing and respecting the integrity of the past, the historian makes the past unrecoverable. Historiography is not a solution but rather part of the problem of Jewish memory.

The problem of memory and historiography is a valuable framework for approaching and assessing certain central features of modern Jewish thought. For one of the central tasks of Jewish thought or theology is to confront and justify the recovery of the past for the present. Indeed, as I shall now try to show, this historical confrontation and recovery is a trope that arises early in the history of modern Jewish thought, with Moses Mendelssohn in the late eighteenth century. We can, that is, understand Mendelssohn's thinking in the context of this problematic, as an attempt to overcome the remoteness and possibly even the irrelevance of the past. But to do so, we need to realize that this problem was itself already present for Mendelssohn in a particularly exciting way. First, then, we shall show how the problem of the remote or distant past was already present in the seventeenth century as a result of early modern historiography and how Hobbes responded to it. Then we shall place Mendelssohn in this framework by clarifying how he takes up a Hobbesian strategy against his own opponent, Benedict de Spinoza.

But to accomplish this task we need to sketch a background to Mendelssohn's thought that is not normally appreciated. We will start far afield, but I hope the following will, in retrospect, seem neither extraordinary nor unnecessary.

In his brilliant study of English historical and legal thought in the seventeenth century, *The Ancient Constitution and the Feudal Law*, J. G. A. Pocock shows that for Hobbes, as well as his contemporaries, Harrington, Spelman, Hale, and Brady, a certain set of ideas and strategies, inherited from the French legal historiographers of the sixteenth century and the common law theorists, framed the debate over the relation between past and present. Pocock features the notion of the feudal law and its role in the debates over law, sovereignty, and parliamentarianism. Most of his subtle, stimulating discussion we can ignore. What I want to focus on is the role of historiography in legal and political debate, the ways in which some sought to make the past relevant to the present, and Hobbes's part in all of this, a part that provides the bridge to Mendelssohn's perplexing argument.

Pocock's subject is the role of certain ideas—immemorial custom, ancient constitution, feudal tenure—in legal and political thought in seventeenth-century England, and the relation of these ideas to the development of legal historiography by such people as Sir Henry Spelman, William Prynne, Sir Matthew Hale, and Robert Brady. But the emergence of legal historiography in the discussion of legal theory had already occurred in France in the sixteenth century as part of the humanistic return to antiquity, and even if the English experience is imperfectly indebted to the French predecessors—Cajus, Bodin, Hotman, et al.—the conceptual terms for understanding Spelman and the others are present in the Continental discussion. Pocock usefully outlines the earlier Renaissance stage.[12]

Unlike the ancient historians, Thucydides and Tacitus among them, who constructed, for largely moralistic reasons, "an intelligible narrative of human affairs" (*Ancient Constitution*, 1), the new historiographers of the Renaissance engaged in research into the past, scrupulously examining texts and eventually other evidence in order to determine regular patterns and to refine the modes of investigation that reveal those patterns and their utility for understanding the past. They realized that commentaries had overlaid old texts with new meanings, and so they sought a return to the original text, in its own setting, and hence to a remote past on its own terms. Pocock calls this stage of humanistic historiography "the threshold of the modern historical consciousness" (4),[13] and it was a threshold that already harbored more than its share of paradox:

> . . . the humanists aimed at resurrecting the ancient world in order to copy and imitate it, but the more thoroughly and accurately the process of resurrection was carried out, the more evident it became that copying and imitation were impossible—or could never be anything more than copying and imitation. . . . In short, the humanists, going far beyond their original purpose, relegated Greco-Roman wisdom inescapably to the past, and robbed it, in the end, of all claim to be applied immediately and directly to modern life. . . . Thus their work raised the whole question of the relation between past and present. Was the past relevant to the present? was there any point in studying it? what was the status of its survivals in the present? and, perhaps above all, how had it become the present? (4–5)

This is the problem of modern historiography and present memory already operative in the sixteenth century. The context for its emergence, Pocock argues—at least one especially challenging context—is the historical school of Renaissance jurists. For with the lawyers, the problem of relevance was urgent, precisely because "the data they were assigning to a past context were simultaneously the principles on which present society was endeavoring to govern itself" (8). In short, once the urge to clarify and secure the historical roots of law was felt, the problem of the irrelevance of the past arose as a vitally practical and not merely a theoretical problem.[14]

In the 1560s there appeared a trio of works by French historians of law, all of which tried to solve the problem of bringing "history and jurisprudence back into concord" (11). Their most consequential strategy, which Pocock takes to be prominent throughout English discussion in the next century, is this: Roman codes were "written and unchangeable," expressions of a remotely past society. But the real roots of contemporary law were not in such codes; rather, they lay deep in the soil of the customary, unwritten law of the past. Here was the bridge between past and present: custom, "the usages of the folk interpreted through the mouths of judges," the relevance of which is confirmed *de facto* by continued acceptance and utility. "Custom was *tam antiqua et tam nova*, always immemorial and always perfectly up-to-date" (15). Indeed, for this reason custom was doubly available as a means of making the past relevant, for it implied both acceptability and adaptability. Law as custom is both "the ever-changing product of a historical process" and "fixed, unchanging, immemorial" (173–74).[15] Its use, when viewed in its English, common law context, was manifest in the acknowledgment of immemorial law and an ancient constitution, incorporating rights that precede all sovereignty and establishment. Law as custom is primordial, aimed at superseding the typical monarchical myths of origin and constitution.[16]

Pocock has a great deal to say about custom and the ways it was employed to solve the problem of the remote and irrelevant past. For our purposes, it is sufficient to realize that law as immemorial custom was one important feature of common law thinking and the constitutional debate in pre–civil war England and that it, together with its opponents, generated increased interest in historiography, whether the historian's purpose was to find continuity or discontinuity in the legal and political past. Custom is authoritative because it constitutes the "accumulated and refined wisdom of many generations" (162–63), because it is the expression of what Sir Matthew Hale called "artificial reason." Its binding force, in other words, derives from continuous reflection, revision, and acceptance. One ought to accept it because history proves that it is right to do so.

Among those who reacted against the idea that "law is law because it is immemorial custom" (162) was Thomas Hobbes, and it is Hobbes who provides the link between the problem of the remoteness of the past and Mendelssohn. According to Pocock, Hobbes's opponent was Sir Edward Coke and his common law views that (a) most law was law because immemorial and (b) law of this kind could not have been produced by one person, since it constituted the "accumulated and refined wisdom of many generations" (162–63). Hobbes's strategy was to divide the question into what the laws were and how they were identified, on the one hand, and by what mechanism they received their binding force, on the other. His famous answers were, respectively, natural reason and the sovereign's command. In other words, reason tells each of us what the laws should be, but only the artificial command of the ruler turns these "theorems of reason" into laws.[17]

> . . . custom alone has no binding force; for custom to become law requires that there should already exist an authority capable of making law by his injunctions. Therefore, no law is immemorial; before there can be law there

must be a sovereign; and every law must have been made at a particular point in time. (163)

Once again we find a view generated by historiography and yet leading to a renewed interest in it. To oppose the weakness of custom, Hobbes introduced sovereign command, fixed historically and continuously effective as long as unrevoked. For custom by itself provides neither the content nor the authority of law.

By the seventeenth century, then, the problem of the continuity of tradition and the remoteness of the past had already been raised and indeed confronted, in both a legal and a political context. Moreover, by the late eighteenth century it was appreciated and appropriated widely, among others by Moses Mendelssohn.

Born in Dessau in 1729, Mendelssohn spent most of his life in Berlin. There, in 1754, he met and impressed Lessing, who became his lifelong friend and collaborator. Indeed, Lessing used Mendelssohn, whose defense of toleration became famous, as his model for Nathan in Lessing's own defense of religious toleration, *Nathan the Wise*. In Lewis White Beck's words, "Mendelssohn was the epitome of popular philosophy at its best," a chief literary and religious spokesman for the ideas of "the Frederician enlightenment," with its moralistic conception of religion, optimistic view of human progress through enlightenment, confidence in the scope and role of philosophy, and indifference to current political and ideological problems.[18] Mendelssohn, whose writings included discussions in aesthetics, epistemology, and metaphysics, was most well-known for two works: the *Phaedo*, published in 1767 and widely translated, and his 1763 essay on the degree of evidence in the "metaphysical sciences," which defeated Kant for the prize of the Berlin Academy. In addition to his defense of religious toleration in response to the challenge of Johann Casper Lavater, Mendelssohn's most important Jewish contributions were his biblical translations and the work we shall be examining, *Jerusalem*, published in 1783. A friend of Kant, Heine, and other leading intellectuals of the 1780s, Mendelssohn died in 1786, during an unhappy controversy with Jacobi concerning Lessing's alleged Spinozism.

*Jerusalem* is one outcome of a series of events that began in 1781. These events have been frequently chronicled in detail;[19] we need only mention the highlights in order to set the stage for *Jerusalem*. When the Jewish community of Alsace solicited Mendelssohn's aid in preparing their plea for civil emancipation, Mendelssohn declined in favor of a young, Christian lawyer, Christian von Dohm. The next year von Dohm published his work *On the Civil Improvement of the Jews*, with Mendelssohn's aid and endorsement. On one issue, however, the two disagreed, for von Dohm still supported what Mendelssohn had long rejected: the right of ecclesiastical institutions to excommunicate nonconformists, dissidents, or whoever was judged threatening to the community's survival and well-being. Mendelssohn sought a vehicle for clarifying his differences with von Dohm; he encouraged Dr. Marcus Herz to translate Mannaseh ben Israel's *Vindiciae Judaeorum*, the century-old plea for the readmittance of Jews into Cromwell's England, and appended his own Preface, in which he made manifest his opposition to the right of excommunication. Amidst the stormy controversy that ensued, one pamphlet stood out. *The Search for Light and Right* was long thought to be the work of August von Sonnenfels, an Austrian diplomat and advocate of liberal, rational religion. We now know that the pamphlet was in fact written by August Cranz, a journalist and someone held in less regard by Mendelssohn. The gist of the pamphlet was twofold: did not the biblical commandments of Judaism require sanctions, without which they would have no continued force? And if the commandments had no force, why did Mendelssohn not ignore them and indeed convert to liberal Christianity, which was hardly other than rational or natural religion, of which Mendelssohn himself was an advocate? Shaken by such a challenge, Mendelssohn set out both to defend his views on excommunication and religious tolerance and to establish the integrity of his commitment to Judaism. The work in which he sought to perform both tasks, *Jerusalem*, was subtitled *On Religious Power and Judaism.*

Early in *Jerusalem*, a work that is centrally about law, Mendelssohn shows us that Hobbes is one of his philosophical predecessors.[20] We can now add that in Part Two, Mendelssohn's response to Spinoza concerning the ceremonial law is in part indebted to Hobbes's response to the rise of legal historiography and its use of the idea of custom. That is, one of Mendelssohn's arguments for the continued authority of the ceremonial law—and indeed a largely unappreciated argument[21]—both responds to Spinoza's *historical* argument for its obsolescence and uses a Hobbesian notion of sovereign command to do so.

One of Spinoza's accomplishments, in the *Tractatus Theologico-Politicus* (1670), is the development of a historical, critical method for reading the Bible and for portraying Judaism in its formative period.[22] In many ways, the *Tractatus Theologico-Politicus* is a work of modern historiography which attempts to understand the biblical world on its own terms as expressed in an ancient text.[23] As one result of this study, Spinoza finds that religion is part of political life; it is an aid to the political enterprise. He distinguishes between inward piety, the moral disposition to acts of justice and benevolence, and the "outward observances of piety and the external rites of religion" (Ch. 19, 245). Here we have the distinction between moral virtue and ceremonial or ritual observance. Regarding the latter, Spinoza says:

> religion acquires its force as law solely from the decrees of the sovereign. . . . the rites of religion and the outward observances of piety should be in accordance with the public peace and well-being, and should therefore be determined by the sovereign power alone. (Ch. 19, 245)

That sovereign is the "temporal ruler," the king or legislative agent. Furthermore, the sole function of public ritual is to aid the moral purposes of the state by encouraging allegiance to and acceptance of the sovereign's rule. Therefore, when the state is destroyed and sovereignty ended, the binding character of the ceremonial laws is nullified; as law, obligatory ritual conduct ceases. For the Jewish commonwealth, this occurred in 70 C.E. Spinoza is unequivocal about this: ceremonial observances "had nothing to do with blessedness and virtue, but had reference only to the election of the Hebrews, that is . . . to their temporal bodily happiness and the tranquility of their kingdom, and that therefore, they were only valid while that kingdom lasted" (Ch. 5, 69).[24]

Viewed against the background of the rise of modern historiography, Spinoza's results echo those of French and English scholars before him. For them, Roman codes or feudal law expressed and defined remote times and places. In the case of those who saw the Norman Conquest as a radical interruption in English political and legal life, the result was the relegation of Anglo-Saxon law and practices to an irrelevant past. For Spinoza, the ceremonial or ritual laws of biblical Judaism are similarly disposed, consigned to a time and place remote and defunct. By tying the ceremonial law to an earthly sovereign and by tailoring its roles to a temporal institution, Spinoza undercut its authority and its relevance to Jewish life in the seventeenth and subsequent centuries.[25]

What is Mendelssohn's response to Spinoza's historiographical assault on the continued relevance of the ceremonial law? In one sense, of course, Mendelssohn's most elaborate response takes shape as a kind of natural law justification of the ritual law. In the second part of *Jerusalem* he argued that the ritual law is a stimulant for recalling those eternal truths without which moral perfection is not possible, a vehicle for enabling moral perfection. In this way, Mendelssohn links the detached objectivity of moral agency to the particular perspective of individuals who have "forgotten" the eternal truths necessary for virtuous conduct and seek to regain them. But the link is a fragile one; in terms of the background we have sketched, we might take this to be Mendelssohn's way of simply *ignoring* Spinoza's historiography, of refusing to give it serious credence, or of seeking to flee it.[26]

But while this argument is Mendelssohn's major one, it does not stand alone. In the course of Part Two of *Jerusalem*, he introduces a second defense of the ceremonial law's continued authority,[27] and here we see him employing a Hobbesian strategy[28] against Spinoza's already Hobbesian attack. This is what Mendelssohn says:

> In fact, I cannot see how those born into the House of Jacob can in any conscientious manner disencumber themselves of the law. We are permitted to reflect on the law, to inquire into its spirit, and, here and there, where the lawgiver gave no reason, to surmise a reason which, *perhaps*, depended upon time, place, and circumstances, and which, *perhaps*, may be liable to change in accordance with time, place, and circumstances—if it pleases the Supreme Lawgiver to make known to us His will on this matter, to make it known in as clear a voice, in as public a manner, and as far beyond all doubt and ambiguity as He did when He gave the law itself. As long as this has not happened, as long as we can point to no such authentic exemption from the law, no sophistry of ours can free us from the strict obedience we owe to the law. . . . If in things human I may not dare to act contrary to the law on the mere strength of my own surmise and legal sophistry, without the authority of the lawgiver or custodian of the law, how much less may I do so in matters divine? (*Jerusalem*, 133–34)

Those born under the yoke of the law are bound to obey it, as long as its sovereign legislator has given no clear and unambiguous sign that it has been revoked.

In many ways this is a strange argument for Mendelssohn to use. After all, he was a liberal and a contract theorist in the natural law tradition. Why not treat the ceremonial law, historically determined and relative to one people, as subject to reconsideration and abrogation by contemporary Jews? Why not question the continued "relevance" of ritual conduct to moral development? Why not accept the contextual, historical displacement of a type of conduct that has the negative effect of distinguishing and separating a people struggling for civil, public acceptance?

Mendelssohn's strategy may be more apparent than his reasons for employing it.[29] What he does is, in a way, dispute Spinoza's historiography by disputing his metaphysics.[30] For Spinoza, God enacted or commanded the ritual law only through the action of a temporal ruler; hence, since the ruler was ruler of a state, when the state was destroyed so was the sovereign authorization of the law. Political demise spells the end of positive law. Mendelssohn's counter is to argue that God Himself was the sovereign power of the pristine and original Jewish commonwealth; it was His command alone that authorized the law and bound His subjects to it. Having accepted Him, the Jews accepted His will, and as long as the law is not publicly revoked, it remains in force. In other words, Mendelssohn denies Spinoza's naturalism, and, in so doing, he denies his historiography. God and not a temporal sovereign, in this case Moses, is the legislator, and in good Hobbesian style Mendelssohn argues that since it is legislative enactment or command that gives the ceremonial law its binding character, only such public action can rescind that authority, for, as Hobbes puts it, "when long Use obtaineth the authority of a Law, it is not the Length of Time that maketh the Authority, but the Will of the Sovereign signified by his silence (for Silence is sometimes an argument of Consent)."[31] How that action might be performed and determined Mendelssohn does not make clear, but that is a minor point. What is important is that the argument takes on a new character when viewed in this way. It is not an inexplicable expression of traditionalism, nor a lapse away from liberalism. Rather, Mendelssohn has read Hobbes carefully, and from *Leviathan* he appropriates a reasonable and serious response to, rather than avoidance of, the historiographical problem of the remoteness and irrelevance of the past. Moreover, Mendelssohn's response calls upon every Jew to play the role of a citizen continuously engaged in a relation of obedience to his divine ruler.

Unlike the earlier and more prominent argument, this one emphasizes the political and historical rather than the moral and timeless relation between God and the Jewish people. Both arguments, as theological justifications, acknowledge the particular individual's point of view, but only to transcend it, the one by treating the agent ultimately as a universal moral agent, the other by treating him or her as a covenanted "citizen." But the important contrast is between Spinoza's effort to detach the experience of obedience to the ritual law and to place it in the distant setting of ancient Israel and Mendelssohn's attempt to show that the experience of God as ruler is as possible for modern Jews as it was for ancient ones. In short, Mendelssohn defends the viability of an individual, subjective "remembering" of the divine-human relation conceived as the relation between a divine ruler and a human subject.

In this chapter I have tried to do two things: first, to clarify the way in which modern historical analysis and writing, what I have called "historiography," forces upon Jewish memory (or the recovery of tradition and the past) and Jewish thought, as it tries to cultivate and justify that memory, the problem of the remoteness of the past, and, second, to show how Moses Mendelssohn, for whom the problem is already present in the person and argument of Spinoza, uses a Hobbesian strategy to deal with it. At the same time, I have indicated that the entire problematic of historiography, historical remoteness, and theological justification of memory and recovery might well provide a valuable framework for understanding modern Jewish thought.

Part of the problem's overwhelming character comes from the fact that in the modern world all forms of traditionalism are widely rejected and denigrated; this is a phenomenon that Yerushalmi himself notices.[32] But part may come from another quarter, from the commitment that genuine Jewish religiosity can neither dispose of nor be enslaved to history. Judaism is about history and transcendence and their intermingling. The problem of the remoteness of the past and its separation from the present is only one aspect of that enterprise, but it is one that cannot be avoided. For this reason, it is a useful framework for understanding Mendelssohn's Jewish thought and also an important backdrop for examining and assessing modern Jewish thought. Such a task would be a valuable and important one, but for the moment it is sufficient to have noticed this much: that the conflict between Jewish memory and modern historiography emerges in earlier centuries as a fundamental problematic for Jewish self-understanding.

TWO

# History and Modern Jewish Thought

## Spinoza and Mendelssohn on the Ritual Law

A sensitive reader of Spinoza's *Tractatus Theologico-Politicus*[1] might conclude that Spinoza anticipates two important Jewish responses to the modern world: liberal Judaism and Zionism.[2] In fact, however, such a conclusion would be false, because it is both too narrow and too wide. First, it is too narrow, for these are not the only responses that Spinoza anticipates. Another, the one that he rejects, is traditional Jewish Orthodoxy.[3] Second, the conclusion is too wide, because the liberal form of Judaism that Spinoza anticipates is not, in fact, identical with what became liberal Judaism in the nineteenth and twentieth centuries. The latter, like Spinoza's liberal religion, the universal faith of mankind, does have rational morality at its center; liberal Judaism has always emphasized ethics and morality as the special concern of the Jewish experience. But whereas Spinoza's liberal religion was concerned solely with morality, the performance of acts of goodness and justice, nineteenth and twentieth century liberal Judaism has always wanted to preserve—to one degree or another—its Jewish character. For this reason, modern liberal Judaism has always struggled with the problem of the status of Torah and the *mitzvot*, the laws or commandments of God.[4] Spinoza's liberal Judaism does not engage in such a struggle, for the moral dimension of Torah has its own justification while the nonmoral or ritual dimension, ever since the destruction of the ancient Jewish state, simply has none.[5]

Reflections like these may lead some to conclude that Spinoza's anticipation of liberal Judaism is a chimera. What he anticipates is in fact not a form of Judaism at all, but, rather, assimilation into the universal faith of all mankind. This view suggests that what Spinoza's *Tractatus* does, by anticipating assimilation, orthodoxy, and Zionism as responses to the plight of the Jew in the modern world, is to leave open the liberal Jewish option.

It would be wrong, I think, to view Spinoza's primary legacy to Judaism in this light. While it may be true that he never did come to grips with the problem of uniting his "moral faith" with the particularity of Jewish ceremonial observance, and while it may be true that his rejection of Judaism occasioned unfairness in his reflections on Judaism,[6] its principles and main figures, still he does contribute a central insight to an understanding of Judaism: the contours of Jewish experience and the reflective comprehension of that experience in thought are fundamentally exposed to historical events in ways that liberal Jewish thought, so wedded to German Idealism, has consistently failed to appreciate. This is what justifies serious reflection on the *Tractatus Theologico-Politicus*.

The first liberal Jewish thinker is Moses Mendelssohn.[7] This is not so because Mendelssohn was a liberal Jew, for he was not. He is, however, the first serious thinker to seek a middle road between assimilation and orthodoxy, to advocate the centrality of rational morality for Judaism (and all religion) and then to try to justify the continuing Jewish obligation to the ceremonial law. In a sense, then, Mendelssohn takes up the Spinozistic gambit. We have already discussed one feature of Mendelssohn's response to Spinoza, now we turn to another: how he solves the liberal Jewish problem of justifying the continuing obligation to ritual law. The solution is, however, a weak one and ultimately unsatisfactory; as a middle road, it lacks the sternness of the two extremes, universal moral religion and orthodoxy. But even more unsatisfactory still is the very attempt, for it develops from too ready an acceptance of Spinoza's alternatives and too narrow an appreciation of the truth in Spinoza's own view. In short, Mendelssohn took from Spinoza the wrong things; he went to the doctor for a cure but caught the illness instead. Mendelssohn radicalized Spinoza's absolutism, his view that all true religion is rational morality, and cleansed Spinoza's view of Judaism of its historical taint. He rejected, or overcame, Spinoza's important concession to history, that the destruction of the Jewish state made the ceremonial laws of Judaism defunct. But Mendelssohn did not see that although Spinoza was wrong in fact he was right in principle. The ceremonial law *was* transformed after the destruction of the state, and not only then and not only in substance but also in status. Vulnerability to history is ruled out by Mendelssohn. Nothing radical occurs between Sinai and the coming of the Messiah, when God, in as public and explicit a fashion as at Sinai, will revoke the law once and for all. In this regard, we learn a greater lesson from Spinoza than from Mendelssohn. The loyal, devoted Jew's defense of Judaism and the ceremonial law is meager and unsatisfying when compared with the rebel's attack on it.

To see this, and to comprehend how Spinoza and Mendelssohn differ, we must look in detail at Mendelssohn's argument in *Jerusalem*.[8] The pamphleteer who had written *The Search for Right and Light* accurately identified the nub of Mendelssohn's view in the Preface to the German translation of Mennaseh ben Israel's *Vindiciae Judaeorum*. If the ceremonial laws of Judaism are obligatory only because, as laws, they are institutionally backed by threats of punishment, e.g., excommunication or *herem*, then, by denying religious institutions the right to excommunicate, Mendelssohn had, in effect, undermined Jewish particularity by undermining the authority of the Torah and, thereby, the justification for particularly Jewish conduct. Such a criticism suggested only two alternatives consistent with "intellectual probity": either to defend the authority of the ritual law or to abandon Judaism for liberal Christianity, which was, for all practical purposes, identical with natural religion. In *Jerusalem*, Mendelssohn chooses the defense.

The central thesis of *Jerusalem*, the goal toward which Mendelssohn's very precise argument[9] is always aimed, is that even without the threat of institutional excommunication, Jews are still *obligated* to perform the ritual law. One way to introduce the argument that leads to this conclusion is to notice a strange feature of Mendelssohn's defense of it. At the time of the writing of *Jerusalem* and shortly thereafter, Mendelssohn frequently addressed himself to this question of ceremonial observance; in his letters and other writings, however, he gave not one justification, but three. He says quite straightforwardly that modern Jews are obligated to obey the ritual law because

(1) that law contributes in a special way to the attainment of moral virtue and ultimate happiness,[10]

(2) observance of that law will serve as a unifying bond, keeping the people of Israel together,[11] and

(3) God, the sole legislator of that law, has not publicly revoked it; hence, it is still in force.[12]

At first glance, these three justifications for ritual obligation do not appear to be the same, nor is it apparent how they are interrelated or even how Mendelssohn might have thought they were. Rather, they seem to be three independent responses to the Searcher's provocative challenge. But this is intellectual overkill; why offer three solutions to the same puzzle unless there is some question about their effectiveness or about their sufficiency or plausibility? Of the three, which is, or which are, the answers of *Jerusalem*? Do they supplement each other, or are they independent and even redundant justifications for ceremonial observance?

Mendelssohn begins *Jerusalem* with a theory of the liberal state, a rudimentary theory that employs the notions of right, duty, and contract to explain the genesis of the state and the scope of its authority. It is a theory of the liberal state because it values highly individual freedom and, especially, the "freedom to think what one wants"—freedom of conscience or belief. Indicative of the state's limited authority is the unrestricted respect that it gives to such freedom. For, as Mendelssohn tries to show, the very nature of belief and knowledge, indeed of thinking, makes it impossible to allow or tolerate governmental intervention. The only genuine justification for constraining individual choice and actions comes as a matter of mutual protection and civil security. Mendelssohn's state is liberal through and through.

Such a state comes into being as a result of a social contract made by mutual consent in a condition of natural need. The debts to Hobbes and Locke are explicit, and there are other debts, too, for example, to Rousseau and to Spinoza.[13] Mendelssohn's strategy is this: first, he must show why religious institutions do not have the right, whereas civil institutions do have the right and hence the authority, to force people to act in certain ways. Then he must show why, even without this authority, Jewish ceremonial law is, nonetheless, obligatory.

In Mendelssohn's view, the state arises as a regulatory agency, to supervise transfers of goods and services. It develops an apparatus for regulating permissible transfers—via bequests, purchases, investments, taxation, and public expenditures, etc.—and another for regulating impermissible ones—for example, theft, injury, kidnapping, rape, etc. Individuals, to reduce the risk of being harmed or robbed and thereby to gain peace of mind, give to a neutral institution the authority to coerce their actions; one gives up the prospect of uninhibited acquisition by whatever means in exchange for security, the freedom from being victimized in just that way.

Although it is not our purpose to examine Mendelssohn's theory of the liberal state and assess its truth or falsity, it is especially interesting to identify in it his abiding rationalism and optimism regarding human nature. The entire edifice rests on the conviction, *pace* Hobbes, that persons in a state of nature do have rights and duties and, also, that they will act on the basis of rational deliberation. Although he never argues for such a view, Mendelssohn sees law as derived from certain primitive, basic, natural moral prerequisites in human nature; in this he shares a good deal with many modern political thinkers. At the same time, this optimism with regard to human capacity is not boundless; the need for law expresses a correlative appreciation for human limitation. And this appreciation for irrational motivation and its results suggests to Mendelssohn that the state views actions and their meaning in a special way.

Mendelssohn gives no theory of action in *Jerusalem*. He does not discuss the notions of reason and cause, intention and desire and deliberation, all of which have been centrally important to such discussions from Aristotle's time to our own.[14] But he does make one important distinction: he observes that law coerces action by threatening punishment, and it does so by distinguishing an action from the intention of the agent and by trying to concern itself only with the former. Insofar as the law is able, it understands actions independently of their agents' intentions and solely in terms of the harm or injury that they would typically cause. For this reason, law may prevent an action that was initiated for noble purposes; it may also permit actions that are ignobly devised. It does, then, run the risk of impeding virtue and permitting vice on occasion, but it does so by trying to discourage the greatest likely amount of harm and injury compatible with the minimal constraint on individual liberty.[15]

All of this—Mendelssohn's theory of the origin of the liberal state, his account of its authority and its limits—might lead one to ask: how does this result in a difference between religious institutions and the state? Surely, if belief cannot be coerced, then religion can no more demand conviction than the state can. And do not religious institutions arise as a result of agreement and consent? Why is it, then, that Mendelssohn denies to them the authority to coerce action? His answers to these objections emerge from attention to two details of his account: (1) the requirements for genuine contract and, hence, for legitimate transfer of authority to a single institution and (2) the separation between intention and action.

First of all, does a religious institution really originate from a contract? Mendelssohn's response is that in the case of religious institutions there is no contract and, hence, no establishment of a regulatory agency to arbitrate disputes, because the relevant parties do not find themselves in a situation of colliding interests. There are, in other words, no conditions that give rise to contracts. And without a contractual arrangement, there is no transfer of authority and, hence, no right to coerce. In a state of nature, the relevant parties are persons with needs that they can fulfill out of their own resources and needs that they cannot fulfill without the help and cooperation of others. In a protoreligious situation, however, the relevant parties are man and God, and the situation is not one of colliding interests. Both man and God want the same thing—human virtue and happiness. To be sure, man does depend on God for his very existence and for the order of the natural world with only its rare interruptions. But these are granted as gifts and require not regulation by a third party as much as grace by the giver. In the relationship between man and God, harm and theft are impossible; neither party has either the need or the desire to overwhelm the other. Religious institutions, then, do not arise as regulatory agencies governing the conduct between man and God.

But this is only part of the reason why religion has no coercive authority. One might respond: perhaps the religious institution is not a "third party" but, instead, a representative on earth of the Divine Power itself. If so, its authority would derive from God, who has that authority as Creator and Sustainer of all things. For Mendelssohn, however, this position is impossible. Whereas the state protects freedom and guarantees peace, the purpose of religion—which is God's purpose, too—is human virtue and its rewards, happiness and human fulfillment. The state and religion, then, complement each other; the state protects freedom, and religion expresses freedom in the life of virtue. Hence, while the state, in order to protect maximum liberty, must separate intention or belief from action and constrain only the latter, religion, in order to encourage virtue, cannot do so. Religion must treat intent and act as a unity; it must encourage right action performed for right purposes. The end of religion is virtue, and virtue cannot be the result of force or compulsion. In terms that Kant will later make famous, moral excellence, to be moral at all, must be autonomous.

There is, then, no way that the church can acquire the legitimate authority to coerce either beliefs or actions. Since the church does not arise from a contract, it cannot acquire that authority from individuals, and since its goal is virtue, the church cannot acquire that authority from God. Mendelssohn's conclusions are precise: neither civil nor religious institutions ought to coerce beliefs, which are immune to all compulsion. And only the state can coerce action.

The first part of Mendelssohn's task is complete; Judaism has no authority to coerce either moral or ceremonial acts—the first because virtue cannot be compelled and the second because no religion has the authority to coerce *any* action. The Searcher's question—why, then, should the modern Jew be obligated to ceremonial observance?—must now be answered. The moral obligation to practice virtue is still present even if—and, in truth, perhaps just because—there is no "legal" obligation in force. But why perform ceremonial acts? Without the force of legal obligation, or something akin to it, is there any obligation at all? Spinoza's answer was no, none at all.[16] But Mendelssohn disagrees, and his disagreement occupies the whole of Part Two of *Jerusalem*.

There is a part of Mendelssohn's account of Judaism and his response to the Searcher's challenge that is very well-known, and I shall not dwell on it. Mendelssohn's rationalism and his universalism are both influential in his threefold description of Judaism as natural religion, historical truths, and revealed legislation. His effort to identify what Judaism has in common with all genuine religion—that is, morality—and what uniquely distinguishes it—in particular, its revealed ritual law—had tremendous impact, both positive and negative, on Jews and non-Jews.[17] In a sense, however, this account is merely background to the central discussion of the authority of the ceremonial law, and the nature of that authority is our prime concern.

Suppose we begin by asking a question of Mendelssohn that is inspired by Spinoza. *Jerusalem* was written in 1782. Is the source or foundation of the Jewish obligation to ceremonial observance different in 1782 from what it was before the destruction of the Second Temple in 70 C.E., i.e., during the period of the existence of the Second Jewish State? Does the Contemporary Jew have the same obligation as the Pristine Jew?[18] Mendelssohn himself seems to appreciate the force of such a question, for he actually discusses the original purpose of the ceremonial acts and why they were obligatory when the state existed. In his *Tractatus*, Spinoza had argued that the purpose of the ceremonial law was the physical well-being and security of the state. Hence, when the state was destroyed, the need for ritual observance was also destroyed. Furthermore, since the need was civic security, the source of authority was political as well. As long as the religious and civil institutions were the same, the religious obligation was, in reality, a political one. When the state ceased to exist, not only did the need for ritual observance disappear, but the very authority to demand it ceased as well. For Spinoza, the break between Pristine Judaism and Contemporary, i.e., Diaspora, Judaism is radical.

Mendelssohn must avoid these conclusions; he must separate the ritual law from the state both in purpose and in the source of its obligatory character. For him, Diaspora Judaism is not radically different from Pristine Judaism; they are, rather, continuous forms of Jewish life and experience. One is the natural successor to the other. Or, to put it in other terms, the justification for, and authority of, the ritual law must be timeless; there must be no sharp break before and after 70 C.E. Now, one way to solve this problem would be to begin by acknowledging, with Spinoza, that in the period when the state existed religious and political authority were united. But Mendelssohn would have to go further and say that this authority was not the only reason why the ritual law was binding. There would have had to have been another source of ritual obligation, a source connected with the morality that has always been at the core of Judaism. Such a twofold scheme would be able to weather the storm of history, for only one of the two reasons or sources would cease to be effective when the state was destroyed in 70 C.E. While that event would have shattered the unity of civil and religious authority, it would have had no effect on the subtle relationship between ceremonial observance and the attainment of moral virtue.

We cannot proceed further without describing what this "subtle relationship" is. For Mendelssohn, the core of Judaism, as for all genuine religion, is natural religion. This religion of nature or reason was thought to have two components: first, a moral imperative that obligated all rational agents to practice moral virtue and to attain as high a degree of self-perfection as possible and, second, a set of eternal truths, the knowledge of which was thought to be necessary to satisfying that imperative.[19] In part, the imperative called on persons to use their reason and thereby to become maximally free, liberated, that is, from the bondage to irrational desire and passion. It called on them to do the right for its own sake, but to recognize that moral virtue would be rewarded with happiness and well-being. Confidence in such a moral imperative, however, required the knowledge that man was free; without such knowledge the attempt to increase one's freedom would have been irrational, if not simply foolish. For such reasons, knowledge of God's existence, of human freedom, and of other eternal truths was considered a prerequisite for moral perfection.

Mendelssohn's conviction was that the peculiar role of Judaism and, especially, its ritual laws arose as a result of the erosion of this moral imperative and of the knowledge of the truths required for it. People had forgotten the eternal truths and were therefore unable to respond to the imperative. For this reason, God provided the Jews with a means for recalling those truths and, thereby, for reviving the aspiration to moral perfection. But the means had to be one that would not, itself, become an object of special reverence; God did not want to run the risk of idolatry. So He instituted no normal, stable system of symbols but, rather, a set of actions that would serve as a "living kind of script, as it were, stirring heart and mind, full of meaning, stimulating man to continuous contemplation."[20] The ultimate purpose of the written and unwritten laws is salvation or moral perfection.[21] Their immediate purpose, however, is to prescribe conduct that would facilitate recollection of those truths, knowledge of which is necessary for that moral perfection. Hence, Mendelssohn's strategy is to tie ritual obligation to the universal obligation to moral perfection and to do so instrumentally, as a means serves an end.

The instrumental role of the ritual law, then, is one source of ritual obligation during the period of Pristine Judaism. If, as Spinoza thought, another source is the fact that civil and religious authority together rested in one sovereign will, that would provide the twofold basis for ceremonial observance. Hence, when the state was destroyed, in Mendelssohn's view neither the need nor the source of authority would cease, for since both are moral, neither is tied to historical change.

It would be convenient if this were Mendelssohn's account, but is it? To be sure, much of Mendelssohn's concern in Part Two of *Jerusalem* is devoted to making the case for ceremonial observance as a "living script"; this seems to be his prime reason for the continued ritual obligation in Diaspora Judaism. But it is not the only reason. In *Jerusalem* Mendelssohn remarks that the law remains in force until the lawgiver publicly revokes it.[22] Such a revocation God has not performed. For this reason, too, the ceremonial law remains obligatory even though the state no longer exists.

And, as if two reasons were not sufficient, in a letter to Herz Homberg, Mendelssohn gives a further one.[23] The ritual law, he says, is no longer the living script that it once was. But amidst atheists and anthropomorphists the Jewish people still has a purpose. The role of the ceremonial law is like a unifying bond, keeping the Jewish people together and alive.

We are encouraged, by the casual way in which Mendelssohn introduces these latter two explanations and by the elaborate development of the first, to think that Mendelssohn did not in fact regard the three as unrelated. Indeed, he may have seen them as different ways of expressing one explanation for ritual obligation in 1782 or as different components of a single explanation.

Many of the same considerations that make Mendelssohn's "living script" account a plausible one while the state existed continue to operate after its destruction. Ceremonial observance may not have the same vitality and force that it once did to revive the memory of those eternal truths; still, the need is there. Indeed, if we keep that need in mind, we can understand how the unity and continued survival of the Jewish people might be instrumental to the achievement of public and private moral virtue. If the purpose and role of the Jewish people is to remind the nations of those requisite eternal truths, then the observance of the ceremonial laws is not only the mechanism for such a reminder but a means of keeping the people alive as well. Hence, the Jew's obligation to ceremonial observance is instrumentally founded in this double sense and derives ultimately from a prior obligation to "love one's neighbor," to charity and benevolence. In this way, the unity account and the "living script" account complement each other.

It is more difficult to understand the role of the other reason, that the law is mandated as long as its legislator has not publicly revoked it. Surely the laws of a defunct nation are also defunct, whether or not the original lawgiver revoked them or even lived to revoke them. It can hardly be a necessary condition of a law's lapsing that the original legislator or legislative body exist and actually revoke it. Legal codes are too adaptive and too flexible for that, as they should be. Presumably, Mendelssohn would have to argue that the case of the *sui generis* Jewish state differs from that of normal states. Perhaps the difference lies in the lawmaker, who, in this instance, is infinite and, hence, uncompromising. But surely this cannot be what distinguishes the present case and thereby maintains ritual obligation, for that ceremonial law *has*, in fact, undergone extensive change.

To understand how all the pieces of Mendelssohn's argument fit together we need to look again at what he says and to identify the questions that he is seeking to answer. A large portion of Mendelssohn's argument involves a justification for the special role of ceremonial law and ritual conduct as God's chosen vehicle for "inspiring contemplation" of the eternal truths regarding God, Divine Providence, and the soul's immortality. This justification features a discussion of the origin and development of language and the rise of idolatry.[24] It is certainly not necessary to review all of Mendelssohn's story, which is a combination of philosophical history, anthropology, linguistics, and natural science, but we should notice some of its foremost features. He begins with the observation that man was first moved "to attach [concepts formed out of external impressions] to perceptible signs, not only in order to communicate them to others, but also to hold fast to them himself, and to be able to consider them again as often as necessary" (105, 107). Mendelssohn affirms prelinguistic conceptualization—"[t]he first steps toward the separation of general characteristics he *can*, and indeed *must* take without making use of signs," but he argues that thinking, which requires recall, must use symbols, natural and arbitrary signs. "For without the aid of signs, man can scarcely remove himself one step from the sensual" (105). Mendelssohn's comments are brief, but they are substantial enough to reflect his sympathy with Condillac, rather than with Rousseau or Herder, both of whom saw natural need as the ground of language.[25]

Mendelssohn suggests the route by which visible sign systems took shape. First, people doubtless used the sense impression itself to draw attention to a distinctive feature of the sensible object, for example, the sensory impression of a lion as a sign of courage (107–108).[26] Then they more conveniently used images on surfaces, then outlines, parts of outlines, and finally "a shapeless but *meaningful whole*," i.e., hieroglyphics (108). The transition from such figures to alphabetic script, however, "seems to have required a leap," a transition that Mendelssohn associates with sound and speech (108–110). Eventually Mendelssohn turns to corruption and the tendency of peoples to mistake the name for the thing named and to worship the sign rather than the thing signified. Hence, he concludes, "the need for written characters was the first cause of idolatry" (113).

Mendelssohn's conclusion is that the ceremonial law of Judaism is an act of Providence (117–120). The Jewish people was "a nation which, through its establishment and constitution, through its laws, actions, vicissitudes, and changes was continually to call attention to sound and unadulterated ideas of God and His attributes" (118). But permanent signs, especially written texts, lead to "superstition and idolatry" and encourage abstract speculation. For this reason, God gave this people the *ceremonial law*. Actions are not permanent and thus do not invite idolatry, and, unlike texts, they do not isolate people but encourage "social intercourse, . . . imitation, and . . . oral, living instruction. Thus teaching and life, wisdom and activity, speculation and sociability were most intimately connected" (119–120).

Originally, then, in the Mosaic constitution, the ceremonial law was the providential bond connecting life and theory (128). It encouraged interpersonal exchange and stimulated contemplation of the eternal truths about God and the soul which facilitated moral perfection and happiness. This is the core of Mendelssohn's argument, a rational account of the original role of ritual law based on a philological, historical, and rational reconstruction.

But Mendelssohn's argument has a final turn. For his object is not to demonstrate historically the existence of a *fact*. Rather, Mendelssohn's goal is the demonstration of an *obligation*. Hence, his argument must have a practical dimension. If it will conclude with an "ought," it must include one in its reasoning.

The standard interpretation is that Mendelssohn's reasoning is instrumental: each person is morally obligated to seek moral perfection; but in order to seek moral perfection one must believe in God, immortality, and Providence. People, however, have forgotten these truths. The Jewish ceremonial law is a constant reminder of these truths. Hence, the Jewish people are obligated to obey the ceremonial law.

There is a grave problem with this argument. Its conclusion binds the Jew to obey the ceremonial laws of Judaism by a particular, nonmoral obligation. Only the Jew, and none other, is so bound. But the argument, in its first premise, enjoins a universal obligation on all people, the moral obligation to moral excellence. How can a universal obligation give rise to a particular one? And how can a moral obligation entail a nonmoral one?

At first glance it is tempting to think that Mendelssohn ignored this problem altogether. But a close reading of the crucial pages of *Jerusalem* shows that at least in part Mendelssohn's argument comes to grips with this problem explicitly and directly and solves it, or purports to do so. That solution can be uncovered by understanding Mendelssohn's important claim, that in the original Mosaic constitution and in the ancient Jewish polity, "state and religion were not conjoined, but *one*; not connected, but identical" (128; cf. 128–134).

The key to Mendelssohn's justification of the continued obligation to obey the ceremonial laws of Judaism is the fact that those laws were once and always remain civil laws, even in 1783, when the state no longer exists. They were never obligatory *as a means* to moral fulfillment, although that has always been their purpose. Rather, they were always and remain obligatory as the civil law of the Jewish state. And even though they are religious legislation, they *could* be civil law in *that* state, because it was a *sui generis* constitution in which civil and religious spheres uniquely coincided and were *one*. Hence, as long as these laws were never revoked, even after the state's destruction, these civil laws, the ceremonial legislation of Judaism, remain in force.[27]

Mendelssohn's argument, then, has two decisive grounds. One is the providential act which established the ceremonial laws as civil laws of the original Mosaic constitution; the other is that even after the state's destruction, God has not revoked the law. "[P]ersonal commandments . . . must, as far as we can see, be observed strictly according to the words of the law, until it shall please the Most High to set our conscience at rest and to make their abrogation known in a clear voice and in a public manner" (134). The *purpose* of the ceremonial law remains the same, to stimulate contemplation, inquiry, and, ultimately, moral perfection and to avoid idolatry. Its *obligation* does not derive from that purpose but is the outcome of divine legislation. It is a legal obligation and not an obligation derivative from moral duty.

There is, however, a question that remains, and it is one that Alexander Altmann has noticed in his magisterial biography. "What Mendelssohn failed to explain was why Providence left the rest of mankind without a comparable legislation that would serve it as a safeguard against idolatry and as a bond between doctrine and life."[28] As Altmann comments, Mendelssohn should have argued for a *universal revealed legislation*. But he did not. The ceremonial law as an act of Providence remains impenetrable to reason; as a historical reality it can only be partially understood. Ultimately the particularity of Judaism rests on a mystery.

Mendelssohn's three reasons, then, are in fact all ways of expressing one, and that one is, in the end, the reason that provides the foundation for Jewish obligation to the ceremonial law *always*—or nearly always. That is why Mendelssohn can differ with Spinoza over the impact of the demise of the Jewish state. For Spinoza, the ceremonial law is a human law, formulated to cope with historical problems of physical well-being and civil security. For Mendelssohn, however, the ceremonial law is divine and, for this reason, is both the civil law of a unique polity, a theocracy, and very much akin to the moral purposes of justice, benevolence, and the pursuit of happiness. For Spinoza the relation between the ceremonial law and the divine moral law is mediated by the state; when the state dies, the relation is broken. But for Mendelssohn the relation is immediate; on this basis he can claim that a Judaism composed of natural religion and revealed legislation is a genuine unity, and the destruction of the Jewish state has no effect on it. Religious particularity and moral purpose are an eternal marriage.

On reflection, then, Mendelssohn, in his relentless rejection of the historical, becomes the godfather of modern Jewish absolutism; his natural heirs include Hermann Cohen and, oddly enough, Franz Rosenzweig, both cavalier in their dismissal of Zionism. Spinoza, on the other hand, arch-rationalist and anti-empiricist that he was, reveals himself as the unexpected ancestor of Zionists like Leo Pinsker and Theodor Herzl. For Spinoza, a vigorous rationalist and opponent of the influence of history on truth, also appreciates the role of history in determining the contours of Judaism and Jewish life. To Spinoza, of course, history corrupts; the experiences of historical man are confused and inadequate. Hence, a Judaism exposed to history is sure to die. But his motives notwithstanding, there may be more truth in Spinoza's denunciation of Judaism than in Mendelssohn's advocacy of it. Mendelssohn's love for Judaism shows itself everywhere, most of all in his dauntless struggle to unite Jewish commitment with rational liberalism. Spinoza's brilliance far exceeds that of Mendelssohn, but, in comparison, his love for Judaism is paltry. Yet, perhaps Spinoza's bequest is greater; what he could not give with his heart he gave with his mind, a paradoxical victory for reason if there ever was one.

THREE

# Liberalism in Mendelssohn's *Jerusalem*

One of the important strategies of recent moral and political philosophy involves paying careful attention to the relation between moral and political theory, on the one hand, and the philosophy of mind, on the other. Bernard Williams, Thomas Nagel, Derek Parfit, Charles Taylor, among others, elaborate and criticize moral thinking in terms of the notions of the self that it requires or excludes.[1] Michael Sandel criticizes John Rawls on the basis of an inconsistency in the philosophical anthropology that underpins his theory of justice.[2] And in a recent study of Hobbes, Gregory Kavka shows how one can develop Hobbes's insights regarding the self and his conventionalist moral and political theory into defensible modern versions of egoism and rule contractarianism.[3] The upshot of these and many other works is that moral and political theories should be understood and assessed in terms of the philosophical anthropology, the philosophy of mind, or the conceptions of the self which underlie them. This seems a sound and indeed old insight worth our attention.

It is an insight, moreover, that is as applicable to thinkers of the seventeenth and eighteenth centuries as it is today. C. B. Macpherson, for example, has argued that with Hobbes and his successors two conceptions of the democratic self arose in modern political thought and that we can assess the development of democratic and liberal theory in terms of these two notions of the self.[4] Sometimes, furthermore, the various conceptions of the self that a philosopher employs are dissonant, and their joint presence in his work is a mark of inner conflict. Such dissonance and hence such conflict can be shown to exist in Moses Mendelssohn's *Jerusalem*.[5] They are a further indication of the problems that inflict Mendelssohn's account of Judaism and especially of the tension between the historical and the unconditional in his thought.

Others have sought to find weaknesses in Mendelssohn's account of liberal government, church, and state, and the viability of Jewish distinctiveness. I will here articulate one weakness of Mendelssohn's thinking by focusing on the conceptions of the self that support his explicit arguments in *Jerusalem*. Guidance for this strategy comes not only from recent developments in moral and political theory; it also comes from an altogether surprising quarter. In the waning moments of the Second World War, Jean-Paul Sartre composed his reflections on the Jewish question, a book less about Jews than about Sartre's plea for genuine, authentic French renewal. In his brief but remarkable second chapter[6] Sartre provides us with a clue for examining Mendelssohn's Judaism and his liberalism and for identifying the discord between them.

The liberal democrat, Sartre says, is the Jew's "feeble protector." He seeks to save the Jew as man but not the Jew as Jew. He treats all men as divorced from their family, clan, nature, group and thrusts them into the crucible of all mankind, from which they emerge naked and alone. Hence, the liberal democrat is only willing to defend the Jew as a man like all others; for the Jew as a distinct individual, particularized by background, community, and so on, he holds no brief. But what lies at the heart of this "feeble" defense, Sartre asks. What enables the liberal democrat to distinguish the Jew as man from the Jew as Jew? The answer, Sartre says, is the liberal democrat's conception of the self, his philosophical psychology. To the liberal democrat the self or the individual is an "ensemble of universal traits," of rights, desires, characteristics, and capacities, all of which are common to all humankind. To this abstract, Enlightenment view, Sartre contrasts his own, according to which the self is an ongoing process of being in a situation.[7] For the moment we can ignore the nuances and indeed the veracity of Sartre's own philosophical anthropology and his claims about that of the liberal democrat. The hint we sought lies in Sartre's strategy, not in his results. If we are to locate a deep dissonance between Mendelssohn's liberalism and his conception of Judaism, we should examine their respective conceptions of the individual, of the self; if we are to evaluate Mendelssohn's attempt in *Jerusalem*, we should seek out the conception or conceptions of the self that underlie that work and ask how well, if at all, the Jewish and the liberal selves coincide.

Any attempt to identify the conceptions of the self that underlie *Jerusalem* must capitalize on a reading of the argument of its two parts. In the first part, Mendelssohn expresses his differences with Hobbes and Locke, states his position on the nature and roles of religious and civil institutions, decries the practice of civil oaths, and makes a plea for tolerance. In the second part, he directly engages the Searcher by giving an account of original or pre-Diaspora Judaism and by defending the ongoing authority of the ceremonial or ritual law.

Thanks to the excellent work of Alexander Altmann, the legal and philosophical background of Mendelssohn's political philosophy is available to us.[8] We need not dwell upon but can draw on that wealth of material when clarification of Mendelssohn's argument requires it. That argument begins with a comment on Hobbes. Hobbes is wrong in two regards: might is not right, and the state of nature is not without a moral component.[9] Mendelssohn stands firmly in the natural law tradition; societies are constructed by human beings, who have by nature certain rights, obligations, capacities, property, and liberties. The task of Mendelssohn's political philosophy is to identify these natural features and then to show how civil and ecclesiastical institutions arise on their foundation.

In the state of nature, man has needs, wants, capacities, rights, duties, and liberties. According to Mendelssohn, who follows the traditional reading, Hobbes identified natural right with power or capacity and identified right with liberty. Man was thereby free to do what he could do, and what he could do was his right to do. For Hobbes, moreover, man's overriding natural desire is for the avoidance of violent death and for peace. But power and fear make anxious bedfellows; so, according to Hobbes, men convene for the purposes of contract. Recognizing laws of nature for their mutual protection and benefit, they agree to constitute a "mortal god," the state, to enforce and administer those laws. In contrast to this picture, Mendelssohn paints another, in which the state arises not as a policeman but rather as a tax collector and distribution agency. Hobbes's state enforces prohibitions, Mendelssohn's regulates beneficence.[10]

Borrowing a traditional classification, Mendelssohn claims that in the state of nature all men have perfect and imperfect rights and duties.[11] Perfect duties, such as not stealing, are enforceable obligations against all others, and perfect rights are the correlative claims on one's own property and person. That property, moreover—what Mendelssohn calls "natural property"—includes one's capacities and abilities, the products of either, and the unproduced pieces of nature that are inextricably bound to one's products, such as, I take it, the land on which one's home is built. Although Mendelssohn never says so in *Jerusalem*, surely *one* function of a state might very well be to protect, à la Hobbes, one's perfect rights. In addition to this function, however, the state has another, more primary one, and that is to regulate the transfer of imperfect rights and the performance of imperfect duties. Imperfect duties are positive rather than negative and include what we would call "acts of charity and benevolence"; imperfect rights are claims directed to another's property, what we would call "petitions" or "wants" or "needs." In the case of perfect duties, each is bound unconditionally regarding what not to do, when, how, and how much. But in the case of imperfect duties, Mendelssohn says, the decisions about what to do, when, how, and to what degree are solely up to the individual in the state of nature; these decisions mark off the distinction between use and charity, and collectively they come to "natural liberty."

At the same time that one has a duty to beneficence, however, one also has a desire for security and even for some degree of luxury. Moreover, while one may be fortunately sated in one regard, one may be wanting in another. In short, life in the state of nature is one of benevolence and selfishness, of rights and duties, and of abundance and want. Such a life is unsatisfying without an opportunity and sufficient desire for beneficence, just as it is threatened by excessive want. Some mechanism is required for regularizing beneficence and fulfilling want, an agency that collects from abundance and satisfies need—fairly and equitably. Thereby arises the state, a "moral person" to whom individuals transfer their perfect rights over selected property and which converts imperfect into perfect rights over needed goods. In other words, the state is given a fixed amount of everyone's natural liberty and distributes fairly civil liberties. While Mendelssohn does not explicitly mention it, the state is created by an interpersonal contract and is given its authority to organize and sanction its collections and redistributive policies by individual contracts between it and the several citizens.[12]

In the domain of actions, then, the state has authority to demand adherence and coerce conformity—as long as the actions in question fall within the state's purposes and prerogatives. Notice, however, that according to Mendelssohn the state only arises because individuals are plagued by natural liberty, abundance, and want. It is only because individuals in the state of nature have conflicting interests—only because you may need and want what I have and vice versa—that the state arises via contract, a transfer of natural liberty from its only source, the individual, to the civil agency. Where no such conflict of interests exists, there is no need and hence no justification for a transfer of natural liberty, a transfer of authority to dispose of property. When the agents are human beings, such a conflict exists, but when they are man and God, Mendelssohn argues, it does not. God and man both want the same thing, human felicity; God wants worship and reverence but only as a vehicle to human happiness and as a constituent of it. Where no conflict exists, no contract is possible, and where there is no contract, there is no transfer of authority. Hence, the church is unlike the state; it cannot demand or coerce conformity of conduct. Its role is to encourage, persuade, stimulate, and console but never to force. Human felicity is a function of virtue, and the latter requires right action performed for right reasons. In order to enable benevolence and guarantee the satisfaction of basic human needs, the state must have the authority to demand and enforce adherence. But ecclesiastical institutions desire more than conformity; they desire virtue and so can only persuade and never coerce.

It stands to reason, then, that the church cannot force conformity of belief, since virtue requires right intention and a good will. But because the right to believe is inalienable and indispensable, it cannot be transferred under any conditions, as little to the state as to the church. One can transfer only one's natural liberty and then only when the capacity or product involved is dispensable. Some capacities or products are inalienable because intrinsic to one's life itself; others, like belief, are inalienable because of what they are. Indeed, one can be coerced to utter a statement, but not to believe it. Believing is intrinsically autonomous.

The results of Part One of *Jerusalem* are clear: neither the state nor the church can demand conformity of belief, and the church has no coercive authority at all. Its role is to support and supplement the state by encouraging right conduct and consoling the guilty. The church is a therapeutic and educational institution the primary goal of which is human felicity.[13]

Mendelssohn, in Part Two of *Jerusalem*, turns to a defense of the particularity of Jewish existence. In order to answer the Searcher, he must show what role coercion has played in Jewish life and how Judaism maintains its integrity and its goals when stripped of the authority to enforce conformity of practice and belief. In short, Mendelssohn must try to show how the account of church and state just given does not destroy Judaism.

What are the elements of original or pristine Judaism, of that Mosaic constitution within which Jewish religious and civil life were uniquely interwoven?[14] Mendelssohn distinguishes eternal from historical truths and the modes of justification appropriate to them. All men, Jews included, have the rational and observational capacities to grasp and verify necessary and eternal truths, such as the truths of logic and geometry, and contingent eternal truths, such as the laws of natural processes. Historical truths, however, depend upon witnesses and the veracity and authority of their testimony. In the biblical text, the trustworthiness of such witnesses is signaled by the performance of miracles; Mendelssohn follows Hobbes and Spinoza in this regard.[15] Original Judaism includes all of these truths and more. Universal providence provides all mankind with the capacity for gaining knowledge of eternal truths, *a priori* truths, laws of nature and those metaphysical truths regarding God, providence, and the afterlife without which human felicity is unattainable. In addition, all men can know the principles of right conduct and have an overriding desire for individual and collective happiness. Particular providence, through the biblical revelation, adds the remaining ingredients, those that distinguish the Jewish people from all others. It conveys, on the one hand, the ceremonial law, and, on the other, the historical record that supports that law, together with the witnesses who transmit Jewish history and the miracles that confirm their authority. As Mendelssohn succinctly puts it, original Judaism includes three components: eternal truths, revealed legislation (i.e., the ceremonial law), and historical truths.

Mendelssohn draws two conclusions: first, that the coincidence of religious and civil authority in the Mosaic constitution is *sui generis* and hence that the relation between civil sanctions and ritual law is contingent, indeed accidental; the ceremonial law is not coerced except under these unique circumstances. Second, that the real authority for the ritual law derives from another quarter altogether, from its role vis-à-vis the attainment of moral virtue and human felicity. The details of Mendelssohn's argument are not here as relevant as is its conclusion, that ritual conduct provides a needed opportunity or stimulus for reflecting upon and indeed recalling those eternal truths—about God, His providence, and the afterlife—without which human happiness cannot be got.[16] The authority of the ritual law, and hence the ground for Jewish particularity, is derivative, an instrumental corollary to the moral goals of natural religion.

Once Mendelssohn has reconciled the original authority of the ritual law with the sanctions incorporated in the Mosaic constitution and with his own rejection of ecclesiastical excommunication, he can turn to the Searcher's further query: why remain faithful to ceremonial conduct stripped of its original sanction? In a sense, Mendelssohn has already proffered his trump—the role of ceremonial conduct as "a living kind of script" stimulating the mind to reflection on the eternal verities that enable the attainment of virtue and happiness. In effect, however, he acknowledges the force of that trump. Given its moral role, he says, and its status as revealed legislation, one would be justified in abandoning the ritual law only if the original legislator Himself rescinded it; only such an act could abrogate its original role and render the ceremonial law superfluous. And because no such act of public recantation has occurred, the Jew has no reason to abandon the rites and ceremonies of Judaism. The only legitimate way for a Jew to advocate rational, moral religion is as a Jew.[17]

At a glance Mendelssohn seems to have reconciled his liberal theory of the state with his account of Judaism by subordinating Jewish particularity to what is universally accessible and laudable in all men. If this conclusion were the limits of Mendelssohn's achievement or his failure, our search for a deeper tension will have been unsuccessful. In fact, however, I think that Mendelssohn's *Jerusalem* reveals more than this subordination of religious particularity to moral universality. If we examine the conceptions of the self, of the moral-political-religious individual, that underpin Mendelssohn's two-part discussion, we shall find not subordination but rather our deep dissonance exposed with precision and stark contrast.

Mendelssohn's conceptions of the self will be more easily identified if we have in hand a model classification to guide us. Such a classification can be extracted from Michael Sandel's very illuminating critique of John Rawls's theory of liberal democracy, *Liberalism and the Limits of Justice*.[18] Sandel wants to show that Rawls's theory of justice, as a deontological ethic and a theory of just political institutions, can be fairly treated and then criticized as a philosophical anthropology. My interest is not with the success or failure of Sandel's endeavor but with the tools he employs. In the course of his critique, Sandel identifies several conceptions of the self, two that support aspects of Rawls's theory and others that are excluded by his theory. By recognizing these conceptions, we can equip ourselves to return to *Jerusalem* and explore the philosophical anthropology contained in that work.

At the poles of selfhood Sandel finds the radically situated self,[19] who *is* his situation—his traits, capacities, desires, attachments, and so on—to such a total degree that such a self lacks continuity of any kind, and the radically disembodied self, who *is* a continuous possessor of all that one can ascribe or associate with it.[20] The former is in constant flux; the latter is contentless, without shape or form. In a sense, the former is a Sartrian "self," all form and no matter, while the latter is a descendant of *prima materia,* without character or qualification, a pure *that* with no what about it. For Sandel, the interesting cases range between these two poles, cases that all involve a distinguishable self that *is* something and yet *has* many traits, characteristics, and relationships. The Rawlsian or deontological self, for example, is a possessor of its capacities and ends, a member of a plurality of selves already shaped and individuated prior to their choices of ends and expressions of capacities. To be sure, such deontological or "lean" selves have needs, desires, and so on, but they are individuated prior to any specification of the latter, and they have no overarching goals and desires in common. Somewhat more robust, then, are the universally constituted selves, with varying short-range desires, needs, or wants and distinguishing capacities but with a shared overarching goal or set of goals that in part constitutes their identity and character. Whereas the lean selves attain or complete their selfhood by choosing their ends, the more robust selves do so by self-reflection, which reveals their simple, overarching common end, for example the welfare of all humankind.[21] For the former, self-identity is a voluntaristic matter, while for the latter it is cognitive and reflective.

To this classification Sandel adds one further variety of the self, the one that he himself favors and the one least well served by Rawls's theory. It might well be called the communally constituted self, an individual that *is* and not merely *has* its relationships to a special group, family, clan, or nation, a self with character and history, whose very identity is already shaped and constituted by its relationships, attachments, commitments, and memory. This sort of self, unlike the others, comes to understand what it is not by reflecting on its ends and those that extend to all mankind. Rather, it discovers who it is by reflection on its attachments, its memory, its allegiances, and all that contributes to its place in a fabric of specific, not wholly generalized, community.[22]

With these conceptions of the self in mind, let us return to *Jerusalem*. What kind of individual inhabits Mendelssohn's liberal state? It is, to be sure, not so lean as Rawls's or even Hobbes's individual. For both, the self is individuated dramatically and comes together for largely prudential reasons. Mendelssohn's individuals, in contrast, have as constitutive of who they are natural duties, rights, and liberties as well as common cognitive capacities, the rational and observational capacities to attain knowledge of eternal truths, moral, metaphysical, and physical. Mendelssohn's individuals are paradigmatically universally constituted, with common abilities, obligations, and overarching goals—individual and social well-being. All have the same rights and duties, perfect and imperfect; all have natural liberty and natural property; all are capable of making contracts and are bound to honor them; all have rational capabilities. Sartre called the liberal democratic self "an ensemble of universal traits"; Mendelssohn's political theory requires such a self, as long as one recognizes a substratum for those traits and ends together with the traits and ends themselves.[23]

This account is rather uncontroversial and unsurprising. The universal self of Mendelssohn's liberal political theory is what one would expect from a contract *cum* natural law theorist. It is indeed what one expects and gets from Locke. Our sketch begins in Part One of *Jerusalem* and borrows elements from Part Two, but our use of Part Two is harmless. No one would deny that the rational and perceptual capacities mentioned in Part Two and associated there with pristine Judaism are also constitutive of all individuals in the state of nature.

As we turn directly to Part Two, however, we realize at once that these universal, rational capabilities are not sufficient to characterize the individual Jew. Such a self is more than a rational and morally directed person; he is a member of a covenanted people, the recipients of particular as well as general providence whose round of life and historical memory, while relevant to moral virtue and human felicity, are interwoven with ritual and ceremonial conduct. In other terms, the Jewish self not merely *has* certain customs and habits, a certain set of affiliations and loyalties and attachments; it *is* that network of communal relationships.

Is this particular providence and the communally constituted self already present in the state of nature? Is it relevant to ask whether such a self would choose a liberal state? Is communal role a supplement to universality, or an alternative to it? There is reason to think that Mendelssohn wanted it both ways, I believe, and therein lies the deep dissonance in his work.

The Mosaic constitution of Part Two is *sui generis*; it occurred once and will never occur again. And just as the state of nature in Part One precedes and fixes the conditions for civil and religious society, so the Mosaic constitution of Part Two precedes and sets the conditions for the separation and cooperation of Jewish society and the state. The Mosaic constitution and the state of nature are analogues at least and possibly more than analogues. Mendelssohn, in Part One, shows how church and state are related, how they complement each other and how they differ. What he does not address is the temporal relationship between the establishment of one and that of the other. Part One ignores history. But Part Two is thoroughly historical, which enables us to ask: is the state prior to, contemporary with, or subsequent to the establishment of the church?

The Mosaic constitution is an ideal state but not *the* ideal. Its relationship to *the* ideal state, one that governs by education and not legislation, is similar to the relationship between the states outlined in Plato's *Laws* and in his *Republic*. The latter is ruled by men and governed through education; the former is ruled by laws and governed through sanctions. The civil state as a state of law arises when the philosopher cannot succeed. Mendelssohn, in the tradition of Maimonides, identifies prophecy of the highest degree, rational prophecy, with philosophy. And prophecy is a matter of both universal and particular providence. Prior to the civil state, then, both kinds of providence occur, which is to say that while some selves are universal, rational persons, others are constituted by communal loyalty, group duties, and specific historical memory.

Another way of seeing this point is to ask why the ceremonial law is binding for the Jew living in 1783. The answer is twofold: because God Himself has not rescinded it and because Jewish ritual still serves to stimulate reflection on and recollection of the essential metaphysical truths. But why, one might ask, is the Jewish people the sole original recipient of the special revelation that dictated these laws? Mendelssohn's answer to this query comes at the very end of *Jerusalem*; it takes the form of an answer to those who advocate the unity of all mankind. Mendelssohn's brief but remarkable response is both an implicit rejoinder to Spinoza[24] and an answer to our question about how original was the particular providence that constituted the Jewish people. "Diversity," he says, "is evidently the plan and purpose of Providence."[25] In other words, communal and religious difference is given; it is natural, indeed as natural as creation and history themselves. We simply cannot know why God separates mankind into groups, clans, and so on; He does, and they are so divided. That is all there is to it. And to defy that separateness, that particularity, is to oppose nature and the God of nature.[26]

One effect of Mendelssohn's final comment is to confirm the hypothesis that special as well as general providence is given in the state of nature. Sinai is a prepolitical event; it occurs in the desert, distant from civilization and civil affairs, and it precedes the establishment of the biblical monarchy. The covenant precedes the contract, and hence the communally constituted self vies with the universal self for prominence in Mendelssohn's political thought.

The tension between the two selves can be exposed by asking whether the communally constituted self would necessarily have chosen Mendelssohn's liberal state. Would such a self's overarching desires have resulted in a state that protects perfect rights, enables benevolence, and ensures against want? The key word here is "necessarily." Surely Mendelssohn's communally constituted self would have chosen a state that acknowledges the self's identity and allows it to flourish, and in the nature of the case, each self must expect that of all others. A state that acknowledges communal identities must recognize too the principle of communal identification. The result of the contract among such selves might be very much like Mendelssohn's state. But what is more likely to emerge than a state that ignores communal identification is a confederation of semiautonomous communities that respects the rights of all individuals and yet works to facilitate the flourishing of all communities. Mendelssohn's state is an individualism; this state would be a communal-pluralism.[27]

There are, then, two types of selves lurking in *Jerusalem*, and while they may learn to live with each other, they must compromise to do so. The liberal self must efface the rich tapestry of community and history that brings that self to life. The communal self must allow permanent, general goals to take precedence over its special hopes and allegiances. Neither self can remain coherent and whole. Nor is this compromise so easily negotiated, for it is wise to recall that the two selves are in fact one and that accommodation is a mere euphemism for inner conflict.

Thus far I have argued that Mendelssohn's *Jerusalem* harbors a serious internal incompatibility, for in it Mendelssohn is committed to two conceptions of the self that resist and compete with each other. But it is possible that I have been unfair to Mendelssohn and that he does incorporate these two conceptions of the self but not with the negative results I have claimed. Rather, it is possible that the conceptions of the ideal or good life associated with these two selves are compatible and do not clash. Such an objection to my argument might proceed in the following way.

Charles Larmore, in a recent discussion of liberalism,[28] develops a dichotomy that will be useful to us. Larmore distinguishes two models for the relationship between the state and the moral theories or conceptions of the good life advocated by its members. One model, political expressivism, treats the state and its political theory as mirroring or reflecting a particular conception of the good life. On this view, then, political theory is also moral theory, and the good precedes the right. There is continuity between citizenship and moral perfectability, for the state is a, indeed *the* primary institutional arrangement for facilitating a particular conception of ideal selfhood. Larmore finds this view in Kant but also, and more important, in Herder, Hegel, and recent communitarians like Taylor and Sandel.

But, Larmore claims, there is a second and, in his eyes, more acceptable form of liberalism that incorporates a second model of the state's relation to the various conceptions of the good life held by its citizens. On this second view, the *modus vivendi* model, the state is organized according to principles and decisions made by citizens who disagree about their ideal conceptions of the good life but seek agreement out of a sense of neutrality and equal respect. Here the state, the liberal state, expresses no single conception of the good but facilitates them all. It is, in short, neutral with respect to ideals of selfhood. Here political theory is *political* but not moral, and the right functions independently of the good.[29] The liberal state promotes no particular conception of the good because it thinks that conception to be superior; it protects a pluralism of such views by adhering to an ideal of neutrality and tolerance. Indeed, Larmore finds this *modus vivendi* view of liberalism already present in the sixteenth and seventeenth centuries, "in the toleration theories of Bodin, Locke, and Bayle, for whom the supreme importance of religion is compatible with the fact that the state should aim at civil peace rather than salvation."[30] And the work of Locke's to which Larmore refers is *A Letter Concerning Toleration*, the very work of Locke's to which Mendelssohn had access and to which he himself refers in the first part of *Jerusalem*.

We can, then, appropriate Larmore's distinction between political expressivism and the *modus vivendi* view in such a way that the two conceptions of the self that we have identified in *Jerusalem* can be shown to coexist rather than conflict. If Mendelssohn adopted the *modus vivendi* view of liberalism from Locke's *Letter*, then it is possible that the universal self is a political conception, corresponding to Larmore's facilitator liberal state that is neutral with respect to substantive conceptions of the good life. The universal self is the citizen, tolerant of all conceptions of moral-religious ideals. The universal self is a *thin* self, with just enough content to advocate public institutions aimed at peace and tranquility but no more. The *thick* selves, those of Jews and others, are protected by the state but not essential to political principle. In short, if Mendelssohn divides political from moral-religious liberalism, then we can save him from inconsistency—and, so this objection would go, his appropriation of a Lockian view of tolerance suggests that he did.

Even if we were to admit, what Larmore suggests, that Locke's *Letter* does express the *modus vivendi* view of the liberal state, Mendelssohn's Lockian association does not prove that he completely separated the moral-religious from the political. And while Part One of *Jerusalem* shows clearly that for certain purposes and in certain ways church and state must be distinguished, it just as clearly shows that for other purposes they must not be. In Part One, Mendelssohn argues that the circumstances that give rise to religion and hence the nature of the contract involved distinguish it, the church, from the state. The matter turns on the authority and scope of legislation determined to restrict action. But the objection just raised concerns not the type of authority the two have but rather whether political and moral-religious goals are the same. It is a matter of whether the moral-religious conception of the good life and hence its conception of ideal selfhood are or are not *expressed* at the political level. Is the liberal self, to put it differently, pervasive? Does liberalism pervade Mendelssohn's view from top to bottom? If so, then at some level the two conceptions of the ideal self, the universal and the communal, will conflict. They will conflict in the Jew, who is expected to be distinctively Jewish and at the same time universally liberal. They will conflict, that is, because the liberal state is expected to be tolerant of the Jew and indeed of all unharmful diversity of conceptions of the good life, while at the same time expressing and advocating one such conception as superior to the rest.

When put this way, the question about political theory and moral-religious ideals in *Jerusalem* finds a direct answer. For in Part One Mendelssohn leaves no doubt that while church and state do have different characters, they also have something in common, the moral virtue and perfection of all. That is, for Mendelssohn the state is not neutral with respect to the various conceptions of the good life held by its citizens. One such conception, that of rational or natural religion, is privileged. It is the theory that gives an account of how the state arises and what it should be like, and it is a moral view that the political organization is intended to advance and reflect. Mendelssohn puts it this way: human beings

> enter into society with those in a like situation in order to satisfy their needs through mutual aid and to promote their common good by common measures. Their common good, however, includes the present as well as the future, the spiritual as well as the earthly. One is inseparable from the other. Unless we fulfill our obligations, we can expect felicity neither here nor there, neither on earth nor in heaven. Now, two things belong to the true fulfillment of our duties: *action* and *conviction*. . . . and society should, as far as possible, take care of both by collective efforts, that is, it should direct the actions of its members toward the common good, and cause convictions which lead to these actions. The one is the *government*, the other the *education* of societal man. . . . Society should therefore establish both through public institutions in such a way that they will be in accord with the common good.[31]

Mendelssohn, then, like Kant, was indeed a political expressivist, to use Larmore's term, and hence his conception of the communal self is independent of but also subordinate to the liberal, universal ideal.

What this means, moreover, is that Mendelssohn's view of tolerance must be distinguished from the version that Larmore finds in Locke. Larmore's conception is that political liberalism is tolerant of all conceptions of the good because it is neutral with respect to them and because it is constructed and functions in terms of an equal respect for all. To be sure, there are times when political liberalism is intolerant and even rejects a certain conception of the ideal life, as in Locke's rejection of atheism, for example, but this is only because the conception in question threatens the state's ability to perform what are largely minimal tasks. But as the state's tasks become maximal, advocating one conception of human flourishing, one good, then more conceptions of the good will be ruled out as adversaries, as inferior and inhibiting to the state's final goal. Mendelssohn's view of tolerance must be torn by his two conceptions of the self. Based on his political expressivism, he ought to expect tolerance of Jews as men but not Jews as Jews, to recall Sartre's indictment of the liberal democrat. That he does not, that he seems to want tolerance for a distinctive Jewishness, communally defined, is just another sign of the weakness we have been trying to identify.[32]

In the end, then, Larmore's dichotomy and the *modus vivendi* view of political theory *could* but *do not* save Mendelssohn. But perhaps there is greater nobility in his unresolved struggle, for there are strong reasons for advocating political expressivism and continuity between the state and the conceptions of the good which its citizens endorse. Liberalism is, for Mendelssohn, both a political and a moral-religious theory. He wants the two selves that he located to be independent and subordinate, but of course they cannot be both. Mendelssohn cannot bring himself to separate political citizenship from his conception of the ideal self. Ultimately, then, *Jerusalem*, for all its grand goals, is a flawed work, and I have tried to show one way in which its flaws can be understood.

FOUR

# The Curse of Historicity

## The Role of History in Leo Strauss's Jewish Thought

A fundamental problem for modern religious thought is to understand the relationship between religious truths or beliefs and history. In what sense, if any, are the meanings of religious beliefs subject to historical determination and alteration? And, once the question of meaning is settled, is the truth of religious conviction open to historical falsification, confirmation, or modification? Indeed, to what degree must these very questions themselves be understood as the result of our own historical situation? What *is* that situation? Is there in fact *just one* such situation that we all share?

Modern Jewish thinkers seem rarely to appreciate this bundle of issues, and yet any serious and fruitful reflection on the nature of contemporary religious experience and purpose can hardly afford to neglect them. For this reason, if for no other, I have come to treat the political philosopher Leo Strauss as one of the most profound Jewish thinkers of our day. Vigorous opponent of historicism, Strauss was thoroughly sensitive to the role that history can play both in life and in thought. And in one remarkable essay he displays that sensitivity in a classic defense of Jewish orthodoxy in the modern world.[1] Although I disagree with its conclusions and am not persuaded by its subtle argument, I am convinced that Strauss's essay is a little-regarded masterpiece of Jewish self-reflection after the Holocaust.

The essay I am referring to was written in the early 1960s and was published as the preface to the English translation of Strauss's book *Spinoza's Critique of Religion*. Ostensibly it is a piece of intellectual autobiography that swings back and forth from the 1920s to the 1960s in order to explain why Strauss had chosen to write a book about Spinoza and his critique of religion.[2] Implicitly it is a precisely argued defense of the following thesis: For a modern Jew who has come to realize that liberal democracy can offer no sanctuary, no home for the Jew, and who for this reason seeks a return to Judaism, the only path open to him and compatible with intellectual probity is to return to Jewish orthodoxy. But this path is available only if Spinoza is wrong in his critique of religious (and particularly Jewish) orthodoxy.[3] This is a complex thesis, and Strauss must argue for each component of it. He must show that the modern Jew who is searching for a place in the modern world is confronted with two complementary problems. The political problem is that there is no place for him in that world. The best political-social constitution, liberal democracy, cannot provide a genuine home for him nor can a separate national state solve the problem of Jewish homelessness. Hence, pressed by historical circumstance and political trauma, the modern Jew turns back to Judaism and is confronted with a second problem, the religious or intellectual problem. For, as he returns to Judaism, the modern Jew comes to realize that only orthodoxy is compatible with "intellectual probity" and then only if it has not been decisively refuted. But the most complete and penetrating attack on orthodoxy or traditional, revealed religion is that of Spinoza. Hence, while there is no genuine solution to the Jew's political dilemma,[4] there is a solution to the religious problem: to refute Spinoza and return to Jewish orthodoxy. To prove this thesis, then, is the task of Strauss's essay.

In 1670 Baruch Spinoza, after five years of labor, anonymously published his *Tractatus Theologico-Politicus*. Its purpose is to plead the case for freedom of thought and speech both against a superstitious religious establishment and against a faulty view of political constitution.[5] Both religion properly conceived and liberal democracy, the best kind of state, ought to acknowledge these freedoms. For one who reads the *Tractatus* with one eye and Spinoza's *Ethica* with the other, the purpose of the former is transparent: to convince the nonbeliever to respect, if not demand, the freedom of the true philosopher. Spinoza, caught in the predicament of a philosopher despised by adherents of vulgar religion and by politicians alike, seeks a way out. Both problems are soluble; both vulgar religion and liberal democracy ought to make room for the freedom of philosophy.[6]

In 1965, nearly three hundred years later, Leo Strauss begins his apologia with this sentence: "This study on Spinoza's *Theologico-political Treatise* was written during the years 1925–28 in Germany. The author was a young Jew born and raised in Germany who found himself in the grip of the theologico-political predicament."[7] Spinoza's *Treatise* is written by a philosopher, a man in general, caught in a predicament that can only be solved by showing how religion and the state are compatible with philosophy and may even in fact require philosophy. Strauss's book is written by a Jew in collapsing Weimar Germany, and because he is a Jew in particular and not a man in general, his predicament is different. Spinoza's predicament is static: How can the philosopher live alongside religion and the state? Strauss's predicament is dynamic: What happens to the Jew who leaves the traditional religion of his fathers to live in the modern world? What disillusionment sends him returning to Judaism? And what Judaism remains for him to return to?

Strauss's theologico-political predicament is the plight of all those Jews who chose the liberal alternative of entrance into the modern world and accommodation to it only to find themselves at sea. But is it really a predicament? And if it is, what makes it both a religious and a political or social one?

Modern society can be repressive and despotic in its treatment of the Jews, and even its occasional hospitality is sharply restrained. Of all the possible regimes, from tyrannies to monarchies to more liberal forms of government, surely the most attractive is the liberal democracy, the standard-bearer of freedom, justice, and equality. If ever Judaism can be at home in the modern world, it would be in such a state.[8] Hence, if the Jew is shown to be homeless even here, then we are justified in concluding that Judaism is incompatible with every political constitution in the modern world. In a sense, if Strauss can show Judaism to be in the grip of an insoluble political or social problem, he will have shown history itself to contain an irresolvable paradox.[9] The result for the modern Jew would be a twofold choice, either to ignore that paradox by continually trying to solve the insoluble or to endure it by returning with vigor and devotion to the orthodoxy of his fathers. This is the first stage of the predicament: Is Judaism homeless even in a liberal democracy? And does this homelessness demand blind indignation, or heroic return? Are there other alternatives? Or are these the necessary limits of the Jewish condition?

Strauss's argument for the homelessness of the modern Jew in liberal democracies is brief and a priori.[10] There is no chance, he claims, that the Jew can be accepted fully even in the most hospitable form of society. For a liberal democracy separates religious from political or civil authority and then stands or falls on the radical division between private and public domains for them. The state and its laws reach only so far into the individual's life, and where the law finds its limit, there the boundary between privacy and public welfare is drawn. The law can forbid injury, slander, evil speech, and evil acts; the law can prohibit overt persecution and publicly expressed hate. But because it guards individual freedom of thought, belief, and conviction, the law is impotent to prohibit individual, private hate. In a liberal democracy, antisemitism is a protected freedom.[11] Hence, according to the very structure of the liberal democracy, coupled with the power of a non-Jewish majority jealous of its privileges and prerogatives, Jews are expected to shed their heritage but without any real chance to become exactly like everyone else.

Is Jewish homelessness a permanent enigma of history? Yes, but only if there is no solution to the political problem of the Jew in the modern world. But, Strauss suggests, surely many have thought that there is such a solution. While it may be true that in a world of majority favor and antisemitic feelings Jews as individuals cannot in principle become like everyone else, why cannot the Jews as a whole—as a people—become like other peoples? Would not this "normalization" bring with it the desired equality and respect? From its very beginnings political Zionism was built on the realization that the state is not neutral with respect to religion, and that the key to who belongs and who does not is power. Hence, political Zionism was convinced that in order to find a home in the modern world Jews must build that home; the only way to solve the Jewish problem and to bring to Jews the equality, dignity, and honor they crave is to create a Jewish nation like other nations. Strauss speaks with utter respect of the deepest meaning of political Zionism. "Strictly speaking," he says, it "was the movement of an elite on behalf of a community constituted by common descent and common degradation, for the restoration of their honor through the acquisition of statehood and therefore of a country—of any country. . . . "[12] Hence, political Zionism confronted the Jewish problem of homelessness as a human problem and set out to solve it, for human problems can be solved by human hands.

Political Zionism led to the establishment of the modern state of Israel. Strauss allows himself a moving tribute; aligning itself with "traditional Jewish thought," political Zionism thereby "procured a blessing for all Jews everywhere regardless of whether they admit it or not."[13] But, he reminds us, blessings are not solutions; they are blessings. The predicament remains; the problem of Jewish homelessness is not solved—blessing or no, state or no.

But why? Why is the Jewish state not a solution to the political problem thus far defined? Strauss's argument is oblique. *We* might notice that even if the state provided a home for every Jew it would not solve the problem of the Jew in the modern world. But Strauss does not notice this. *We* might notice that the Jewish state, like any state, has limited power and resources, and hence will be fraught with external dangers and internal strife. But Strauss does not notice this either, or not, at least, explicitly. What he does notice is that the state as a political entity can give people equality and prestige as citizens. But the state can solve the Jewish problem only if it is a Jewish state, and once it acknowledges its Jewish rootedness, it cannot see itself as that solution.

Consider political Zionism as honestly recognizing and acknowledging its own narrowness. The state will solve no Jewish problem unless it is rooted in the Jewish heritage. Hence, political Zionism requires reconciliation with Jewish culture; the truth of political Zionism reveals itself as cultural Zionism. But, Strauss continues, even this recognition is not sufficient to satisfy honest self-examination. For when cultural Zionism truly understands itself, it realizes that the culture it endorses does not see itself as a human creation but rather as a divine gift. When cultural Zionism reaches full self-recognition, then, it turns into religious Zionism. But, Strauss says, religious Zionism is primarily Jewish faith and only secondarily Zionism. What this means is that it is committed to the state but only as it sees that state within the framework of traditional Jewish hopes and expectations. And, according to those hopes, there are no wholly human solutions to the problems of history; the Jewish state is a profoundly important event *in* history, but it does not mark or approximate history's end. The founding of the state, as Strauss puts it, is a "profound modification of the Galut" (exile), but it is not redemptive. In sum, then, the truth of political Zionism reveals itself as its own denial, not as the denial of its achievement but rather as the denial of its own *assessment* of that achievement. When Zionism understands itself, it becomes humble and modest. And its self-understanding suggests the only response left to the modern Jew caught in the grip of this problem of homelessness, in the Galut or in the state of Israel, the only response left to one who desires self-respect and dignity—a return to the religion of his fathers.

The dialectical result of modern Jewish "emancipation," then, is return, or, as Strauss calls it, using the provocative and ambiguous Hebrew term, *teshuvah*.[14] But such *teshuvah*, a return to the religion of the fathers and hence to the God of the fathers, is fraught with risk. And the core of that risk is what Strauss calls again and again "intellectual probity," an honesty of the heart that is at the same time an honesty of the mind. The political problem creates a "vital need," but this need cannot but make peace with intellectual probity. If the core of the religion of the fathers, of traditional Judaism or Jewish orthodoxy, has been refuted by the modern world—by Feuerbach or Marx or Freud, by modern historiography or modern science—then even that vital need cannot be satisfied without rejecting an honest reconciliation with that refutation. And so Strauss sets out to prove that the refutation has not been made.

His defense has four stages. First, he shows that Jewish thought has only inadequately defended Judaism against the attacks of science and scientific historiography. The defense of those such as Hermann Cohen is in fact self-destructive. But, and this is the second stage, while science can explain away the old revelations, it is harmless against the new. Whatever effect theory may have as it coopts the "reports" of ancient revelations, it cannot explain away current experience; rather, it must incorporate such experience with justice and impartiality. This is the essential insight of Buber and Rosenzweig: revelation is a permanent and hence contemporary possibility. To accept the real possibility of such experience, moreover, is to replace an old style of thinking with a new. The return to the orthodoxy of the fathers, then, must be mediated and thereby qualified by the experience of the children. But, as Strauss argues, this qualified return to orthodoxy is itself flawed, and once its flaws are uncovered, it becomes apparent that such a qualified return is itself disqualified. And so finally the return becomes a matter of all or nothing, the only obstacle being Spinoza's attack on all revelation (*simpliciter*), new and old alike. If the attack is persuasive, then the return is blocked; if not, then unqualified *teshuvah* reveals itself as the dialectical truth of Jewish emancipation in the modern world. If Spinoza can be refuted, then Strauss will have demonstrated that while Jews and the Jewish people are forever historical, their essence is forever eternal.

In the course of this four-stage argument, Strauss watches Jewish orthodoxy weather a series of storms. Of these storms, the most revealing for our purposes is the confrontation between Strauss's orthodoxy and Rosenzweig's neoorthodoxy. How does Strauss distinguish between the two and why is the latter not preferable?

Strauss's strategy is to show how Rosenzweig's new thinking replaces an old thinking that either abstracts from the experience of God or excludes it altogether. The new thinking is essentially nonreductionist and so does not run the risks of materialism or idealism. Both forms of the old thinking, when employed to save orthodoxy, are self-destructive; traditional Judaism lives with a God forever distinct from both man and the world. What is miraculous is not that this gap is dissolved but rather that it is bridged in such a way that both poles retain their integrity. Such a bridging is at the heart of the Jewish experience and hence of traditional Judaism.

This line of thinking suggests, however, that Rosenzweig may have simply reaffirmed orthodoxy in the face of weak efforts to defend it against science and historiography. But such is not the case. As Strauss puts it, Rosenzweig's return to orthodoxy is "qualified." Strauss notices four significant differences between traditional Judaism and Rosenzweig's neoorthodoxy and in each case shows the deficiencies in Rosenzweig's account.

First, the two differ in their starting points. Traditional Judaism begins with Torah; the primary experience of the Jew is that of commandment, and the primary reality is conduct oriented by commandment and obligation. According to Rosenzweig, however, the core of Jewish experience is chosenness and peoplehood. Torah is derivative. In reality, Strauss argues, traditional Judaism is correct, for the people is constituted by the Torah and not vice versa. The performing of the commandments and the acceptance of the divine yoke, the Torah as obligatory, are what make this people a particular nation, a *goi kadosh* and *mamlechet cohanim*. There is no people without Torah.

Strauss wonders about Rosenzweig's deviation from what he, Strauss, takes to be the natural and traditional priority of Torah. It is a result, he thinks, of Rosenzweig's desire to identify a starting point for Judaism that corresponds to the role of Jesus as the Christ in Christianity. Both chosenness and Jesus as the Christ serve to particularize the roles of Judaism and Christianity in history, and both become irrelevant at the culmination of history, when the two religions will merge in their common purpose, the Kingdom of God. Hence, in Strauss's view, Rosenzweig's understanding of Judaism and its core is modified as a result of the need to accommodate Judaism to a Christian model. The result is distortion, not only for Judaism but also for Rosenzweig's own principles. The purported "absolute empiricism" begins not with that which is experienced but rather with a necessary presupposition of what is experienced. Orthodoxy turns out to be more empirical than neoorthodoxy.

Here a modest corrective is in order. If indeed all of this were true, then Rosenzweig's treatment of peoplehood and chosenness would surely seem to be inauthentic, a distortion at best, dictated by systematic accommodations. But there is another plausible explanation for Rosenzweig's treatment of Torah and his implicit claim that the experience of chosenness, of being "singled out," is primary—at least logically, though doubtless not temporally.[15] This explanation takes revelation and the experience of it to be the core of Rosenzweig's Judaism, a revelation that amounts to an address, a calling, and one that issues in a hearing that is a responding in part constituted by interpretation and hence articulate Torah. This is no time to elaborate Rosenzweig's account of the nature of revelation and the divine-human encounter. It is sufficient to recall that for him that encounter is at the center of *The Star of Redemption*; it is the center of Judaism, and it is in itself without the content of articulate Torah. Torah is a response and a result, mediation after immediacy. Strauss knows this about Rosenzweig but does not choose here to acknowledge it. If Rosenzweig's account is necessary in order to ward off the modern attacks on revelation,[16] then the fact that Torah is, in some sense, posterior to election is not only justified but also necessary.

Second, traditional Judaism and Rosenzweig's neoorthodoxy differ in the ways they appropriate the Torah (the Bible and the tradition built on it). The Torah of traditional Judaism takes itself to be absolute and unqualified; it is to be appropriated by others as it appropriates itself. Not only does Rosenzweig differ with this view, he does so self-consciously. He realizes from the start that what the biblical author or compiler meant is one thing and what the modern believer understands and appropriates is another. Torah is like a quarry, to be mined according to a principle of individual selection that Rosenzweig calls "inner power" or "force." The materials have a common origin, but the selection procedure is subjective. And the result is that the Torah, which takes itself to be absolute, is radically relativized and historicized. For Rosenzweig there is only one absolute, and that is God. Ways to God, on the other hand, are radically subjective and historical. The route or path to a fixed point is in every case relative to one's starting point; the historical contingency that infects the latter also infects the former. Strauss's conclusion, then, is that Rosenzweig errs by not understanding the Bible as it understands itself.

Third, traditional Judaism and Rosenzweig, orthodoxy and neoorthodoxy, differ in their conception of Torah not only with regard to its content but also in terms of its nature and purpose. Orthodoxy tends to treat Torah as Law and hence as prohibition. Rosenzweig, on the contrary, treats it as liberation. For him, Torah is the result of transforming Law into Commandment, thereby bringing man and God together. There is an optimism in Rosenzweig's view, both about the nature of Torah and about the nature of those who "create" it. Strauss's judgment is brief: "It is not immediately clear, however, whether the orthodox austerity or sternness does not rest on a deeper understanding of the power of evil in man than Rosenzweig's view. . . . "[17] Perceived as a constraint on the human capacity for mutual harm and injustice, law is a necessary device for civilized society. Without it the Hobbesian state of nature would engulf us all. But when law is viewed as constraint and yet man is viewed as naturally benevolent, the need for law is restricted, if not altogether obviated, and its acceptance is given over to human choice. Strauss's oblique allusion to the Nazi extermination of European Jewry warns against such an overly optimistic view of human nature. Indeed, Rosenzweig's failure to estimate or appreciate, if not foresee, the "power of evil in man" infects his system in many ways; Strauss is here noticing but one of them.

Finally, orthodoxy and neoorthodoxy differ about miracles. Rosenzweig was unable to believe in all the biblical miracles or to believe in some of them all of the time. For him, belief was in part a function of one's capacity to believe. But orthodoxy would reprimand him for his doubts; if God was able to create the universe out of nothing, then no scriptural miracle is ruled out. Once again, Rosenzweig's historicism and his subjectivism bring him to read the Bible in a way different from the way it "reads" itself.[18]

Let us suppose that Strauss's four-stage argument against neoorthodoxy and the qualified return to traditional Judaism is compelling. What then is the result? The result is twofold: first, that orthodoxy and neoorthodoxy are not the same and were never intended to be; second, that since neoorthodoxy is flawed, the only way to return to the religion of the fathers, traditional Judaism, is an unqualified way. What is required is an unyielding, unhindered giving over of the self to the power of God and the life of His Torah. This is what is required by historical need and by intellectual probity—if, that is, there exists no final, dramatic refutation of that orthodoxy and the revelation that is central to it. Orthodoxy is right only if Spinoza is wrong.

In the final paragraphs of his essay, Strauss turns to Spinoza: has Spinoza refuted orthodoxy? Strauss answers no.

Spinoza's major systematic work is the *Ethica*. Why not study it to determine whether or not Spinoza has refuted orthodoxy and the notion of revelation necessary to orthodoxy? Because, Strauss says, like any theoretical system, that is, any axiomatic one, the philosophy of the *Ethica* is based on definitions, axioms, and assumptions of all kinds. These are the most basic premises of its demonstrations. But these premises say from the beginning that there is no God, indeed no substance or being, outside of the natural world. Hence, the truth of the premises already implies the impossibility of revelation and thereby the falsity of Jewish orthodoxy.

Strauss's claims about the *Ethica*, however, are not strictly true. The definitions and axioms of Part One in particular do not explicitly say that there is one and only one substance, that that substance is God, and that God and nature are in some sense the same. But in *Ethica* 1, propositions 1–14, Spinoza does purport to prove that there is one and only one substance, that that substance exists necessarily, and that that substance is God, and those propositions are intended to be proven or demonstrated using only the definitions and axioms of Part One. Hence, the conclusions are already in a sense contained in those axioms and definitions at the outset. To accept the axioms and definitions is already to accept what they imply—if one holds, of course, that one is committed to accepting not only one's beliefs but also what is implied by what one believes. In short, then, Strauss is right that to begin with the *Ethica* would be to beg the question against orthodoxy from the start.

The *Tractatus Theologico-Politicus* was written in an interlude during the preparation of the *Ethica*. Yet it does not and indeed cannot presuppose the *Ethica*. This is clear from its purpose, for that purpose is to convince those who believe in revelation, those members of "vulgar religion" whose convictions are burdened by prejudice and superstition, not only that free philosophizing is possible for religion and the state but also that the welfare and security of both may even require it. The *Tractatus* is an *apologia pro philosophica*; it is dialectical,[19] then, and must begin only with premises to which the superstitious believer is willing to assent. If in his treatise Spinoza tried to refute orthodoxy, it is only on the basis of Scripture, traditional authorities, and common sense. Hence, it is at least true that in the *Tractatus* Spinoza does not assume that orthodoxy is false. Whatever arguments he gives to defend the role of philosophy may, for this reason, incorporate an honest attack on revelation. Strauss's task was to see whether or not there is such an attack and whether or not it is persuasive.

Strauss's conclusion is this: Spinoza does not refute orthodoxy. Rather, there is a "moral antagonism" between him and Judaism. Spinoza's system is an alternative to Jewish orthodoxy.[20] To accept or to reject Spinoza's system, indeed to choose one or the other, requires an act of will, a will to believe. Both systems are internally consistent; they satisfy the conditions which they set for consistency and coherence. Hence, Strauss says, orthodoxy survives the critique only by means of the self-destruction of rational philosophy.[21]

For Strauss, a genuine refutation of orthodoxy would require an account of the world and human life that is known to be true. For only then could we infer that any account different from it must be false. But Spinoza's account is hypothetical; it is an account consistent with its own assumptions. These assumptions are not known to be true but only believed to be so, and it is similar for Jewish orthodoxy. Hence, the cognitive status of both is the same. Spinoza cannot deny that revelation is possible. All he can say is that on his assumptions it is impossible. But orthodoxy depends on the assumption that God exists as other than man and the world, and on such an assumption revelation is possible. Spinoza has not refuted the orthodox assumption; rather, he has shown what would happen if one were to reject it. Hence, the choice between Spinoza's naturalism and orthodoxy is not one between what is known and what is merely believed. It is instead a choice between different, competing systems of beliefs. But rational philosophy is based on distinguishing knowledge from belief by giving reasons relevant to the truth of the propositions in question. When all reasons have run out and the choice is then a "moral one," rational philosophical discussion is no longer relevant.[22]

Strauss, writing in the 1960s, is aware that this victory for orthodoxy is not an "unmitigated blessing."[23] For he is keenly aware of the centrality of rationality to the Jewish experience.[24] But it is not necessary here to unravel his final remarks and the hints he gives about his own return to premodern philosophy, especially the political philosophy of the medieval and ancient traditions. We have canvassed the basic contours of his argument, and it is time to reflect on certain of Strauss's own assumptions employed in it. I do not want to ask how successful an argument Strauss has constructed. Its weaknesses should be apparent. What I want to consider instead is the role that history and Strauss's antihistoricism play in his essay. How does Strauss, in his Jewish thinking, bear what Rosenzweig once called "the curse of historicity"?[25]

Strauss ultimately defends Jewish orthodoxy, a life of Torah, of Jewish faith, and the Jewish way of life. The return to this orthodoxy is historically motivated, but it is at the same time an unqualified return. That is, it is a return to a timeless Judaism, a Judaism whose essential nature lies in adherence to Torah and not to working in the world. Strauss's orthodoxy is not decisively transformed by historical events nor does it invest itself in transforming the world and its history. The evidence that this is Strauss's view is, I think, conclusive.

First, let us recall, with Strauss, the motto of Leo Pinsker's *Autoemancipation*, taken from Hillel's famous saying in *Pirke Avot* [The Sayings of the Fathers].[26] "If I am not for myself, who will be for me? And if not now, when?" In quoting Hillel, Pinsker omits the sentence, "And if I am only for myself, what am I?" Strauss comments: "He saw the

Jewish people as a herd without a shepherd to protect and gather it; he did not long for a shepherd, but for the transformation of the herd into a nation that could take care of itself."[27] This view, this exchange of trust in God as the shepherd of his people for a new self-reliance, Strauss calls a "profound modification of traditional Jewish hopes" that is in fact a "break with these hopes." This is a clue to Strauss's own view of Judaism and history. For Pinsker, the Jewish problem is a historical, social problem, and historical problems are human, capable of human solutions. Hence, what is appropriate is not hope for the Messianic coming and for divine redemption but, rather, self-reliant action. For Pinsker and for Herzl, historical problems are humanly soluble; for traditional Judaism—which Strauss ultimately defends—only God can solve these problems. Human effort can never transform history in any decisive way; only divine acts can do so. Small wonder that for Strauss a return to a timeless orthodoxy is the dialectical result of the problematic of emancipation.

This same view of Judaism as essentially ahistorical, without a singular investment in history and historical-political problems, is reflected in Strauss's moving yet restrained tribute to the modern state of Israel. It is, recall, a "blessing for all Jews everywhere regardless of whether they admit it or not."[28] But it is a blessing, not a solution, and one on which the final judgment must be that it is a profound modification of and not the end of the Galut. Israel is the result of self-reliant action taken in the hope of solving the human problem of Jewish homelessness. Grand as it is, however, this hope strikes Strauss as sharply incompatible with traditional Judaism. In support of the incompatibility—at least in support of his own judgment of that incompatibility—Strauss quotes Spinoza's remarkable sentence: "If the foundations of their religion did not effeminate the minds of the Jews, I would absolutely believe that they will at some time, given the occasion (for human things are mutable), establish their state again."[29] What are these "foundations" but the "traditional Jewish hopes" for divine redemption from historical predicament and political woes and the conviction that Jews must ultimately rely only on God and not on themselves.[30]

Strauss wrote his essay in the early 1960s, in a Jewish world defined by the twin realities of Auschwitz and the rebirth of the Jewish state. Yet neither of these events seems to influence how he, in the 1960s, views the theologico-political predicament which "gripped" him in the waning days of Weimar. There is, however, good reason to think that they should have.

We can approach this problem of historical interpretation and personal reflection only obliquely, via Strauss's critique of Rosenzweig's neoorthodoxy. The underlying theme of all four stages of that critique is the same: Rosenzweig's historicism infects his account of Judaism throughout and distorts it. Why does Rosenzweig's neoorthodoxy find a starting point at odds with the self-conscious starting point of Jewish experience? Why does it understand the Bible only relative to individual need and capacity? Why does it relativize miracles to its own cognitive capabilities? It does all of these things because it is controlled by its situatedness in history—by the needs, desires, and overall world of each "returning" Jewish individual. In all these ways Strauss judges that the "curse of historicity" sabotages the qualified return to Jewish tradition.

Furthermore, just as in his critique of political or secular Zionism, Strauss acknowledges the rebirth of the Jewish state only to mitigate its historical importance and role, so here, in his criticism of Rosenzweig, Strauss calls on the reality of Auschwitz—though obliquely, to be sure—only to ignore its potential impact on the very thesis he is defending. Why, he asks, is Rosenzweig's positive, optimistic understanding of Torah and Commandment less satisfactory than the traditional view? Because it appreciates too little the "power of evil in man." But while Rosenzweig may be overly optimistic about human capacity, is Jewish orthodoxy and traditional Jewish hope not overly optimistic about God? Strauss feels free, in 1965, to use the evidence of Auschwitz and Israel to defend a timeless, ahistorical Judaism that is unchanged since the 1920s. At the same time, however, he is reluctant to use the same evidence to criticize the same Jewish orthodoxy of the 1960s.

Rosenzweig once characterized his view of Judaism as an eternal people and the account of Jewish life appropriate to that life of eternity in time as a "hygiene of return." In a slightly different sense, Strauss's essay also provides in part a hygiene or strategy for returning to Judaism. And although the return Strauss conceives differs significantly from Rosenzweig's, they do have this in common: both ultimately view Judaism as uninvolved in any essential way in solving the problems of historical, political life. And yet, one wonders whether Rosenzweig would have altered his ahistorical conception of Judaism if he had experienced the rise of Hitler, the extermination of his Jewish world and the world of eastern European Jewry, which he loved and admired, and finally the rebirth of the Jewish state.

About Strauss we need not wonder. He wrote in the 1960s about a theologico-political predicament that had led him, forty years before, to seek a return to Jewish orthodoxy in a way that satisfied his sense of intellectual honesty. And there is little doubt that for him the orthodoxy of the 1920s is still the orthodoxy of the 1960s.

The core of Strauss's thoughts about Judaism and its modern predicament is the conviction that the truth of history lies outside of history, and this conviction is best expressed by Strauss's conclusions that the political problem of the Jew in the modern world is humanly insoluble and that its proper outcome is a return to—not a reappropriation of, but rather a "going back to"—a timeless Judaism. It is no surprise, then, that

Auschwitz and Jerusalem move the heart but not the mind. Openness to the impact of these events, however, suggests a revision in Strauss's conclusions, a revision that is of tremendous significance.

Let us imagine Strauss, in 1965, faced once again with the option of return and hence with the need to prepare a new study of Spinoza's critique of orthodoxy. Once again he turns to ponder that remarkable passage in which Spinoza foresees a renewal of Jewish national autonomy, a rebirth that would occur only if the foundations of Judaism were to cease to emasculate the minds of the Jews. How might Auschwitz and Jerusalem alter his reading of that passage?

Strauss's theologico-political predicament of the 1920s was the result of a dialectical interplay between two problems, Jewish homelessness in the modern world and a modern intellectual critique of revelation. One of these he takes to be insoluble, driving the modern Jew to the other problem, one that can be solved. What, in forty years, has changed about these problems? How have the trauma and triumph of history transformed them and the way they must be understood?

To begin, each dimension of the predicament helps to expose for defense and for criticism a variety of Jewish alternatives, from an emancipated liberalism to a traditional orthodoxy. But surely these sharp divisions among a religious orthodoxy, a secular Zionism, and a historicist neoorthodoxy, for example, no longer dominate our thinking now as they did Strauss's in the 1920s. Nor should they. For after Auschwitz and the rebirth of the Jewish state, can there be a traditional Jewish hope that stays unflinchingly with an abiding trust in God's power? And after these events, can there be a secular Zionism that does not see itself just as devoted to religious purposes as it is moved by secular self-confidence?[31]

Auschwitz and Jerusalem, then, have weakened the sharp contrasts that run through Strauss's argument; they have bound together the secular or political and the religious or theological into a new unity. The result for the modern Jew is that the dialectic between historical contradictions, secular freedom, and self-confidence, on the one hand, and religious purposes, hope, and trust, on the other, has dramatically changed. For Strauss this dialectic involves two temporal stages, where the second is the negation of—because a reconciliation with—the first. For the Jew of today, in contrast, the dialectic involves a simultaneous tension, where each pole, the religious and the secular, supports and yet, at the same time, strains against the other. In place of an either-or, we have a both-and. The truth of history lies not outside of history but rather within it; the theologico-political predicament of the modern Jew leads not away from but rather into the world.

But why has history had this effect on the predicament Strauss describes? Why has a two-stage development become a permanent, simultaneous dialectical tension? The answer concerns that feature of "traditional Jewish hopes," and hence of Jewish orthodoxy, that Strauss returns to again and again. Why is it that "finite, relative problems can be solved: infinite, absolute problems cannot be solved"? Why is it that "human beings will never create a society which is free of contradictions"? Why is it that "the foundations of [the Jewish] religion . . . effeminate[s] the minds of the Jews"? Strauss criticizes Rosenzweig's optimistic view of Law as liberating, renewing Commandment. Such a view, he says, is too little aware of and sensitive to the genuine capabilities of human beings. "The orthodox austerity or sternness . . . rest[s] on a deeper understanding of the power of evil in man."[32] That deeper understanding has two aspects. First, orthodoxy realizes that radical evil is possible and hence that man needs constraints in order to live in peace and security.[33] Second, it realizes that the power of evil is permanent in history, that evil is as much a part of human nature as is goodness, and hence that human nature alone is incapable of eradicating pain and suffering, thereby perfecting life in history and in the world. Absolute problems require absolute solutions; in the end, Jewish orthodoxy is based on an abiding trust in God, His compassion and love and saving power. There is an openness to the reality of Auschwitz here that is profound and deep, but it is an openness at one level that becomes an escape at another.

To Spinoza this abiding trust in God emasculates the minds of Jews. To Strauss it represents a profound recognition of the limits of human nature, of human finitude; it is, for him, a necessary article of the Jewish faith, immune to change, immune to historical modification or refutation. But it is an article of faith with two parts. Need the conviction in one require the conviction in the other? It is as least possible to believe that events in our day, while they confirm the reality of evil and caution against any easy optimism, at the same time call this abiding trust into question. Consequently, once Jews everywhere accept ultimate responsibility for the survival and future of Judaism and the Jewish people, then the problem of Jewish homelessness requires not flight but rather political action. And it is an action authorized by need and not by blind overconfidence until a renewed trust can overcome the realistic fears of the Jewish people. In this way, the modern Jew comes to live with both the political and the religious problems at once; this is his theologico-political predicament.

Clearly Strauss recognizes the subtle ways in which history and thought interact. It is a theme, if not *the* theme, of his entire intellectual corpus. And that recognition is apparent here, in the essay we have been studying. It is a profound reflection on the Jewish situation in the modern world, one that is moved by history to transcend it, in ways that show Strauss's deep sensitivity to the interplay between history and Judaism, time and eternity, life and thought. But this transcendence, wrought out of a keen awareness of the evils of radical historicism, may today be an unwarranted indulgence. Though Strauss would surely demur, for some the curse of historicity has today become a Jewish necessity, if not—dare we utter the word—a blessing. Surely Strauss would have to agree that while curses and blessings can be avoided and rejected, all one can do with a necessity is to endure it or perhaps even appropriate it with resignation if not with joy.

FIVE

# Leo Strauss and the Possibility of Jewish Philosophy

Regarding Judaism, Leo Strauss argues that in the modern world only orthodoxy retains its integrity and can be defended. But our understanding of the human condition and modernity is philosophical and political. Hence, should not our general response to the contemporary situation be guided by an understanding that is both Jewish and philosophical? It should, but only if Judaism and philosophy are compatible. According to Strauss, however, they are not.

## STRAUSS'S JEWISH THOUGHT

In his impressive reflection on Strauss's life and thinking, Allan Bloom has said that "Leo Strauss' thought . . . had its source in the real problems of a serious life. His intellectual odyssey began with his Zionism."[1] Bloom's judgment carries the important truth that Strauss's thinking has its origin in his reflection on his situation as a Jew and his attempt to come to understand his own Jewish life. And it may be true, biographically speaking, to locate the nub of Strauss's Jewish reflection in his Zionism. But in order to understand his Jewish thinking fully one must begin not with a solution but rather with the problem, for Zionism, in one form or another, was surely that, a solution to a problem, and it was in this way that Strauss saw it. Bloom sees this too, for he notices that "assimilation and Zionism were the two solutions to what was called 'The Jewish Problem'."

In the famous Preface which we examined in chapter four, Strauss himself is more precise about this and less precise. There is a Jewish problem, which concerns the possibility of Jewish life within the world. Traditionally, Jews took that problem to be insoluble by human means; ultimately God would have to solve it. With Spinoza, however, two modern, human solutions revealed themselves: political Zionism and what Strauss called assimilationism. That is, the problem of exile and suffering for Jews could be solved by abandoning the impotence of a completely other-worldly trust and by assuming the responsibilities and challenges of self-government or by "assimilating" to the state religion, the civil religion, of a liberal democracy. The Jewish predicament, therefore, could be resolved by human means, or at least seemed to be humanly resolvable, either by the establishment of a Jewish state or by total participation in a liberal democratic state. Both would put an end to exile, in a sense, and to Jewish suffering—or so one might have thought.

Ultimately Strauss will identify several options for Jews in the modern world. Along with assimilationism and political Zionism, he will notice cultural and religious Zionism, modern rational Judaism, Jewish existentialism, and orthodoxy. He outlines a Jewish intellectual itinerary: he begins with an account of the modern Jewish situation, the predicament of modern Jews, and spells out the possible strategies for coping with that predicament and for resolving the Jewish problem, tracing options as they arise as possible solutions, identifying their weaknesses, and ultimately finding his way to a return to premodern Jewish rationalism and ultimately to traditional Judaism and its confrontation with philosophy, by which Strauss means that type of moral and political thinking rooted in the Greek philosophical tradition. As Strauss shows, the outcome of this reflection, this dialectical line of thinking, is no comfortable resolution. Rather, it is the recognition of a fundamental opposition in Western thought between two conceptions of the good life and its foundations. He frequently remarks that the very life of Western civilization is "the conflict between the biblical and philosophic notions of the good life" and hence "a fundamental tension" that cannot be resolved as much as acknowledged and lived.[2]

There are a number of things to be said about Strauss's conception of the Jewish predicament and how it gives rise to Jewish reflection on its solution. The key texts are the Introduction to *Philosophy and Law* (*Philosophie und Gesetz*) and the Preface to the English edition of Strauss's Spinoza book.

In his Introduction Strauss sets out the quarrel between the Enlightenment and orthodoxy in order "to arouse a prejudice in favor of" Maimonides' form of medieval rationalism.[3] That is, Strauss delivers a critique of Enlightenment rationalism based on the notion of the self-sufficiency of reason in order to expose the strengths of medieval rationalism. First, he tries to show the effectiveness of the Enlightenment commitment to reason in opposition to Creation, miracle, and revelation. Then, Strauss shows that the existential disposal of rationalism and its return to orthodoxy is only a qualified one. In the end, one comes to realize that the attack of Enlightenment was a failure; one set of presuppositions confronted another. Traditional thought was based on belief in a set of ideas that could never be refuted by reason alone. As beliefs they could be discredited only by a complete system that excluded them, and the complete system turned out to be idealist.

But, if Strauss is right, idealism in the end historicizes even the new science on which the Enlightenment is based; "it understands modern natural science as a historically conditioned form of 'world interpretation' along with others."[4] Ultimately, then, the upshot of these reflections is the realization that the controversy over revelation and orthodoxy becomes a quarrel between systems of belief. The modern existential response involves the recognition that life involves a special kind of response to one's natural situation and its threats and risks, a new kind of bravery; religion is opposed as a palliative device. This new form of bravery is called "probity" and "it forbids every flight from the horror of life into consoling illusion."[5] This, Strauss says, is the truth of the quarrel between Enlightenment and orthodoxy, between reason and revelation; this existential recognition, that is, incorporates the "intellectual probity" that refuses any mediation between the two and that recognizes the two as revelation and atheism. If these are the only alternatives, then either there is no resolution or one is forced to ask whether modern rationalism is the only form of rationalism. Must reason always oppose revelation? Isn't medieval rationalism, such as that of Maimonides, outmoded just as Aristotelian cosmology is outmoded? Strauss suggests an alternative, that the centrality of Law might make Maimonidean rationalism retrievable and hence true. In short, is a Judaism rooted in Torah true and recoverable?

In the Introduction, written in 1935, there is a suggestion that the Judaism of Maimonides, based on Torah, might be true and immune to the subsequent attack of modern rationalism. In the Preface, written in 1962, this suggestion is deepened. Later, I think, it is abandoned in favor of the view which I set out earlier and will elaborate later, that there is a permanent, fundamental tension between reason and revelation, between philosophical and biblical conceptions of the good life.

The Preface is Strauss's attempt to explain the intellectual route that led him to an examination of Spinoza's *Tractatus Theologico-Politicus*. Strauss tells us that his sustained reflection led him to understand existentialism as a voluntaristic rejection of transcendence, of religiosity, on the basis of "intellectual probity." It is, he says, an act of will that disposes of religion while also disposing of philosophy. The "atheism from intellectual probity" is the final and deepest justification of Spinoza's critique of religion. Hence, the final victory is orthodoxy's, for philosophy can only dispose of it through an act of self-renunciation, whereby rational reflection takes its stand against revelation but only as an act of will based on belief. Strauss then makes an ominous remark: "Other observations and experiences confirmed the suspicion that it would be unwise to say farewell to reason."[6] First, the outcome of this suspicion was the thought that premodern rationalism may not have succumbed to self-destruction the same way that modern rationalism did, and this led to a new study of old writings with a view to how they were written. Second, this suspicion also led Strauss to read Spinoza's *Tractatus* in a new way. Finally, it leads us to ask how differently Strauss understood the theologico-political predicament that initiated these reflections. I want to focus now on this last point and on the various ways in which Strauss came to understand this notion of the modern Jew's theologico-political predicament.

Strauss's remark is ominous, I think, because it focuses on the difference between his situation in 1925–28 and his later situation, one over which Nazism cast its dark and dominating shadow. Strauss begins the Preface with these famous words: "This study on Spinoza's *Theologico-political Treatise* was written during the years 1925–28 in Germany. The author was a young Jew born and raised in Germany who found himself in the grip of the theologico-political predicament."[7] One is moved to wonder what exactly that final phrase means, and Strauss immediately begins to say something about it by identifying the regime, the Weimar Republic, as a liberal democracy with certain features, among them its weakness. Weimar, contrasted with the epoch of classical Germany, was a weak advocate of human rights, of freedom and tolerance, impotent to withstand any resurgence of German national longing and will. As Strauss believes, Weimar is a victim of the crisis of modernity, of a notion of the diminished state that honors private differences and convictions but is unable to withstand the power of vital, national will and all the animosities and hatreds it brings. Existential voluntarism, historicism, and relativism poorly equip people to withstand such tendencies. Perhaps reason can do better. It is no wonder that after the fall of Weimar and when the desires and capabilities of Nazism became apparent Strauss came to worry about the abdication of reason.

What, then, was the "theologico-political predicament" of this young Jew in the liberal democracy of Weimar? It was, I take it, the predicament of being a Jew in a liberal democracy in the modern world. It was the problem of reconciling his religiosity with his world, a world of reason, freedom, tolerance, but also of weakness.

Was this also *Spinoza*'s theologico-political predicament? In a sense it was, for Spinoza sought a conception of religion that was compatible with his conception of the best state, a civil religion suitable for a liberal democracy. But Strauss came to see the weaknesses of liberal democracy and the crisis that Weimar especially suffered; his predicament was more complex than Spinoza's, for, in subsequent years, he could not risk a reconciliation that would ill-equip the citizens of the state to oppose Nazism and totalitarianism. He could not be satisfied with modern liberal political philosophy and its implications; nor could he be satisfied with modern forms of Jewish self-understanding.

In the end, Strauss's theologico-political predicament is the "fundamental tension" between philosophical and biblical conceptions of the good life and the holding of one view while being open to the challenges of the other; it is, in other words, the very character of the vitality of Western civilization. It is unresolvable and yet endurable. Hence, for the young Strauss the predicament was one thing but for the older Strauss it was another, indeed two other things. The theologico-political predicament was, for Strauss, threefold: first, it was a problem of understanding Judaism in a way that met the demands of the crisis of liberal democracy and of modern rational critique; second, it was one of doing this while safeguarding oneself against the threats of Nazism; and finally it was one of recognizing that, through and through, the biblical and philosophical views of the good life, their moral and political conceptions, are distinct, incompatible, and in conflict.

The Preface is a subtle piece of argumentation, closely reasoned, and intricately dialectical. In it, Strauss begins with his account of the predicament, with special attention to the weaknesses of Weimar and the nature of the Jewish problem. He then considers a variety of Jewish responses to that situation, from the creation of *Wissenschaft* to political Zionism to cultural and religious Zionism to rational religion to religious existentialism à la Buber and Rosenzweig, and finally to an "unqualified return to Jewish orthodoxy."[8] Indeed, Strauss's reflections lead him to "wonder whether an unqualified return to Jewish orthodoxy was not both possible and necessary—was not at the same time the solution to the problem of the Jew lost in the non-Jewish modern world and the only course compatible with sheer consistency or intellectual probity." But doubts began to occur, and they began to take the shape of Spinoza, so that Strauss, in the 1920s, had come to the conclusion that "orthodoxy could be returned to only if Spinoza was wrong in every respect."[9] But, as he asserts in the Introduction to *Philosophie und Gesetz*, Strauss comes to see Spinoza's attack on orthodoxy as unsuccessful, or, to be more precise, only successful in existentialism, in the atheistic will to reject traditional religious belief as incompatible with "intellectual probity," a courageous confrontation with human anxiety that does not flee into illusion. But, as we earlier noted, Strauss's judgment is that the Spinozist refutation, then, succeeds only by self-renunciation or self-destruction. Hence Strauss's early study of Spinoza had taken him to be successful; later he came to see him as less so and came to feel compelled to return to premodern writings to see if reason could not be retrieved.

A close study of Strauss's Preface, then, involves and uncovers most varieties of serious modern Jewish thought and does so at a subtle and deep level. But most important, it poses the question of what the "theologico-political predicament" of the modern Jew is, in all its diversity and depth. And it raises the question of how Jewish thought, Nazism, and an understanding of modern political and moral philosophy are importantly interrelated.

## POLITICAL PHILOSOPHY AND THE CRISIS OF MODERNITY

Strauss, in a variety of places, characterizes what he called "the crisis of modernity" or "the crisis of Western civilization," to which the crisis of modern political philosophy is closely related.[10] The nature and existence of this crisis, as Strauss elaborates it, have been the subject of much discussion,[11] and that discussion intensified with the publication of Allan Bloom's controversial *The Closing of the American Mind*, a critique of American higher education largely based on Strauss's critique of Western civilization and American liberal democracy. We need not engage in either a detailed description of Strauss's critique or an evaluation of it. The issues—the nature of political philosophy, its relation to political science, to the history of political thinking, and to moral philosophy, and Strauss's intellectualist account of the impact of modernity via Machiavelli, Hobbes, Locke, through Nietzsche—are important but complex and would take us far from our concern. My reason for introducing this cluster of issues at all is that they are importantly related to Strauss's Jewish thinking on the one hand and to his return to the classics on the other.

Strauss takes Machiavelli and Hobbes to be the founding fathers, as it were, of the modern crisis of Western civilization and ultimately of liberal democracy in the West. A host of crucial shifts characterizes this crisis. They include the shift from the primacy of the notions of duty and obligation to the primacy of the notion of rights, from the primacy of whole to that of the parts, from the state or nation to the individual, from teleology to mechanism, from nature to history, from finitude to infinity, from truth to meaning, from an expressive relation between the state and a conception of the good life to an instrumental relation between the minimal, protective state and a variety of conceptions of the good life, and so on.[12] The fundamental failings of modern political thought and modern civilization concern its relativism, historicism, and ultimately its moral diversity. Strauss's criticisms, variously discussed in his articles and books, are not unlike those of Hannah Arendt, the Critical School, and others, including Alasdair MacIntyre. The chief villains, for whom Strauss nonetheless has a deep respect, are Nietzsche and Heidegger.[13]

Strauss's understanding of modern political philosophy and of the crisis of the modern world led him to seek a return to the premodern or classic political writings of the West. His dialectical assessment of the possibilities for modern Jewish life and thought and his critical assessment of modern society and political thinking suggested to him the same strategy, an inquiry into classical thinking about Western moral, political, and religious life. On the one hand, Strauss the Jew was led to reread premodern Jewish rationalism and its source, the Bible. On the other, Strauss the political philosopher was led to reread the classics of political philosophy. For our purposes, we can conceive of this two-pronged program as a single one.

Not only did these two routes lead to the same program, a rereading of the classics; the routes are also closely related themselves. What we have said about Strauss's Jewish thinking suggests three points at which his critical understanding of his Jewish situation and his modern political situation overlap.

First, they overlap because for Strauss his reflections begin in a predicament that is precisely the predicament of someone with religious attachments and commitments in a twentieth century liberal democracy, and the liberal democracy, with its significant strengths but outstanding weaknesses, is the highest point of Western civilization. That is, a central feature of Strauss's predicament is the fact that it is located in a liberal democracy, in a state that stems from Machiavelli and Hobbes, through Locke and Rousseau and Kant. One might put it schematically. The modern liberal democracy is based on the notions of tolerance of a variety of conceptions of the good life, of the centrality of rights, of the primacy of the individual, and of the separation of political conduct from moral purpose and frequently from moral assessment. These and other ideas are the legacy of these thinkers. They contribute to the crisis of liberalism, its relativism, its separation of the public and the private, and its vulnerability to hatred and domination. Modern liberal democracy promotes the surreptitious use of power behind the facade of rationality and persuasion. In short, the origin for Strauss's Jewish reflections incorporates the presuppositions of just that liberalism that is in the midst of a crisis of its own. No successful Jewish reflection can ignore this context.[14]

Second, Strauss often says that the continued existence of the Jewish problem, the problem of the Jew in the modern world, of suffering and persecution, of integrity and assimilation, is an indication that the human condition remains unredeemed. It is an unsolved problem, a sign of incompleteness, of flaw. One is reminded of Rosenzweig's justification for Christian persecution of the Jews, that the Jews are a constant reminder of the church's unfinished task and hence of the church's failure. The synagogue, the distinctiveness of the Jewish people, is a historical emblem of being on the way, of not yet, of failure of achievement, of a redemption still to come. Strauss appropriates this teaching and makes it his own. Moral-political thinking from the Jewish point of view is, by Strauss's lights, fitting; the Jewish point of view is a peculiarly appropriate perspective from which to view the predicament of moral and political life.

Finally, Strauss notes that the historical locus of the crisis of Western civilization, of liberal democracy, and hence of political and moral philosophy is that regime of total negativity, Nazi Germany.[15] That is, Nazism displays one outcome, perhaps the most appalling outcome, of relativism, scientism, and historicism. It is no wonder that Strauss links Nazism with Nietzsche and Heidegger, albeit in no simpleminded, simplistic way. One might be tempted to accept the existentialist disposal of religion and revelation as dishonest or lacking in "probity," that new kind of bravery, until one realizes that existentialism reduces alternatives to matters of will and power. One should not, Strauss cautions, be too quick to win the rejection of religious orthodoxy if the cost is the self-destruction of reason. Is it surprising that Strauss worries about the replacement of duty and obligation and law with rights and freedom and positivism, of all varieties?

Strauss associates the decline of Western civilization with the loss of the modern concept of progress:

> . . . the idea of progress in the modern sense implies that once man has reached a certain level, intellectual and social or moral, there exists a firm level of being below which he cannot sink. This contention, however, is empirically refuted by the incredible barbarization which we have been so unfortunate as to witness in our century. We can say that the idea of progress, in the full and emphatic sense of the term, is based on wholly unwarranted hopes.[16]

At least one of the implications of Auschwitz, then, is that human hope is undone. More was actual than was possible. Hannah Arendt and Hans Jonas were right. Moreover, as Strauss goes on to show, this barbarization is the outcome of "a gradual corrosion and destruction of the heritage of Western civilization." Nazism is one outcome of modernity, of a revision of Western civilization that has destroyed the notion of progress; there is no such thing as betterment. Political and social institutions are instrumentalities, available as tools of domination for those with will enough and power enough to commandeer them for their purposes. Nazism is the epitome of a world that has three characteristics: it is anthropocentric rather than theocentric; all meaning and purpose originate in the human subject. It is a world with a new moral orientation, centered on rights which are rooted in freedom and passion rather than reason and virtue and obligation. And finally, it is a world that has discovered history, where all truth is bound to situation and context, where the only determination is temporary and historical, and where the eternal is replaced by the temporal.[17]

Hence, it is not accidental that Strauss came to believe that the predicament of the modern Jew in a liberal democracy and the crisis of modern political philosophy and Western civilization both pointed in the same direction. At one point, Strauss puts it this way: "the crisis of modernity . . . leads to the suggestion that we should return. But return to what? Obviously, to Western civilization in its pre-modern integrity, to the principles of Western civilization."[18] At another, he indicates why such a return is necessary; adequate contemporary analysis of our social and political life requires understanding our presuppositions, assumptions, and hypotheses, and these are illuminated, brought to light, by an examination of classical political philosophy.[19] To assess our current understanding of political and moral life and the social sciences that provide our access to it, we need a prescientific understanding of social, political, and moral life. This, Strauss argues, can be got from the ancients, where we can see at work the "common sense understanding of political things."[20]

On the one hand, then, in order to uncover the truth about moral and political life one needs to return to the ancient political and moral writings, where the commonsense understanding of political-moral phenomena is exposed. On the other hand, in order to arrive at an acceptable understanding of Judaism and Jewish life, one needs to return to pre-modern Jewish writings and the primacy of Torah in Jewish life and thought. What is the conception of the good life articulated in the biblical world, and can we today return to it?

## THE BIBLICAL AND PHILOSOPHICAL CONCEPTIONS OF THE GOOD LIFE[21]

Thomas Pangle, in his introduction to *Studies in Platonic Political Philosophy*, focuses on the theologico-political predicament as the center or nerve of Strauss's thinking.[22] In a letter written in response to Myles Burnyeat's critical review of the volume,[23] Pangle makes a special point of registering as a shortcoming in Burnyeat's treatment that he omitted any discussion of this issue, of the role of Athens and Jerusalem in Strauss's thought. Burnyeat never really responded to this criticism. But Pangle is surely right, as we have tried to show; the result of a return to the classics, for Strauss, is a profound recognition of the tension between philosophy and religion, Athens and Jerusalem. Pangle's analysis focuses on the role of Socrates and Plato with regard to this issue. My own perspective is somewhat larger and pays special attention to the role of Strauss's Jewish roots.

At one level, Strauss was vitally interested in and concerned about the relationship between politics and morality. Morality, broadly conceived, is about the good life, its constituents and goals. Different moral views, some religious and some not, have differing views about what the good life is, whether it should focus on actions, personality and character, relationships, goals or purposes, and so forth. And political philosophy, broadly conceived, is about morality when it is elaborated within a social context. Hence, a primary question that should be raised by political philosophy is how political arrangements, roles, and institutions are related to moral views. Is a given political arrangement committed to and even expressive of a particular moral view? Or is it neutral with regard to a variety of moral views and organized to facilitate their implementation? To use a terminology from Charles Larmore, who has discussed these issues with regard to Locke, Rawls, and others,[24] sometimes moral views are also political views, sometimes they are not. At times, that is, civil and political institutions express a certain moral view and conception of the good life; at times they do not, but rather facilitate the citizens' implementation of a variety of such views or conceptions. With respect to morality, as Larmore puts it, some states are expressivist, some are simply facilitators.

In Strauss's view, the modern political enterprise, insofar as it sponsors liberal democracy, is committed to the *modus vivendi* view of the state; it is not itself committed to any particular conception of the good life but regulates affairs so that its citizens can, in private, engage in their lives under their own conception of the good life. In antiquity, the situation was different. There, in the Greek polis as well as elsewhere, there was a continuity between the individual and the state. Morality and politics were part of the same cloth, or, to put it differently, morality was diffused throughout the individual's life, at every level. In Larmore's terminology, the ancient state was an expressivist state; it facilitated and represented one conception of the good life and the good for humankind.

In terms of this distinction, Strauss adds a further discovery. A careful reading of the philosophical tradition and of the Bible reveals two conceptions of the good life that share certain features—for example, a concern for justice—and yet are significantly different. Their difference concerns the role of speculation, study, knowledge, and openness. In the Greek tradition, the ideal is speculative, exploratory, and theoretical; in the biblical tradition, the ideal is practical and active, even legal. The outcome is two distinctive conceptions of the good life, of the human ideal, but both within a general understanding of the political as expressive and not merely facilitating. Strauss's conclusion, or one of his conclusions, is that in the modern world, liberal democracies, when properly organized and administered, may be the best that we, in history, can do, given this insoluble and irreconcilable disagreement between the biblical and philosophical conceptions of the good life. But the conflict remains; it is the fundamental tension which I referred to above. It is, I believe, the deep sense in which we live and have always lived in a theologico-political predicament. What this phrase really means, then, is that we live in a civilization in which (1) biblical and philosophical conceptions of the good life are permanently in conflict and (2) political life can either express or remain neutral with respect to one's moral view, one's conception of the good life. Clarity and self-consciousness about these matters brings the best form of life of which we are capable, a life of vitality but also of irresolvable tension. It is this that Strauss means by the conflict between Athens and Jerusalem and this that is the most profound theologico-political predicament that he finally comes to recognize.[25]

A careful reading of Strauss reveals, I think, that this is what he has in mind. Pangle's point is that Strauss finds the whole business present in Socrates' life as portrayed by Xenophon and Plato, and I agree. But I think that Strauss already sees it reflected in the Bible in his account of the early chapters of Genesis in "Jerusalem and Athens." That is, Strauss believes that an open and honest reading of the classics of both dimensions of our tradition, the biblical and the philosophical, yields the same message, the perennial tension between Athens and Jerusalem, between reason and revelation, between "a life of autonomous understanding" and one of "obedient love."[26]

The three Chicago lectures of the early 1950s certainly reflect this sort of picture. There Strauss says that "the one thing needful according to Greek philosophy is the life of autonomous understanding. The one thing needful as spoken by the Bible is the life of obedient love." In other words, philosophy conceives of the best life as independent and cognitive, the Bible sees it as dependent and affective. Now, as Strauss then proceeds to argue, both agree concerning the importance of morality or justice, although they do tend to treat morality somewhat differently. But

> they disagree as to what completes morality. According to the Greek philosophers . . . it is understanding or contemplation. Now this necessarily tends to weaken the majesty of the moral demands, whereas humility, a sense of guilt, repentance, and faith in divine mercy, which complete morality according to the Bible, necessarily strengthen the majesty of the moral demands.[27]

And Strauss then associates this difference with the difference, as Maimonides portrays it, between a commitment to Creation and divine omnipotence, on the one hand, and a commitment to eternity, on the other. In the one case, one's way in the world is ultimately dependent upon one's own knowledge of the world's way, i.e., Nature as it is. In the other, it is dependent upon a relationship with God, i.e., a covenant with Him. This, Strauss says, is "the core, the nerve of Western intellectual history, Western spiritual history . . . the conflict between the biblical and the philosophic notions of the good life . . . this unresolved conflict is the secret of the vitality of Western civilization." The result is that

> No one can be both a philosopher and a theologian nor, for that matter, some possibility which transcends the conflict between philosophy and theology, or pretends to be a synthesis of both. But every one of us can be and ought to be either one or the other, the philosopher open to the challenge of theology or the theologian open to the challenge of philosophy.[28]

Philosophy grounds itself on a commitment to epistemological certainty, while revelation is rooted in a classic revelation confirmed by reliable tradition, prophecies, and miracles. One is open, critical, and active; the other closed, obedient, and passive. In the end, there is no way that the two can be reconciled, no matter how vigorous the attempt. "It is impossible for reason, for philosophy, to assent to revelation as revelation."[29] Indeed, as Strauss comes to realize, the two, revelation and reason, Jerusalem and Athens, are so dissimilar that all mutual refutations are question-begging: "all alleged refutations of revelation presuppose unbelief in revelation, and all alleged refutations of philosophy presuppose already faith in revelation. There seems to be no ground common to both, and therefore superior to both."[30]

But Strauss then makes an admission reminiscent of a point we discussed earlier, of the way in which existentialism comes to appreciate orthodoxy as an alternative but less honest and less courageous system of belief. That is, Strauss points out that ultimately philosophy "must admit the possibility of revelation" and that this means that philosophy must admit that it "itself is possibly not the right way of life." But under these circumstances, "the choice of philosophy is based on faith. In other words, the quest for evident knowledge rests itself on an unevident premise."[31] This admission, moreover, has a twofold impact. First, it shows that the fundamental and permanent conflict between philosophy and the Bible, when acknowledged by philosophy, seems to be catastrophic for philosophy, which is based on reason and not on faith. Second, it should lead us to probe more deeply exactly how philosophy requires reason, for as long ago as Aristotle it has been recognized that all knowledge cannot be demonstrative, which is another way of saying what Aristotle, Descartes, and others have recognized, that reason is heterogeneous and that all reasoning need not rely upon faith of one sort or another.

Centrally, then, Strauss raises the question whether one can be a religious thinker and a philosopher at one and the same time. Moreover, his recovery of the ancients and his rereading of the tradition suggest that this dual role is simply impossible without a deep inner tension. Hence, in the end, Strauss himself can be either a Jewish thinker or a philosopher but not consistently both, that is, not a Jewish philosopher, for the latter is an oxymoron pure and simple. This might be our conclusion, or alternatively we might have doubts. Rather than take him at his word one might be lead to reengage the traditional texts and the issue itself and ask once again this fully serious and deep question about the relationship between philosophy and religion, between Athens and Jerusalem. Doing this, however, might already implicate us in opting for philosophy and not for biblical faith.

SIX

# Judaism and Peter Berger's Heretical Imperative

During the past two decades, major events have regularly served to test the relationship between Jews and Christians. There are of course many kinds of Jews and even more varieties of Christians, so the changing nature of their interaction has been complex. At times, events stimulate modest differences, but at other times the gulf between the church and the synagogue seems vast and deep.

In the Cold War years, Jewish theologians responded to American culture—with its acquisitiveness, technological fanaticism, materialism, and more—by attempting to define a plausible notion of faith and arguing in its behalf. Without a receptivity to transcendence, they believed, American life and Jewish life were sadly lacking. This fideism, however, has come to seem controversial. At least in Jewish life, there are various routes to spirituality or transcendence and various assessments of the importance of faith to Judaism today. There are those in Jewish and Christian circles who defend it still, as a primary focus of religious attention and energy. One of those is Peter Berger, a sociologist of knowledge who explores insightfully our secularized modern society and attempts to define the modern consciousness corresponding to and interacting with that society. Berger's method enables him to diagnose those problems that confront any seriously religious person in such a world and to offer a solution—if not for how to live religiously in a secular, modernized world, at least for how to think religiously in such a world.

Berger works at the intersections of phenomenology and social theory.[1] In a variety of books he has developed a ramified theory of how our subjective views, attitudes, and perspectives develop in subtle, dialectical relation to an objective reality that is both an independent given for consciousness and intentionally constructed by the social self. On the basis of this theory of individual consciousness in the social world, Berger and his collaborators have analyzed the peculiarly modern situation as a complex result of secularization, technological change, pluralization, and the attendant loss of traditional norms and fixed points of reference.[2] Of particular concern to Berger are the implications of this understanding of social reality for two domains of experience, the political and the religious. In two works, for example, he assesses the impact of modernization on political ethics and Third World societies.[3] In Berger's anthology *Facing Up to Modernity*, a variety of essays aim at disclosing the implications of modernization for American politics and religion.[4] *The Heretical Imperative* applies the same analysis to describe the situation of modern religious life and thought, to diagnose its "disease," to display a variety of alternative "cures," and to defend one of these cures as the most desirable.[5]

The plot of *The Heretical Imperative*, as Berger himself notes, is straightforward and undisguised. First, he uses the tools of the sociology of knowledge to characterize the modern situation. Increased technological sophistication has brought with it a proliferation of institutions, roles, and the alternatives that attend such pluralization. For religion this means that old authority structures are undermined; more of life is open to selectivity and decision. For modern man in general, a religious world is an alternative, not a given, and for those who choose it there is a wide variety of religious options. In short, modernization has led to extreme pluralization of opportunities, and this in turn has brought with it not only the possibility of choice but also the necessity to choose. Modern man, in Sartre's ironic words, is "condemned to be free." Berger calls this the transition from fate to choice. He notices, among other things, that it results in uncertainty and anxiety as well as increased freedom. The outcome is heresy, not in the old sense of a choice against orthodoxy but in the new sense of the necessity of choice itself. The old heresy—the word derives from the Greek verb *haireisthai*, to choose—was a possibility; the new is a necessity. The old was heterodox, aimed against a taken-for-granted view; the new operates in a world in which there are no orthodoxies, for no view is authoritative or taken-for-granted.

Berger then turns to an account of the nature of religion as a social phenomenon. At its core religion is a human experience of the supernatural that breaks into or shatters the everyday world. That experience resonates in the lives of those who have it and in the lives of others by means of an aggregate of reflections, beliefs, attitudes, and interpretations that constitute a religious tradition. Religion, then, is a combination of a tradition and the experiences on which that tradition is based. At times the authority of religion clings to the experience itself, at times to the tradition. In the past the core experience, however, was taken to be an experience of a supernatural reality, of a Divine Other. Hence, at such times the tension of religious authority was a tension between divine authority transmitted through a core experience some time in the past and the authority of the historical tradition that interpreted and mediated that experience to every age. Today's tension is different, for secularism presses modern man to dispense with the Divine Other and to adjudicate between the past tradition and the present experience, an experience which is itself cut off from the transcendent.

Berger outlines three models for coping with this situation, three methodological options for a serious religious thinking confronted with the secular threat to transcendence and the dialectic between religious experience and religious tradition, and then criticizes these alternatives. The first he calls the deductive model, for its basic structure requires modern man to submit himself totally to the original core experience and to deduce the articles of one's faith from the content of that experience and the tradition that sacralizes it. The reality of the Divine Other is not only accepted; one gives oneself to it unconditionally, and the tradition that stems from it is acknowledged as absolutely authoritative. Berger's example here is Karl Barth. His chief criticism of Barthian neoorthodoxy is that even a submission is a choice, and one for which we cannot explain either why it is made or why the peculiarly Christian option was chosen. Berger neglects to take seriously, however, the natural neoorthodox response, that in reality no human choice is made but rather a human acknowledgment of a divine new choice. If this is incompatible with Berger's phenomenologico-sociological analysis of religion in the modern, pluralized world, then so much the worse for that analysis.

The second model Berger calls reductive. His example is Rudolph Bultmann, but could have been any modern theologian or religious thinker who translates the original, core experience and the resultant tradition into one or another contemporary secularizing language. Reductionists, then, interpret tradition in terms of modern secularity; the authority of the core experience and the tradition that mediates it is subordinated to the authority of modern consciousness and its understanding of the modern situation. Berger calls this a bargain in the face of cognitive pressure, pressure applied by the modern world and its conflict with religious consciousness. In the end, however, reductionism is self-liquidating, for the cognitive gains can just as easily be got without accommodating to religion at all. Berger's chief criticism is sober: modern, secular consciousness is a given of our historical situation. In and of itself it warrants or deserves neither ridicule nor idolization. For like any structure of consciousness it should be examined, understood, and coped with but not absolutized. To do the latter is to take one's stand against religion, which essentially signals transcendence and cannot endure total bondage to this world. Reduction, then, turns out to be an option, to be sure, but not a *religious* option as much as a choice against religion.

Berger wants the third possibility to emerge as a persuasive mediation of the extremes of deduction and reduction, of completely ignoring the authority of the modern world and completely submitting to it. The former failed to do justice to the modern situation and the necessity of choice; the latter failed to do justice to the autonomy of tradition and the core experiences of the transcendent enshrined by it. The inductive model is intended to look as if it overcomes both of these shortcomings, doing justice to both present and past, to modern freedom and transcendent authority. Induction requires that one take seriously the human experience of the Divine Other as the core from which religious tradition springs and the center to which it returns again and again. Religious experience, that is, must be both the source and the goal of religious life. By using historical methods, one can examine human experience in the world and discern in that experience signals, hints, intimations of encounter with the transcendent, Divine Other. The inductive focus is on experience; its goal is to uncover the ongoing, recurrent reality of revelation in everyday life. Neoorthodoxy announces a submission to a mediated Word of God; liberal theology—Berger's paradigm of the inductive method—affirms revelation as a permanent possibility and searches for signs of it everywhere. Tradition must give the nod to the human experience of the Divine as the core but also the goal or center of religious life and religious thought.

Berger endorses this third model despite criticisms often leveled against it. One such criticism is that liberal theology frequently lapses into reductionism. Indeed, even when it preserves its integrity, such a theology can neither justify its preference for one particular revelation nor explain how true religious experience is to be distinguished from false. When revelation is taken to be an immediate divine-human encounter, authenticity and historical discontinuity become serious problems. Berger's ideal is Schleiermacher, but Berger might have noted that Martin Buber's dialogical concept of revelation appears to be plagued by similar problems. In the inductive method, then, freedom is preserved, but it is a freedom to encounter God, to rediscover transcendence, and hence it involves a search for those experiences in which such encounter has taken and can take place. It is no wonder that induction has problems of authenticity and justification, for it treats tradition and past experience as a resource to be used and not as an authoritative source to be heeded.

Having defended the centrality of religious experience for modern religious life and thought, Berger turns to the implications of the inductive model for the Christian future. For Berger, the core of Christian theology must be a search for the true nature of religious experience. The primary structure of religious experience in the West has been confrontational. That is, in the West religious experience of the transcendent is a matter of finite man confronting the Infinite in a moment of history. Berger, I think, takes the agenda of Christian theology to center on the truth of this view and the tradition that surrounds it. Hence, the appropriate strategy for testing that truth is to encounter openly and honestly religious traditions with alternative conceptions of religious experience, traditions such as Buddhism and Hinduism. This Berger calls contestation, an activity which he defines as an open-minded encounter with other religious possibilities on the level of their truth claims. To contest, Berger believes, requires that one be prepared to change one's view of reality. For too long Christianity has been contesting—if at all—only with secularity and modernity. The new agenda calls for taking a stand in favor of transcendence and against secularism and, from that starting point, to contest with Eastern faiths concerning the truth of the Christian message. The modern world is exhausted with secularity and hungry for redemption and transcendence (*Heretical Imperative*, 184). The responsibility of Christianity is to focus once again on religious experience as the core of religiosity and to test the Christian message about God, man, and the world against alternative views. Berger encourages a contestation first with Judaism, then with Islam, and finally with Indian religions—all on the basis of what seems like a shared openness to the possibility of experiencing the Divine in one's life.

Berger's approach is one of diminishing generality. A Christian himself, he claims that his phenomenologico-sociological accounts of modernization and religious experience are value-neutral and hence completely general. As his argument proceeds, however, its generality shrinks. While the outline of theological alternatives is the product of religious openness, Berger claims that his descriptions, when generalized, might reasonably apply to all religious points of view. In short, for nearly the entire book Berger maintains a kind of neutralist triumphalism; the heretical imperative, with all it entails, applies as surely to Jews and Muslims and Hindus as it does to members of any Protestant denomination. Hence, if Berger's sociological account is accurate and his diagnosis and cure completely persuasive, the results should be vital to future Jewish thought. In place of the traditional *mitzvot* we are offered the heretical imperative and how to satisfy it. These are results worth taking seriously if they are true, and refuting seriously if false.

First, there is an ambiguity or confusion in Berger's provocative expression for the modern religious situation. By the "heretical imperative" Berger means the necessity that secularization and pluralization impose on all modern persons to choose for one religious worldview over any other. What kind of necessity is this? It is what we might call a factual or descriptive necessity: we must do what the situation makes us do. Berger need not be a determinist, of course, for his sense of necessity here is selective. We may be free to do or not do a good deal, but apparently we are not free to ignore this necessity to choose. Berger calls this an imperative, suggesting that it is not only a factual necessity but also an obligation. It is, one might be led to think, a new "commandment," the commandment to choose between religion and secularity and then to choose one religion or another. But Berger has given us no good reason to think why this need be so. For such a prescriptive imperative would require a commander or at least a source of obligation, while all that is present here is at best an illicit inference from "is" to "ought."

With respect to Berger's use of such an expression, this ambiguity or confusion about two senses of necessity—a familiar distinction to philosophers of law or science and to moral philosophers—may in fact be harmless. It suggests, however, a more general and deeper problem about Berger's argument and the role of factual or sociological analysis in it. Does Berger adequately guard against the fallacy of inferring obligations from his sociological description of the modern religious situation? Is he careful not to allow his Christian commitment to bias his sociological analysis and not to permit his sociology to infect his descriptions, criticisms, and defenses of the three options for religious thought? In a person who is both a creative social scientist and a religious thinker, this self-control is bound to be a problem. And I am not convinced that Berger, his constant caveats notwithstanding, succeeds in solving it.

In the course of his sociological analysis of secularization and modernization, Berger intends his Christian commitment, indeed his religious commitment in general, to be bracketed. But his analysis of religion in terms of experience and tradition may not be so neutral. For the phenomenological sociologist religion is described as the religious person experiences it and hence as a received tradition stemming from and oriented to experiences of a transcendent Other, that is, experiences of revelation. To be sure, Berger makes no claims about the truth of these experiences. Some religious options will acknowledge that truth; for them the experienced Divine is a real supernatural being that has confronted man in the past and may continue to confront him in the here and now. Other options will deny that truth and treat such experiences as projections; Feuerbach is the prince of the secularizers of the Divine, though he is neither the first nor the most vociferous among them. It is one thing, however, to make religious experience essential to one's descriptive account of the nature of religion, and another to indict and convict a religious option because it does no proper justice to this phenomenon. One need hold no brief for secular reductionism to see here an injustice being done to it. Reductionism may fail to acknowledge the *truth* of religious experience of the transcendent; it does not or at least need not fail to respect the phenomenon of religious experience itself. Berger slides from what is experienced as transcendent to the reality of the transcendent, as if his sociology of knowledge required both. But, as he realizes, it does not, and for this reason the secular reductionist can agree with Berger's account of religion without endorsing the reality of the supernatural.

One genuine puzzle about Berger, then, is whether or not he is really a secular reductionist in disguise. Another concerns the novelty of his whole approach and its relevance for Jews today. In effect, Berger sets up a well-known tension between the religiously hungry and open self in the modern, pluralistic situation and religion as core experience together with an authoritative tradition. Neoorthodoxy subordinates the former to the latter and is thereby otherworldly. Secular reductionism subordinates the latter to the former and is thereby self-liquidating. Only liberal theology saves both, for it enshrines not an authority but a goal and hence preserves individual autonomy. The individual chooses his own route to God; he uses tradition as a resource, a route of access back to the core religious experience of his tradition, ultimately coming to understand the nature of such experiences and aiming to appropriate them for himself as a permanent possibility in his own life. All of this is by now common fare for Jewish thinkers of the 1950s and 1960s.[6] *Mutatis mutandis* the inductive model fits one of the intellectual heroes of modern Jewish theology, Franz Rosenzweig, and his "hygiene of return." According to Rosenzweig, individual Jews, reappropriating traditional texts and conduct for themselves, can gain that special divine-human intimacy that is the hallmark of the eternal people and indeed of eternity itself. In short, then, Berger's route has already been traveled by Rosenzweig before him, and in a slightly different way by Buber too and by many Jewish thinkers of the past several decades.

By itself the mere fact that Rosenzweig is an example of Berger's favored inductive approach is not remarkable. Surprise comes only when we realize that the situation that gave rise to and supported Rosenzweig's thought has so radically changed that his thinking may no longer suit the *contemporary* Jewish situation.[7] And if it does not, then the Jewish relevance of Berger's argument and its purported generality would be seriously in doubt.

Until the late 1960s Jews and Jewish thinkers had spent much time and effort struggling over the nature and role of revelation in Judaism and over the tension between the present and the past, between the autonomous self and the weight of tradition and divine authority. Buber and Rosenzweig were the chief intellectual heroes of those engaged in these struggles. In the same spirit, Berger suggests that the serious options for *all* religious persons are options between the autonomy of the modern situation and that of religious tradition.[8] Berger opts for signals of transcendence and the search for them, a historical quest through legend and lore to uncover intimations of the Divine in the experiences of men. This may or may not be the central imperative for contemporary Christianity; I am inclined to think that it is not so for Jews. And if not, then Berger has gone astray; the generality he claims is refuted, and a certain fissure opens in his program for Jewish-Christian unanimity.

What is the contemporary Jewish imperative? Why is it so decidedly different from Berger's heretical imperative? And how do Judaism and Berger differ on the role of any descriptive account of the modern religious situation?

In one sense or another, most Jews would agree that the imperative of Jewish life today is spiritual and physical survival—the maintenance of the Jewish people, of Judaism, and of all that these have meant and can mean for Jews today and in the future. We do God's work in spite of Him and serve Messianic goals without abiding transcendent trust. To do so requires a reappropriation of Jewish tradition—its literature, history, and structured life-style—insofar as we are capable of recovering them. For some, this imperative is rooted in an unreasoned, instinctual allegiance to the Jewish people. For others, it is founded on a more abiding, indeed absolute obligation. But for all it is an imperative that emerges from our situation in history, a situation defined by Auschwitz as much as by secularization and by Jerusalem as much as by pluralization. Contemporary Jewish life is now beyond a time of necessary choice for or against religion, for or against fideism and naturalism. We live in an age when such differences make virtually no difference and when Judaism is—in an almost ironic and surely dramatic sense—something to be taken for granted. Certainly some Jews are losing touch with Judaism and the Jewish people. While for such Jews there are only weak Jewish imperatives and perhaps none at all, for the ones who remain steadfast the imperatives are strongly present. For them the options are political strategies and alternative Jewish styles of living, not abstract theological positions. This is as true for Jewish thought as it is for Jewish life, for the task of the former is both to reflect on and direct the latter.

In the Jewish world signals of transcendence reveal themselves even and perhaps most of all in secular places—on battle lines, in protest marches, in letters to the editor, and at private conclaves of world leaders. Shaking a *lulav* during Sukkot may be an act of piety and faith; so is writing a letter of protest, signing a check, and denouncing the hypocrisy of free speech in the service of resurgent evil. Much Jewish action today is the result of a thoroughly secularized intention, but, in the eyes of some, such secular intention hides and expresses a deep, transcendent, divine purpose. Not all see this; not all should be expected to. *Now* it is sufficient that all act in behalf of the Jewish imperative; *some day* it may be necessary for all to see, to acknowledge, even to extol the source of that imperative. But now is not some day; it is merely now. Hence, the Jewish imperative is different from Berger's heretical imperative because the Jewish situation is not simply the modern one. To put this in different terms, Berger's diagnosis and cure would have been relevant to Jews before 1967 but is so no longer; this is not because his theological options are no longer present but rather because history has made the choice among them virtually insignificant for contemporary Jewish life.[9]

The Jewish imperative, then, arises in a historical moment for those living at the moment. I believe that its source is divine; many do not. Some disputes will go unresolved; so be it. That imperative expresses itself only in the mediate understanding of people responding in life to longings, needs, drives, passions too deep to bear their fragile justifications. The authority of the imperative is ultimate; the autonomy of the mediating understanding is finite and yet undeniable. And so the contemporary Jewish imperative is a dialectic of command and articulation, an articulation that expresses itself as individuals search for ways to keep

Judaism and the Jewish people alive in our world. Viewed in this way, the Jewish imperative is an acknowledged mingling of the divine and the human, the religious and the secular. The heretical imperative is a factual necessity masquerading as a moral obligation, and its aim is divine while its source and substance are human. What Judaism holds together, Berger strains to keep apart.

Berger's Christian agenda serves the purpose of truth: what is the true and genuine human experience of the Divine, the transcendent? For this agenda contestation is cathartic; tested against alternative traditions, the Christian message is about what faith is and how one can arrive at the experience of that faith. The agenda of contestation is an agenda dictated, if not demanded, by a modern situation described as the phenomenological sociologist sees it. But Berger's standards are ultimately in tension: as a sociologist he is bound to describe the human experience of God but to remain neutral concerning God's existence and influence. As a Christian, he is open to transcendence if not attuned to it—the life of faith is the life of craving after faith. But in shaded moments Berger's commitment to his sociological description controls his theological critique and vice versa. He attacks neoorthodoxy as implausible, in conflict with institutional structures and modern consciousness. Sociological truth outstrips the Word of God. And then he chastises secular religiosity as in essence not religious at all, a total submission to the modern situation—secularized, modernized, pluralized, and then sterilized. Can Berger cope with his dual roles? Only the inductive striving for religious experience seems to satisfy his twin allegiances.

Jewish thought sees things differently. Like Jewish life, it is historically situated, neither immune from history nor enslaved to it. For Jewish thought human freedom and divine command are a paradoxical, subtle unity. The command is a command only when freely received and the freedom a freedom only when divinely given. Berger cannot keep the religious and the secular properly apart; Jewish thought does not try to keep them apart. The human and the divine, the secular and the religious—what to Berger are separate domains in at best dialectical interrelation—are for Jews today unities, fragile and explosive but unities nonetheless.

The differences between Berger and Judaism, then, are not superficial. It is not merely that the heretical imperative is not the Jewish imperative. Nor is it merely that the Jewish historical situation is a postmodern situation. It is more than that. For Judaism no phenomenological sociology can do justice to an experience that is secular and religious, human and divine all at once. For Berger such a descriptive account can truthfully tell part of the story—as long as it does not prejudge the remainder. Christianity tells that remainder; the two fit, and although it is difficult to avoid trespass, the fit can be neat. For Judaism no such fit is possible, because no partial story is even partially true. Berger's sociological analysis is true as a Christian sociological analysis, true, that is, as a view of the modern religious situation importantly defined by Christian interests (as Berger sees them). Berger's inductive option is true only insofar as it harmonizes with and is supported by this sociological analysis; it is, in short, defined by the needs uncovered by that analysis. Lurking in the background here is a distinction between fact and value, "is" and "ought" that is troubling, both in the application and in the breach. Jewish thought sees the Jewish experience differently.

To be sure, descriptive sociological analysis is appropriate to wholly secular experience. But in the case of Jewish religious experience it misconstrues and distorts. For here, as Jewish thought sees it, the secular and the religious are not two sides of the same coin but rather an indissoluble unity. One cannot simply assume that value-neutral social science can do justice to the Jewish experience. Berger is convinced that sociological truths are compelling, for while sociology brackets the reality of the object of religious experience, it does not deny it. For Jewish religious experience, however, revelation cannot be understood without taking seriously the reality of the Divine Presence; after Feuerbach and Marx and Freud it is an understanding shot through with risk and uncertainty but one that reaffirms the reality of the Divine Other after doubt and is not satisfied to defer the question of truth altogether.

Furthermore, even in the everyday experience of Jews, a sociological understanding is inadequate. To describe the Jew as condemned to autonomy in the face of radical pluralization is to misperceive. The truth is that secularity is both a historical given and a religious imperative. The failure to see this may be what leads to Berger's confusing use of "imperative" in the title of his book. The Jewish imperative to secular self-confidence is, however, not simply—if at all—a historical, social necessity. It is most importantly an imperative, an obligation to rely on human capacity and human ingenuity. Here Berger's conclusions differ most radically from Jewish thought. Rejecting Barthian-style neoorthodoxy, Berger rejects not only what he takes to be an implausible option. He also alienates himself from the very notion of obligation; moral necessity collapses into factual necessity, and the only weight to be felt is that of the modern, pluralized, secularized world. Berger himself chooses to search for transcendence, but his choice is not a response to that transcendence. He chooses a goal and a strategy for achieving it, but he identifies no responsibility to seek it. The God of Judaism demands a response in the world. Berger's God can make no demands. At its core, then, the heretical imperative is a naturalistic fallacy coupled with a confusion about descriptive and prescriptive law: we must choose because we do, and we do because we must. The Jewish imperative is different. Freedom is made possible by secularity, but its exercise has prescriptive roots. For some Jews those roots are ethnic allegiance, for others a Commanding God, but for all they introduce responsibility and obligation.

Berger forces us to rethink and reassess the nature of the contemporary religious experience and hence the Jewish experience. But his thinking, of great interest sociologically, is inapplicable to that Jewish experience. To realize this is also to realize something important about much current Jewish thinking and about the role of Jews in the world today. If Berger is accurate about the Christian experience and its current state, then Jewish-Christian conversation must begin by appreciating a significant divergence of interests, goals, and imperatives. Such an appreciation can be beneficial but only appropriate if Berger is right at least about the new agenda for Christian life and Christian theology. It would be valuable to know whether or not he is right; my own intuition is that for the church, as for the synagogue, survival is a much more historical, worldly business than Berger seems to think.

# SEVEN

# Jewish Ethics after the Holocaust

## SITUATION AND CRITERIA

In his collected responsa (*teshuvot*), Rabbi Ephraim Oshry records Halachic decisions, made in the Kovno ghetto during the Nazi Holocaust, that adjust the Jewish legal tradition in order to oppose the deepest purposes of the Nazi state. In a rare case, for example, in which permission to commit suicide is sought before the fact, Oshry overturns the dominant Halachic prohibition.[1] He permits the act. But to advocate suicide is to encourage a lack of trust in God and thereby to encourage the Nazis in their attempt to eradicate the Jewish soul together with the Jewish body. And so he forbids the publication of his decision, and his grounds are at once profound and moving. There is a subtle dialectic in Rabbi Oshry's judgment, for a once-secure trust and hope in God, negated by the decision to permit the suicide, is reaffirmed in the refusal to allow a Nazi victory. And a self-reliant acceptance of human initiative and need, affirmed by Oshry's permission, is negated by the reason for that permission, the uncompromising opposition to Nazi purposes. And finally the religious conviction, recorded in the will to confide in Halachah and compromised by the intrusion of an utterly historical purpose, is ultimately reaffirmed by the nature of that purpose, to oppose evil by embracing its object, by clinging to God, tradition, trust, and hope.

Jewish law and Jewish integrity should characterize any serious, authentic foundation for Jewish moral thinking today, but they will not be its starting point. Rather its beginnings will be the intellectual and historical situation of contemporary Jews and Judaism. This is one of the lessons of Rabbi Oshry's experiences in Kovno. To be sure, there is an initial, almost intuitive presumption in favor of recovering the past and, in the domain of Jewish moral thinking, that means, among other things, examining the tradition of Jewish law or Halachah and taking it seriously. However, even that presumption must itself be ratified, and that ratification must be historically situated. Furthermore, once it is agreed that it is necessary to recover the Jewish legal tradition for the present, that recovery—whether it is by an orthodox *posek* in New York, a member judge of the Israeli supreme court, or a Reform rabbi in Chicago—is determined by the historical and intellectual world of the contemporary Jew. History, on this account, intrudes itself both at the fundamental level, where the obligation to recover the past is ultimately moored, and at the derivative level of interpretation and appropriation. Contemporary Jewish thought as a whole should begin with that history and a sense of which events in it are determinative or orienting.[2] I would like to propose that by starting with the Holocaust, we can formulate an account of Jewish obligation and particularly of Jewish moral obligation that responds in a profound way to the deepest Jewish intuitions and to the most serious criteria for Jewish moral thinking today.[3]

Among modern discussions of Jewish ethics, there is an overriding uniformity. Natural law theories, Kantian-style rationalisms, and traditional divine-command moral theories—all rest on the conviction that the heart of a moral theory is its principles or obligations and that these principles ought to be universal and unconditional.[4] From Moses Mendelssohn to Hermann Cohen, from Samuel David Luzatto to Marvin Fox, Jewish moral thinkers have viewed ethical imperatives as immune to historical considerations. I take issue with this fundamental assumption. In this chapter I attempt to develop the foundation of a historically situated moral theory that in its own way attempts to mediate the extremes of relativism and absolutism.[5]

In a preliminary way this mediation can be characterized as follows. Like every divine-command theory, the ethical theory I shall sketch holds that moral imperatives derive their obligatory status from their source, God and the divine will.[6] It is because this source is an ultimate authority that obligations which express His will are themselves authoritative. But while the *status* of moral principles is fixed by their source, the *content* of such principles is determined by their formulation and articulation. And, on the view of revelation presupposed by the theory, that articulation is wholly human.[7] This content is human interpretation that arises out of the historical situation of people who respond verbally and nonverbally to the Divine Presence. Hence, for the theory I shall outline, the ground of obligation is absolute but the specific obligations are historical, conditional, revisable, and relative. Language, like action, does not constitute the revelation of the Divine Presence; the latter is given to man in itself and immediately.[8] Rather, language emerges as a human response or interpretation which articulates the meaning of the event of revelation for those who receive and accept it.

The more distant one is in time from an event of revelation, the more complex is the network of action and interpretation that serves as the bridge between those who directly and originally encountered the Presence and those who seek to respond at a later time. For one who comes after a religious tradition has grown up, then, the problems of appropriating the event and receiving the tradition are complex. In part, the moral theory here developed tries to explore how that appropriation and reception work in a particular case, the moral case. From this point of view, the study of Jewish ethics is a study of the continuity of the Jewish legal tradition insofar as it is a tradition that crucially depends on its reception and the conditions for that reception. At the same time, it is a tradition that shapes and determines, to one extent or another, the situation out of which that reception occurs and the character of those who receive it. In short, the study of Jewish ethics is in part a study of the nature and development of Jewish tradition.

What criteria must our moral theory satisfy? How shall we know if the theory is acceptable and authentically Jewish? These are very difficult questions. Only a fully developed account of the nature of Jewish tradition and the character and conditions for its change, with a special eye to its deontic component, could begin to provide answers.[9] Still, insofar as the theory arises out of a historical situation, it ought to encounter and successfully meet the needs of that situation. It cannot ignore modern challenges to God and revelation; nor can it neglect claims about human freedom, motivation, and purpose. In short, it cannot reject, without thorough examination, modern philosophy and thought. At the same time, it cannot ignore those events and situations that have shaped the experience of Jews today—Jewish history, literature, and practice; the Holocaust; the rebirth and defense of the Jewish state; and the changing character of Jewish life in America and of Western culture generally. All of these factors must be engaged and understood and either accepted or rejected, in part or as a whole. While we cannot perform these tasks here, we can offer a pragmatic alternative. Our theory ought to satisfy certain intuitions that contemporary Jews might be expected to have about any acceptable Jewish moral theory and without which such a theory would simply not be compelling at all.[10] These intuitions might be captured in the following criteria:

I. An authentic Jewish moral theory must not ignore the past or the present. For to ignore the past is to cut oneself off from the historically developing destiny of the Jewish people, and to ignore the present is to court irrelevancy and anachronism.

II. An authentic Jewish moral theory must not neglect God or man. For Jewish ethics is by its very nature rooted in a Divine Command that is imposed and yet freely accepted.[11] To ignore or deny God is to cater to a thoroughgoing relativism that is pernicious or to pander to our failings and frailties rather than to take a stand in opposition to them. And to ignore man is to show disrespect for a liberal truth that Judaism itself has always endorsed, that Torah, at once divinely given, must be freely received in order to enrich and not stifle human living.

III. An authentic Jewish moral theory must not ignore the Jewish people or the needs of humankind. For to ignore the former is to lapse into an abstract universalism that is as insufficient in theory as its effects have been painful in fact.[12] And to neglect the latter is to deny to others the concern and respect one wants and expects for oneself and thereby to lapse into a parochialism at least as pernicious as the universalism it opposes.

IV. An authentic Jewish moral theory must be a part of a larger theory of Jewish existence and Jewish destiny today. For the moral ideals and imperatives that fall upon Jews should take their place among the variety of obligations and opportunities that shape and structure contemporary Jewish life.

V. An authentic Jewish moral theory must provide both an account of what Jewish obligations are—how they emerge, what their sources are, and how they are affected by history—and a strategy for identifying, interpreting, and communicating those obligations.

A Jewish moral theory that satisfied these conditions would be rich and fruitful. It would recognize the dramatic importance of the Holocaust for Jewish self-understanding today. It would furthermore appreciate the significance of Israel to that self-understanding and would, at the same time, confront with a proper sense of realism the moral sense of Jews outside of Israel. Such a theory would be continuous with the past, drawing on the riches of biblical, Halachic, and Midrashic literature, and yet it would recognize a central role for both Divine Command and human freedom. It would be a distinctly, unapologetically Jewish theory, for which the contemporary historical situation of the Jewish people is essentially determinative. Hence, such a theory would sacrifice the security of moral absolutes and the comfort of an easy universalism to its own essential historicity, opening up honest access to others by shutting off the routes of a disingenuous brotherhood. This theory, in short, would found a Judaism that had learned to live with itself because it will have ceased avoiding its own flesh and blood reality.[13]

## THE PROGRAM FOR THE THEORY

The framework for such a theory is available.[14] The Holocaust and the historical situation of Jews in the modern world are its starting points, and they define the terms and method whereby the past is to be appropriated for the present and future. The Holocaust as part of the theory's historical center authorizes that very appropriation and gives it shape, for by its very character the Holocaust has altered our views about human nature, moral psychology, religious purpose, hope, trust, and resolve. The theory I have in mind develops from its core, with due caution, a reserve that suits all too well the horror, the trauma, and the irredeemable evil that surely shatter the serenity of any sane person.[15] But once the theory finds its way beyond the Holocaust, not by negating it nor by diminishing its priority but rather by acknowledging its depth in a profoundly honest way, it emerges as a strategy for Jewish life today and in the future.[16] Jewish moral thinking finds its place within such a theory and develops as an attempt to provide an account of how moral imperatives arise for Jews, on what basis their moral force is founded, and how they are determined.

The reasoning in support of the theory begins with an initial desire to understand or comprehend the meaning of the Holocaust. What shape does the reasoning take? To be sure, it is neither deductive nor inductive in any standard sense. Rather, it begins with an attempt to explain the Holocaust and, once that attempt breaks down, proceeds to ask what significance the event might still have for subsequent Jewish history and Jewish life. The strategy will be to invite the possibility that there *is* such a significance for subsequent Jewish life, to interpret Jewish conduct in terms of this significance, and finally to elaborate that significance by means of a "transcendental deduction" of the conditions within Jewish life and within the Holocaust without which this interpreted significance could not exist. This latter stage, moreover, develops as a series of responses to four questions: What are Jews now doing? Can Jewish conduct be interpreted as responsive to the Holocaust? What is the precise character of that responsiveness? And what is the ground of that action as so interpreted and understood? This procedure is an example, in a sense, of the kind of interpretative enterprise one might engage in at any time in order to try to understand the role of a compelling event in its historical setting. Presumably it is reasoning initially motivated by a sense that the event *is* compelling and pursued when the event's significance becomes elusive and problematic. The reasoning proceeds as follows.

(1) The Holocaust is *unique*.[17] This statement is neither trivial nor absurd. It is not trivial because it means more than that the Holocaust differs from all other historical events. And it is not absurd because it does not make the Holocaust *sui generis* in every respect, unlike every other event in every way. What the statement of uniqueness does mean is that the Holocaust is sufficiently different from all *preceding* events—in terms of ideological purpose, technological manipulation, calculated administration, the character of the criminals, the dehumanization of the victims, and so on—to identify the time thereafter as a new stage in history.[18] Its claim on us, moreover, depends not on the event's uniqueness *per se* but rather on the particular features or constellation of features that make it unique.

(2) These features are so horrifying, so traumatic that they paralyze our capacity to explain them. To be sure, this paralysis is not going to

be obvious or acceptable to all. Surely our attempts to explain and understand the Holocaust will have to be examined and assessed. But for those who accept this judgment of paralysis, no matter how much we come to understand about the Holocaust's antecedent conditions, about the events that follow it, about human nature, or about religious doctrine, the Holocaust defies comprehension. No philosophical, theological, psychological, or historical theory adequately explains a sufficient number of its central features to leave us with a confident sense that we have understood this event or have grasped its meaning.[19] The Holocaust, in short, is as recalcitrant to intellectual resolution as it is to emotional satisfaction. It permits no complacency of thought.

(3) But explanatory meaning, comprehending why events occur, does not exhaust all meaning. A failure to locate an event within a theory, be it theological, historical, or whatever, does not entail that the event has no meaning at all for any or all of us.[20]

(4) Indeed, all Jewish life subsequent to the Holocaust can be understood with respect to it. Some Jews have acted and do act in conscious response to the Holocaust. Others do not respond consciously or intentionally, but their conduct too can be interpreted as responses to it. The meaning that an event has for an agent differs from and may be independent of the meaning of the event as understood, by a third party, with respect to that agent. The former depends on the agent's beliefs and intentions, while the latter is the result of an independent interpreter's reflective comprehension. Indeed, actions can be described and interpreted in many ways; when actions are interpreted as responsive to a given event, whether or not that event is a conscious component in the agent's intentions, we can say that the event in question has a meaning with respect to that action.[21] This is the case with the Holocaust. Having no *explanatory meaning* for it, we nonetheless have discovered its *descriptive* or *interpreted meaning* for subsequent Jewish life. And since all description is situated, is determined by the presuppositions, prejudices, and conditions of a time and a place, our description of Jewish conduct and Jewish life as responsive is not discredited by our reasons for describing them so. Indeed, our reasons authorize and authenticate that description.[22]

(5) These responses reflect an uncompromising opposition to the destructive goals of the Nazi regime. This is the answer to the third of the series of four questions that we listed earlier and now must proceed to answer. First, we notice that Jews today cling to Jewish survival and identification; they underwrite Jewish hope; they show guarded optimism in human goodness or at least in human capacity but an optimism nonetheless.[23] This conduct can be interpreted as responsive to the Holocaust, in the way we have just described (4). All in all, then, the very

strength of this responsive and responsible opposition to Nazi purposes makes one wonder about the *basis* for such stubbornness. It is not whimsical or arbitrary to understand this uncompromising opposition as a response to an obligation that is itself uncompromising, unconditional, and absolute. Indeed, in order to understand this action seriously, nothing weaker than such imperative force will do.[24]

(6) Absolute imperatives come only from absolute sources, and in Judaism there is only one such source, the Divine Presence of the Commanding God who spoke at Sinai and who speaks still.[25] This is the answer to our fourth question. Now, to be sure, positing such a source, we resist seeing the Jewish responsiveness as conditional. We resist too identifying a human or natural source for the obligation, be it qualified or unqualified.[26] Our resistance, however, while it may be premature, is not wholly unjustified. Indeed, it can be understood as an example of the very opposition which it in a sense grounds.

To this point, then, our account has identified the source of post-Holocaust Jewish imperatives as a Divine Commanding Presence situated within the Holocaust itself. However, for those interested, as we are, in understanding how Jewish moral thinking develops its imperatives in response to such a Presence, we have not proceeded far enough. How, then, does this program for a "transcendental deduction" of the Divine Commanding Presence at Auschwitz lead to a mode of Jewish responsiveness that is structured by moral imperatives of this Commanding God?

(7) If we couple our conclusion with a concept of revelation as an immediate relation between God and man and if the content of such a relation takes the form of a *command* and a *response*, both conceived not as divine contributions but rather as human interpretations of the *meaning* of the divine-human encounter, we can begin to see how particular obligations emerge from that encounter.[27] Jewish moral obligations, like all obligations understood to emanate from that Presence, are, in one sense, absolute in their source but, in another, relative, human, and historical in their determinate content. The force or impact that founds them is divine; the interpretative responsiveness that articulates them is human. The latter is a finite receptivity that is revisable and provisional, the former an Infinite Presence that unconditionally demands that *some* response be made. Hence, because the response is imperative, it cannot be a response to the *mere* event, which, even though unique, is still but an event in the world, but must be a response to a Divine Voice. And because the response and the Voice are related only in terms of the event itself, the Voice must be present *there*.

(8) For those who seek to identify the moral obligations of contemporary Jews, one must proceed to interpret what it is that the Commanding

Presence at Auschwitz commands of us. This is no easy task. Since the articulation of such commands is a matter of human interpretation where the individuals, the situations, and the moments of revelation differ, there are no uniform formulas for how to proceed. Still, one needs some guidance, and our theory would be seriously wanting if it did not attempt to provide it.

## OBJECTION, REVISION, AND GUIDANCE

In a sense, we have already begun to articulate the commands in step 5 of our reasoning.[28] There we described the responses of Jews subsequent to the Holocaust not as responses to the event itself but rather as responses to an imperative or a set of imperatives. We proceeded with such a description on the grounds that the uncompromising character of the responsiveness was only properly understood if we posited an obligation to mediate, as it were, the relation between the Holocaust and the Jews of today. If this were satisfactory and if the kinds of responses we had in mind—acts of opposition, whether conscious and intentional or not—were acceptable, then indeed we would already have begun to define Jewish obligation even prior to arriving at its source.

There are, however, questions about steps 4 and 5, and only when these questions are noted and answered can we actually begin to see how the imperatives of contemporary Jewish life properly emerge.

Step 5 arises after we turn to Jewish life subsequent to the Holocaust and, having understood that life as responsive to the Holocaust, try to discern the imperatives that ground that responsiveness. Clearly, however, even a casual consideration shows that contemporary Jewish life only poorly supports such a judgment. To be sure, it is *our decision* to interpret or describe Jewish experience as responsive that is at issue here and not a matter of empirical fact. Hence, one looks not for proof or evidence but rather for encouragement, support, or reason sufficient to justify such a choice and interpretation. But even this eludes us. Increased intermarriage, weakened formal affiliation with the Jewish community, and population depletion hardly encourage an interpretation of Jewish life as being in dramatic opposition to Nazi purposes, nor do they reflect an uncompromising will to survive. Even a distinction between actions intended as responses and those only interpreted as responses does not save steps 4 and 5 as they are presently stated. For while any action or inaction could conceivably be interpreted as a response to the radical evil of Auschwitz, it is hardly satisfying or comforting to be restricted to interpreting actions or trends that so obviously seem to capitulate to that evil. Furthermore, such a strategy, if it did not fail for these reasons, would surely fail if the responses were *largely* unintentional. Some small justification, beyond our own aborted quest for meaning in the Holocaust, ought to recommend treating Jewish life as responsive to that event. This justification can only come with *intentional response* and, as we suggested earlier, with intentional, dedicated response that is as well intentional, dedicated opposition. As we look around us, however, too few models, if any, of such opposition come into view. Thought, paralyzed by the Holocaust, cannot seek refuge outside of that event. Perhaps, then, we are at a loss because we are looking in the wrong direction.[29]

These worries about steps 4 and 5 extend to step 6. Having derived and located a Divine Commanding Presence—even if somewhat prematurely—we confront a bewildering dilemma. A Divine Presence is present to persons in history. If *we* are those who hear, then the Presence must be present now, and one wonders what links it to the events of forty years ago. On the other hand, however, if the Commanding Voice we have identified speaks at Auschwitz, as we have argued, then how can we, now, some forty years hence, hear that Voice? If the Presence was there, then the event was there and the divine-human encounter as well. But how then can we, here and now, be participants in that encounter? How, indeed, can that Voice speak to us?

A moment ago we looked for paradigms of dedicated, intentional opposition to Nazi purposes and were disappointed. Now we find ourselves alienated from the very Presence whose force is to be the ground of our imperatives. What we seek is a solution to both our difficulties, and that solution must be a bridge between now and then and also between us and the Voice of the Commanding God. We seek a model of opposition whose actions are a listening to that Voice and a speaking to us; we seek a link between us and the Divine Presence at Auschwitz, a mediator who encounters God in the immediacy of the moment and, at the same time, makes possible our own mediated appropriation of that Voice today.

The stories of such mediators are being told and retold with increasing frequency.[30] They include the tale of Yossel Rosensaft and his fellow inmates in Auschwitz, who, in December 1944, celebrated Hanukkah with a wooden menorah, carved with spoons, and with candles made of old cartons. Together they sang the traditional Hanukkah song "Maoz Tsur Yeshuati," a song of praise for God's salvation, for the redemption from Egypt, for the relief from exile in Babylonia, for the foiling of Haman's plot, and finally for the miraculous victory that Hanukkah itself celebrates. A traditional song, to be sure, but a setting that is so untraditional as to make the singing of that song an act of transcending opposition to the masters of Auschwitz and their purposes. There is too the frequent repeating of the injunction of Rabbi Yizhak Nissenbaum, who, in the Warsaw ghetto of 1940–41, acknowledged that the tradition of Kiddush Ha-Shem, martyrdom as a sanctification of God's name, had been replaced by an imperative to sanctify not death but life. "In former times," he said, "when the enemy demanded the soul of the Jew, the

Jews sacrificed their bodies 'for the sanctification of God's Name'; now, however, the oppressor wants the body of the Jew; it is therefore one's duty to protect it, to guard one's life."[31] The true Jewish vengeance, a Holocaust victim once wrote, is the power of the Jewish soul and its faith, an abiding trust that cries out "Hear, O Israel" in the face of guns and gallows and that cultivates dignity in the face of every imaginable assault on it.[32] The cases are myriad, cases of dedicated, intentional opposition, but for our purposes it is their common core and not their number that matters. Indeed, in the midst of such hell even one such act would be sufficient encouragement for us.[33]

When we look around ourselves for a paradigmatic opposition that is a responsive listening to the Divine Voice, we look in the wrong place. The right place is not here but there; the paradigmatic opposition is during and not after. We should look not at ourselves but rather at Rabbi Oshry and all those who wrestled dignity and nobility from chaos itself. If anyone heard the Voice, it was they, and if anyone's response ought to guide and direct our own, it is theirs. Indeed, it is only because of them that we can respond at all and only through them that we can begin to see how to interpret the meaning of the Divine Presence for ourselves.

How utterly unsurprising and unremarkable this is. It is the lesson of reception, tradition, and transmission, a lesson so integral to Judaism that it seems hardly necessary to draw attention to it. But because that reception must occur after a determinative event such as the Holocaust, it is indeed necessary to do so. Consider Sinai. The encounter between God and man was and always will be direct, but for Moses it was an origin, for those who followed him both an *origin* and a *goal*. For him it was once and for all an immediacy that resulted in responsive action and speech; for others, that encounter incorporates an impact to be felt only as it is appropriated through a tradition initiated by Moses and for which a new responsiveness is required to build on the old. And what is true for Sinai is true, in a more complex way, for every subsequent encounter between man and God within Judaism. Hence, it is true for the Divine Presence at Auschwitz. The bridge between us and Sinai includes the vast, ramified, intercommentative network of prophetic, rabbinic, and philosophical reflection that is called "Jewish tradition." But that link is rooted in Moses, in him who alone confronted that Presence *panim el panim*, face to face, and whose original response, whose words and actions, constituted the earliest Jewish life. That bridge includes as well all those epoch-making events when the same Voice was again heard and when new responses confronted and transformed the old.[34] The utterly momentous Presence during the Holocaust was Itself encountered, and those who experienced that encounter are the vital link, bringing together our imperatives, the event itself, and all of Jewish experience prior to it. Only through the actions and words of people like Rabbi

Oshry do we hear the Voice that spoke at Auschwitz and, beyond that, do we hear the dim but certain echo of that same Voice in its original encounter with the Jewish people.

## THE IMPERATIVES OF THE MORAL THEORY

For articulating contemporary Jewish imperatives, then, there are no ready formulas, but there are models and mediators. Rabbi Oshry is one; there are many others, exemplars and advocates of an overriding imperative, a principle of opposition to Nazi purposes and of resistance to those purposes.[35]

Oshry himself is especially remarkable, for he enunciates that principle, celebrates it, and gives it quasi-legal status.[36] On November 3, 1941, the Jews of the Kovno ghetto (in Lithuania) had recently survived Nazi actions against the inhabitants in which 10,000 were killed. Those who remained asked Ephraim Oshry whether they were permitted to thank God for their deliverance by reciting the blessing *Ha-gomel* (the Bestower). The Talmud explains that *Ha-gomel* is said by the sick who recovered, the prisoner who was released, the seafarer who landed, and one who crossed the desert. But Maimonides and Joseph Karo, in the *Mishneh Torah* and *Shulchan Aruch*, together with later commentators, disagree about exactly *when* the blessing should be recited. Some permit it even when the deliverance is only temporary; others require that it be complete and permanent. This is Rabbi Oshry's conclusion:

> It is quite possible that the cruel murderers had already condemned these who had escaped that particular *aktion* to death. The reason they let them remain alive was because they deliberately conducted their murderous operation in "cat and mouse" fashion, always allowing some Jews to remain alive for a time. They did this in order to delude them with false hopes so that their despair might be all the greater when the truth became known to them.
>
> Time after time they would lead the ghetto residents astray with all sorts of false rumors of salvation and deliverance in order to instill in them the vain hope that the destroyer's hand had finally been stayed. So, too, when they took them out to be killed, the Germans would lead them to believe that they were simply being transported from one point to another so the Jews should not try to escape or resist.
>
> Therefore, one certainly ought not to instruct those who escaped to recite *Ha-gomel* after having been saved from destruction in this one *aktion*. For these unfortunate ones may begin to imagine that the threat of death is truly over and that salvation is at hand. *In this fashion we would be helping the cursed murderers in their foul plot and would simply be making it easier for them to destroy our sisters and brothers.* Therefore, I ruled that they must not recite *Ha-gomel*. [my italics]

Based on a meticulous consideration of Jewish legal texts and precedent cases, Rabbi Oshry's decision suggests a principle of opposition that is remarkably present and indeed dominant in his mind. And that principle recurs in other of his Halachic judgments.[37] When, for example, a group of students from a nearby rabbinical seminary are threatened with execution, Oshry encourages a Jewish official to risk his own life to intercede in their behalf. These students, he says, are the bearers of the Jewish spirit and the Jewish soul. To try to save them—even at the risk of one's own life—is especially meritorious, for to do so is to oppose the Nazi plot to destroy not only Jews but Judaism itself. Recall too Oshry's unusual decision to permit a suicide with the proviso that his authorization not be publicized. Together these decisions reveal a conviction that Halachah must be served but only when it is made to satisfy a fundamental obligation to oppose what Hitler sought to accomplish—to satisfy, that is, an imperative to keep Judaism alive, to maintain trust and hope, dignity and honor.[38] The spectrum of cases of resistance during the Holocaust, widely and increasingly documented and recalled, here finds both an explicit formulation and, more importantly for us, a role within Halachic reasoning itself. Moral-legal decisions, on which permissions and obligations are based, themselves incorporate the principle of opposition to Nazi purposes and indeed give it priority.

The role of Rabbi Oshry's Halachic decisions in our practical reasoning as Jews—indeed, the role of the vast, rich reservoir of observations, judgments, insights, and decisions by victims and survivors in general—is a complex one. On the one hand, this testimony helps us to appropriate the urgency and impact of an encounter, at least a sense of obligation and necessity, which we can only appropriate through such mediation. In addition, however, these decisions and comments become a guide for us as we try to identify the imperatives of Jewish life today and a component in such interpretative articulation as well.

Oshry's sensitivity to the Nazi objectives, for example, reveals itself in the obligation to preserve the tradition of law and lore and the imperative not to endorse the abandonment of an other-worldly hope and trust. In the very act of studying the legal literature, carefully collecting precedents from the literature available to him, interpreting their sense and applicability, Oshry attempts to satisfy this obligation. To confront the complexity of moral-legal dilemmas without recourse to the Halachic tradition is to serve the Nazis and not to oppose them. As is clear from Oshry's own reasoning, this is not an obligation to adopt the Halachah as it presents itself, even if a specific obligation is uniformly endorsed. It is rather an obligation to consider this tradition, to study it and incorporate its judgments and reflections as components in one's own deliberation. To appropriate the Halachic tradition so far as one is able, then, is part of what it means to accept the obligation to keep Judaism alive, to maintain the continuity of a historical tradition of moral and legal reasoning that stretches between the Jew of today and the Voice that spoke to Moses himself. And that obligation is a fragment of an imperative of opposition to the Nazi plot.[39] That imperative here expresses itself in a particular way by the conviction that the survival of Judaism is jeopardized if the deliberations and decisions of the past are not given due respect in the deliberations and decisions of the present. This is the weight of the obligation to take the Halachic tradition seriously; it is an intermediate position between neglect and complete submission. Indeed, I think that Rabbi Oshry himself, whatever his *formal* commitment to the authority of the Halachah, in those years in the ghetto felt the weight of just this obligation.[40]

One role of Oshry's decisions and testimony akin to them is to show us the way to an understanding of the primary obligation that arises out of the Holocaust. A further role is to help us elaborate its ramifications, to clarify what opposition to Nazi purposes means and how one might set out to enact that opposition. But there is a further role still and one of profound, immediate importance. For since we, confronting the complexities of Jewish life today, seek to act, having considered the Halachic tradition as a component in our deliberations, we must realize too that we can only appropriate that tradition as it existed prior to the Holocaust *in terms of* the way its content was, on the one hand, appropriated during the Holocaust and, on the other, transformed at times by the event itself. Not only do Oshry's Halachic reflections and decisions guide our interpretation of the general obligations of Jewish existence; they also contribute to the specific ways in which we can and should appropriate that tradition in order to arrive at precise imperatives for our own lives. The meaning of the Halachic tradition is mediated for us by Oshry's understanding of it and even by the very situations which Oshry had to confront.

Among contemporary moral problems that have generated widespread discussion both in scholarly journals and in popular publications and forums, the problem of abortion holds a special place.[41] Notwithstanding its controversial nature, however, the abortion question is agreed to turn on two issues: the status of the fetus as a moral person, and the boundaries of justifiable homicide. The discussion of both of these matters in the Halachic literature is complex and provocative; yet out of this variety emerges a dominant view and several minority views.[42] According to the former, the fetus is a person at birth and indeed, for certain legal purposes, only thereafter. Nonetheless, taking its life, the act of feticide, is serious enough to require substantial justification. The dominant view is that only mortal threat to the mother will provide that justification, but minority views allow greater leniency, even to the point of permitting abortions in order to save the mother mental anguish and social disgrace. Throughout the Halachic literature, then, attention is focused on the mother and her needs and thereby on the needs of the present.

If, however, we are to take with utter seriousness the obligation to sustain the Jewish people and, in so doing, to oppose a fundamental Nazi purpose, we ought to consider with equal concern the welfare of the fetus and its future, a future that represents the future of the Jewish people itself. To be sure, such a requirement by itself can produce no precise picture; no simple resolution of cases is forthcoming. But appreciating the primacy of the obligation to oppose Hitler and his designs, we notice that certain considerations relevant to a moral decision play a more important role than they might otherwise have. This is starkly highlighted by the following incident.

On May 7, 1942, the Nazis passed a decree prohibiting pregnancy among the Jews in the Kovno ghetto. It was a law aimed at killing hope and joy among the Jews of Kovno and a law aimed at cutting off the Jewish future as well. Punishment was to be immediate and absolute; any Jewish woman found pregnant was to be executed on the spot. On August 9 of that year Rabbi Oshry was confronted with the following problem: given the Nazi decree, could a Jewish woman who found herself pregnant abort the fetus in order to save her own life? Oshry's response is a moving testimony to the power of law to preserve dignity and order where chaos threatens. Carefully examining the legal literature, he chooses to permit the abortion, for to forbid it would be to accept the deaths of both mother and fetus as a virtual certainty. The point to notice here, however, is not Oshry's decision but rather the diabolical purpose served by the Nazi decree. In effect it forced the Jews of Kovno to cancel in advance their own future and hence the future of the Jewish people. And for those women unfortunate enough to become pregnant, it forced them to cut off their own future in order to save the present. In short, the Nazi cunning was not satisfied to annihilate the Jewish future, to instill fear and remove joy; it enrolled the Jews, the victims themselves, in its terrible plot. And more awful still, in cases where pregnancy did occur, it enlisted Jewish women as the assassins of their own hopes and joys, indeed, of their future. The effect of this realization on those who take seriously the obligation to oppose Nazi purposes must be profound. Who now can fail to consider the future as well as the present? Who can neglect the importance of the fetus together with the needs of the mother? To be sure, there is no ready formula that will tell us how this important consideration will or should influence particular decisions. What is nonetheless clear, however, is that no facile appropriation of the lenient Jewish tradition is any longer possible. To abort without serious threat to the mother may very well be to betray that woman whose case Oshry was asked to consider and to betray too all the Jews of Kovno.[43]

## COMMENTS AND PROBLEMS

Having said this much in sketching a theory of moral obligation for contemporary Jewish life, we have not yet said enough. The reasoning that supports this theory and the procedure for its application are not without difficulties.

First, the derivation of the obligation to recover the Halachic tradition as a component of moral deliberation for the contemporary Jew depends on one's understanding of the connection between *Jewish survival*, in particular the survival of Judaism, and *the recovery of the tradition*. Some may take that connection to be accidental and arbitrary; they may see no obstacle to a Judaism completely severed from the traditional round of Jewish conduct and the laws that define it. Indeed, to some the interpretation of this connection may seem to be a factual matter and one not easily decided. It is, of course, not a factual matter; nor is it a matter of simply defining Judaism in such a way that traditional Jewish law, even if not authoritative, is essential to Judaism. Rather, the justification of the imperative to secure Judaism by recovering Jewish legal literature rests in the paradigmatic opposition to Nazi purposes expressed self-consciously in the actions of Rabbi Oshry and many other Halachic authorities and in the respect given those authorities and their decisions by those who solicited them. To ignore that literature is to impugn these individuals as our only link to the Divine Commanding Presence and hence to cut ourselves off from any authentic response to that Presence. Indeed, it would be to cut ourselves off from any *need* to respond at all, at any rate from a sense of the uncompromising imperative that issues from the Holocaust itself. In short, then, we are bound to accept Oshry's respect for the Halachic tradition unless something decisive supersedes it, i.e., unless we have some good reason for thinking that Judaism today can survive without any respect for Halachic decisions and the legal tradition.

Second, we ought to notice that since specific Jewish obligations derive from a single principle or, perhaps more accurately, are nonhierarchical determinations of this principle, conflicts are bound to arise.[44] One can easily imagine being bound to oppose injustice or to advance the maintenance of human dignity in a situation where the necessary action would compromise the Jewish people. In such cases, there can be no neat resolution of the conflict.[45] Contemporary Jewish ethics does not try to avoid the reality of genuine moral conflict or indeed of conflict between any pair of Jewish obligations. Nor does it venerate such conflicts. Rather, Jewish ethics acknowledges the authenticity of such paradoxes, when they occur, and respects the courage and the anguish that mark our encounter with them.[46]

Third, insofar as the real substance of Jewish obligation reveals itself only when the principle of opposition to Nazi purposes is ramified and given its precise interpretation, it is manifest that this ramification produces a collection of moral, religious, and prudential commands that all have a common source. There is a sense, then, in which the moral and prudential obligations are themselves religious and the religious obligations at least prudential, if not moral as well. For reasons deeper than those we can point to here, then, our account of Jewish ethics rejects any sharp distinctions between religion and morality and between religious imperatives and prudential, political, secular necessities.[47] While we can only notice this feature of our theory here, it is a feature well worth careful scrutiny. By appreciating the ways that the Holocaust has markedly altered our very conceptual tools, we reinforce our original conviction of its momentous importance.

Fourth, the Jewish ethical theory I have sketched takes the interpretation of Jewish moral commands to be the result of the historically situated deliberation of individuals, appropriating the Jewish legal tradition as they consider the needs and requirements of their own situation. These commands, therefore, are always in principle revisable, although in fact they are, when accepted, treated as unconditional. But, one might ask, by treating them as absolute, are we not just deceiving ourselves? Why not simply accept the historicism of our theory? Why indulge in counterfeit absoluteness when an honest relativism waits in the wings?

Perhaps no hasty resolution to this objection will satisfy. But we can certainly caution against accepting it too uncritically. For the objection assumes that no moral obligation can be both divine in origin and human in formulation and hence that none could be both unconditional and revisable at once. But the Jewish moral theory I have sketched is founded on a conception of divine-human encounter that permits, indeed invites just that cooperation of wills. For this reason, the status of the obligations we have been discussing can only be understood when that conception of revelation is critically considered. Others have done this, and we can only hope that their treatment begins to cope with at least some of the reservations noted here.[48] It is nonetheless worth observing that the historicism and relativism of our theory are not self-liquidating. For we view the articulated commands as human interpretations of what is in itself a Presence that no words or concepts can capture. It is hardly surprising, then, that such interpretations, historically particularized both in source and in application, are in fact taken to be unconditional even when they are in principle subject to modification and even rejection.

Fifth, our theory must pay the price of historical situatedness in yet another way. Consider once again the reasoning that supports the theory and especially step 2 of that reasoning. It is crucial to the account as a whole and to that step in particular that explanation of the Holocaust fail and that explanatory failure eventually lead to a different kind of meaning. But explanation is contextual; given a certain phenomenon, an explanation of it is satisfactory or not relative to a given person in a particular situation at a certain time and for a certain purpose. This relativity of explanation infects the argument at least in steps 2 and 3, and this means that the move to step 4 and beyond is justified only for individuals who accept 2 and 3. The purpose of the reasoning, however, is to identify the source of a general obligation for all Jews and then to show how that obligation can be formulated and articulated. In short, the argument wants to derive a general obligation, but, as it stands, it simply cannot do so.

This objection rests on a deep misunderstanding. To be sure, the argument is subjective in the sense that the dissatisfaction that leads from explanatory failure to descriptive meaning is relative to subjective needs. But the result is nonetheless general and objective, for the obligation's ontological status is not impugned by the method through which we come to perceive it. What is impugned is the recognition of the generality of the obligation: for some a much weaker explanation will account for the character of resistance both during and after the Holocaust. Not everyone, that is, will agree with Rabbi Oshry that opposition is an obligation, especially one based on Divine Command. To expect a generally recognized obligation seems far too ambitious to me. It is one thing to claim that an obligation is objective; it is quite another to require that everyone acknowledge and accept it. Indeed, since the proof for the obligation, and for its specific articulation or interpretation, is admittedly human, historically influenced, it is not reasonable to expect that everyone will recognize such an obligation or indeed any obligation holding for all Jews. What is reasonable, however, and also possible, is to know that there is such an obligation, and this knowledge our reasoning provides.

## CONCLUSION

The Jewish moral theory which we have sketched does, I think, satisfy the intuitive criteria we set down earlier. It is responsive to the past and to the present, to God and to man, to the Jewish people and to all humankind.[49] As a theory that issues in particular moral imperatives, it is part of a larger theory of the imperatives that define Jewish existence today. In short, this is a moral theory that a post-Holocaust Jew, immersed in Western culture yet sensitive to the needs of the Jewish people, of the Jewish state, and of their faith, could endorse.[50]

In the modern treatment of religious ethics there is sometimes a tendency to want the same universality and objectivity for religious ethics that many have found in popular rationalist moral theories. I doubt that in the case of an authentic Jewish ethics such unanimity can be discovered. Many will surely find this result unsettling, if not simply wrong. They would prefer a moral theory that begins with a transhistorical Torah and imposes itself uniformly on Jews of all times and all places and indeed on all people as well.[51] This is not the place to debate their preference. What I have done instead is to offer an alternative with the hope that its virtues will impress the discerning reader.

# EIGHT

# Historicism, Evil, and Post-Holocaust Moral Thought

There is an irony about post-Holocaust Jewish thought that is well worth addressing. Like most ironies, it gains in power and surprise by simple formulation. There are two groups of post-Holocaust Jewish thinkers, those who recognize the event's unique, radical evil and those who do not. The latter, while agreeing that Auschwitz was an event of extreme horror and intense suffering, do not believe that it or any other historical episode can alter the theological and moral truths of Judaism. The former, on the other hand, are persuaded that the unprecedented atrocities have altered the very shape of Jewish self-understanding, for Judaism is rooted in history and is always revisable in terms of it. For one group the moral resources of Judaism are decisive and unalterable; for the other they are rich but constantly in flux. The result is irony, for those who take the Holocaust most seriously are without the unconditional moral resources to oppose it absolutely, while those who reject the event's unprecedented character are more able to oppose it unqualifiedly even while they refuse to treat its evil as distinctive. In short, the more transforming the event, the less decisive one's ability to oppose it; the less transforming, the more unconditional one's capacity for opposition.

Perhaps this irony is, like so many, more apparent than real. One would like to think so. For the irony concerns large and important questions about morality and relativism, truth and history, and the very nature of Jewish faith, moral thought, and Jewish life. Let me propose, then, that we use the irony as a way of exposing these problems and examining them. Our goal will be to determine if the particularly powerful *moral context* of post-Holocaust religious—here Jewish—thought may result in an especially profound attempt to resolve the dispute between realism and historicism and to understand the relation between thought and history in the sphere of religious and moral life.

It will be useful to clarify this goal at the outset. Recently philosophers, literary critics, and others have inclined away from some form of objectivism or realism toward what has been called historicism, idealism, or pragmatism. Nietzsche and Heidegger are, among others, the forebears of this movement, but its current practitioners include analytic as well as Continental style philosophers, historians, students of anthropology, science, and religion, literary theorists, and many more. What they share is a refusal to admit invariable standards of value and judgment and a penchant for interpretation and understanding rather than explanation, truth, and certitude. For them acting, thinking, and writing are context-bound activities, events to be understood against a background of discourse, purpose, and reception. History and community determine thought in the sense that all thinking emerges out of the discourse of historical communities. Transcendence is never totally complete; all thought is moored in and emerges from the individual subject's point of view and is subject to historical alteration, confirmation, and revision.

There are many motivations for holding the views incorporated in this way of thinking—doubts about the universality of logical principles (like bivalence), about traditional distinctions (like that between *a priori* and *a posteriori* knowledge), about the objectivity of moral principles and judgments, about translation and communication, about skepticism and its presuppositions, and on and on. The results of these motivations and the arguments they generate are a variety of kinds of antifoundationalism. The question I am raising is this: if the context that gives rise to thoughts about historicism and these issues is profoundly moral and historically particular, as the Holocaust is, then does it yield any hope for a result that is *historically serious*—and hence antifoundationalist or historicist—and at the same time *morally deep and responsible*? In other words, can we show some reason to think that the irony with which we began is in fact only apparent?

We should begin with a thinker who is sensitive to the moral dimension of human and specifically Jewish existence but who cannot bring himself to think that post-Holocaust Jewish theology is substantially transformed by Auschwitz. Here, I think, Eliezer Berkovits is an excellent example. *Faith after the Holocaust*, published in 1973, is a morally impassioned attempt to confront the event with utter seriousness and honesty while at the same time identifying and holding to a transcendent yet historically relevant conception of God, the Jewish people, and their covenantal relationship in history. For Berkovits, Auschwitz is a psychological, not a theological problem for the Jewish people; it is an event that both represents the nadir of human moral development and threatens the Jewish commitment to moral mission, to spearheading the moral redemption of creation. The theological conception that lies behind this twin judgment is *not* threatened, revised, or destroyed. As historical event, the Holocaust has an impact on historical creatures, on the Jewish people, and it does *threaten* them and their level of allegiance to their moral-religious responsibilities. But it does not threaten the philosophy of history and the conception of Divine Providence which these people hold. What is shaken is not the theory itself but rather their ability to accept it, to believe it, to act in its behalf.

This is what Berkovits says:

> The question raised by the holocaust that concerns man most directly is not, "Where was God?", but "Where was man?" The presence of God in history or his absence from it is a complex theological problem; the presence or absence of man as an ethical and moral agent is a matter of experience. The Jewish experience in the ghettos and death camps made manifest in our days the collapse of man as a moral being. . . . In terms of the spirit . . . it was a world catastrophe on the widest possible scale.[1]

Berkovits argues that the event implicates, in addition to the Nazis themselves, the Christian churches, the Allied nations, the Germans, indeed the entire West. "The plight of the Jew became the point for the crystallization of moral direction in history" (36), and it was a point of "disintegration" and failure. For Berkovits, then, the Holocaust is the moment when the moral bankruptcy of Western civilization exposed itself, and at least for this reason it is an event of world-historical significance.

In our post-Holocaust world Christianity is in disarray, and the Jewish people ought to be. But the Jewish thinker must avoid an inauthentic questioning of God. "The inexplicable will not be explained" (70), but it can be endured. "The question of faith for the Jew is . . . not to explain why God was silent while the crematoria were consuming a third of the Jewish people. The question is whether within the frame of reference of Judaism it is possible to take cognizance of the tragedy and promise of existence and whether one may hold on to the promise in spite of the tragedy" (85). After Auschwitz, there is every reason for the Jew to give up, to forgo his sense of purpose and abandon hope. But, Berkovits argues, a secure self-understanding of history, Providence, and the role of the Jewish people, together with a recognition of the significance of the reestablishment of the state of Israel, should enable him to endure.

We need not examine Berkovits's account of a genuine Jewish conception of history and God's involvement in it. Suffice it to say that he takes innocent suffering to be a biblical and rabbinic problem and that he uses a notion of paradox in which free will is given, as is moral command, by a divine presence that is also paradoxically a divine absence, and he thereby sees God's impact as issuing in a millennial task to bring moral perfection to the created world, a task enabled and hindered by the gift of human freedom.[2] The result of this view of history and the Jewish covenantal responsibility is a distinction between two histories, that of the nations or power history and that of Israel or faith history. It is the twin outcome of Nazism that power history seems to have become overwhelmingly victorious in the modern world and that the Jewish people, witness to faith, has become utterly demoralized. The question of urgency, then, concerns not God's role; rather, it is whether the Jewish people can remain at their covenantal post, witnessing to "God's elusive presence in history" (131).

It is not necessary to complete Berkovits's story, for its relevance to our inquiry should already be clear. Berkovits is willing to give the Holocaust a central role in his understanding of contemporary Jewish life. It is the nemesis of power history, the outcome of nature victorious over faith and moral purpose. But Auschwitz "does not preempt the future course of Jewish history" (134), by which Berkovits means that rabbinic faith must not be consumed by the Shoah. Rather, the event must be understood as part of a history whose character is defined by the biblical and rabbinic teachings. *Theologically* speaking, the enormity of the *hurban* (destruction) is insignificant.[3] *Psychologically* speaking, the level of suffering and atrocity is overwhelming. What Berkovits calls the Jewish "philosophy of history" and "concept of divine providence," established in the biblical text and developed by rabbinic interpretation, are unconditional and unrevisable in their basic design. It is faith, subjectively rather than objectively speaking, that is at issue, and the Holocaust puts it in jeopardy. Furthermore, the event is the outcome of all those natural forces—desire, need, power, etc.—which faith and moral purpose are an effort to control, shape, and direct. In short, Berkovits is a kind of Manichaean; in his eyes the Jewish people are mandated by goodness to oppose the sources of evil in nature. Hence, the evil of the Holocaust is rooted in the forces of nature, while goodness is the banner of the Divine carried by human freedom. An original irony, then, is mitigated, for the evil, particularized in its object, is reduced to power and its associates, while its motivational effects do, to some degree, influence the career of faith, albeit not in content. In the end, Berkovits cannot submit to any form of theological historicism, nor does he give evil its complete due. He employs powerful moral weapons but against a compromised enemy.[4]

Berkovits incorporates the Holocaust into a preexisting pattern of Jewish thought. Neither the latter's conception of evil nor its conception of the divine-human relationship is altered by the evil. Yet Berkovits is sensitive to the suffering and the atrocity, to the Holocaust's impact on contemporary Jews, Christians, and others. Hence, in moving away from his position, we seek one that is at least equally sensitive to the event's impact, is respectful of the transcendent character of Jewish self-understanding, but is more responsive to the event's theological significance. This position, I believe, is held by Irving Greenberg in his important essay "Cloud of Smoke, Pillar of Fire: Judaism, Christianity, and Modernity after the Holocaust" (1977).[5]

First, Greenberg is keenly attentive to the historicity of Jewish experience. Judaism applies to history and indeed emerges from history, from the "basic orienting experience" of the Exodus. God cares about human life; in the end human life will be redeemed from suffering, poverty, indignity. The result of these facts is that "events happen in history which change our perception of human fate, events from which we draw the fundamental norms by which we act and interpret what happens to us. One such event is the Holocaust" (8). Greenberg then says that it is impossible to isolate the Exodus from "further revelations" and counterexperiences. In principle, then, for Greenberg the original Jewish understanding of the divine-human encounter and its meaning for Jewish life can be reinterpreted and revised. It is historically exposed.[6]

With respect to the Holocaust, then, how does this exposure occur? Greenberg proposes that Judaism "stand[s] or fall[s] on [the] fundamental claim that the human being is . . . of ultimate and absolute value" (9). Then, as a "counter-testimony" to this affirmation of human worth and dignity, he cites a powerful piece of testimony from the Nuremberg trial record, of the burning alive of Jewish children at Auschwitz, purportedly to save the minuscule cost of gassing them. This pit of burning, screaming children now represents the atrocities, the evil of the Holocaust, and in terms of it Greenberg does two things:

(1) he formulates a criterion of acceptability—perhaps even of authenticity—for all statements, theological or otherwise, that deal with post-Holocaust Jewish life (the criterion of the burning children);

(2) he claims that as a result of applying this criterion, all responses to the event will be dialectical (the dialectical criterion).[7]

It is not clear how Greenberg sees the relationship between these two criteria. On the face of it, he seems to be reasoning this way: the Holocaust is incomprehensible; so our existing standards and concepts cannot deal with it fully, simply, or adequately. There is no way of combining sufficient sensitivity to the event's horror and our categories of thought and action, for these latter reflect our sense of human value. Greenberg draws from this fact of *incommensurability* or *incompatibility* the conclusion that all attempts to deal with or respond to the Shoah are dialectical, where this seems to mean 'complex', 'partial', torn by "irresolvable tensions." Hence, if one theorizes after the event, one's theory must be dialectical, i.e., without complete or final resolution, involving a tension of thought that moves from pole to pole. This characteristic, then, is the "verification principle" for post-Holocaust thinking (see (2) above).

Greenberg proceeds to formulate what he calls a "working principle," what I have called the "criterion of the burning children": "No statement, theological or otherwise, should be made that would not be credible in the presence of the burning children" (23).[8] Now this is a bit confusing. Which is the adequacy criterion for theological thought—this working principle, or the dialectical condition, or both? Let us set aside the objection that the Holocaust is not the only motivation for dialectical thinking. Then I think that what Greenberg means is this: authentic post-Holocaust theology—we omit for convenience other types of thinking—will be partial, tense, and complex, in a word "dialectical." But this is a result of the fact that no complete solutions or simple answers can be held at the same time that one is sufficiently moved by the horrors of the Holocaust. To check to see if one's thought is dialectical would be formal and insufficient. To check to see if one could affirm a claim while wholly conscious of and receptive to the pain, the horror, the atrocity—this will not only expose the flaw in one's thinking but will also direct one's thinking through the dialectical process of affirmation, denial, qualification, affirmation, and so on. In a sense, then, Greenberg wants the two principles to be coextensive. In effect, the principle of the burning children (see (1) above) actually generates dialectical thinking and does so by never allowing thought to escape the utter concreteness and particularity of the event. The tension between universal categories, principles, and so on and the precise horror of this collection of concrete episodes arises in the mind of the thinker when his thought is not allowed to escape the particular episode.

In terms of profundity of insight, this attempt to ensure that the encounter of thought with the Shoah never be permitted to escape the concrete particularity of its episodes of horror marks a high point in Greenberg's discussion. His thought quickly becomes less powerful. For example, he asks, what about faith after Auschwitz? His answer, that it must be dialectical and momentary, is riddled with problems. "Neither classical theism nor atheism," he says, "is adequate to incorporate the incommensurability of the Holocaust." This may be true, but his brief, critical comments about and classification of Berkovits, Emil Fackenheim, and Richard Rubenstein fail to understand any of the three. Berkovits may be a classical theist but hardly a self-satisfied one; Fackenheim simply is not, and Rubenstein is too complex to be cast simply as an atheist. Furthermore, as Greenberg turns to describe "dialectical faith," he weakens his own conception, for he treats dialectic as a movement from moment to moment, from belief to skepticism, from conviction to doubt (27, 33). But surely a strong view of dialectic would treat every moment as simultaneously a moment of faith and insecurity, of hope and despair. Indeed, Greenberg's earlier discussion of Elie Wiesel's Sarah, both saint and prostitute, suggests this notion of a simultaneous dialectic, as does his later account of secularity and religiosity (45–52).

In principle, for Greenberg, all of Judaism can be revised. In fact, however, much resists revision. He argues against the utter destruction of faith, explores biblical models for a post-Holocaust understanding of the divine-human relation, and mines traditional texts for testimony in behalf of human worth and dignity. Greenberg derives this multifaceted commitment to Jewish faith and its traditional expressions from a general notion of moral necessity against the "idols of the age," secularism, idolatry, humanism, rationalism, and so forth. If the dialectical character of authentic response is the hallmark of Greenberg's historicism, this unqualified opposition to the failures of modernity signals his moral absolutism.

From a moral point of view, then, Greenberg has a good deal in common with Berkovits. The Holocaust is a signal of the moral bankruptcy of the modern world, of a secular culture framed by "science, philosophy, and social science," "rationalism and human liberation." "Modernity fostered the excessive rationalism and utilitarian relations which created the need for and susceptibility to mass movements and the surrender of moral judgment" (28). Greenberg argues that secular civilization, after Auschwitz, hardly warrants our commitment. We must resist the "absolutization of the secular" (29). To be sure, what Greenberg advocates is no simpleminded return to a spiritual traditionalism. Remember the mandate to dialectical positions—secular and religious, self-reliant and submissive, and so forth. But nonetheless his doubts about modernity and his respect for the resources of the Jewish tradition do reflect a bias, for to Greenberg the Holocaust is the supreme counter-testimony to the millennial Jewish commitment to human dignity and value.

In the end, Greenberg falsifies our irony but only with an ungrounded, essentially unconditional act of opposition. Once he has admitted the historical openness of Jewish theological thought to the Holocaust, he can recover so much of Judaism only by an act of allegiance to a way of thinking and acting that has always stood for human dignity and value. By seeing the Holocaust as the nemesis of modernity, Greenberg gives a slightly more subtle, more dialectical version of Berkovits's traditionalism, but it is a traditionalism nonetheless.

To a traditional Jewish reader Greenberg's thought must seem threatening or perhaps utterly misguided. From Berkovits's point of view, the lapse into historicism surely must be seen as an error. Berkovits tried but could not completely treat the Holocaust as an unprecedented case of evil, but he could oppose it and its conditions unconditionally, as the outcome of a timeless divine mandate. Greenberg is more receptive to the Holocaust's concrete particularity, to its theological impact, but he can only call upon the resources of Jewish moral purposes as if nothing had changed. If, in addition, Jewish obligation does make a claim upon him, he must at some point ask why and how this is so.

In this context, Emil Fackenheim's articulation of a 614th Commandment and his recognition of a Divine Voice that spoke at Auschwitz look like answers. The struggle between historicism and transcendence has been a central theme of Fackenheim's work for thirty years or more. In *Metaphysics and Historicity* he argued that even an existential account of man as radical self-making in a situation included an element of philosophical transcendence.[9] In the late 1960s he altered that conviction by admitting that even Jewish religious thought, at every level, was not immune to historical alteration.[10] Religious self-understanding is always a matter of an interpretive recovery of the past, for and in the present; no doctrines, principles, or even categories are beyond historical impact. In principle, everything is negotiable, and after Auschwitz in particular, everything is on trial.

The question is, when the verdict is in, what resources are still available to oppose the evil? We focus on Judaism: what Midrashic teachings are recoverable? What kind of opposition is there to the "demons of Auschwitz"? What is the ground of that opposition, i.e., what makes it necessary and what makes it possible? How can that ground make the opposition more than arbitrary or subjective or whimsical or temporary or conditional or . . . ? And how, given the overwhelming nature of the evil, does the ground make it possible, conceivable, humanly willable?

These are serious questions, and Fackenheim's attention to them has become more and more thematic and self-critical over the years. His first real attempt to deal with them comes, for our purposes, in the third chapter of *God's Presence in History*.[11] Here he argues for the following conclusions: First, that when religious thought fails to comprehend the Shoah, it turns to the task of identifying a response that can only be understood as the response to an imperative of opposition to Nazi purposes. Second, that the ground of that imperative cannot be a humanly created or humanly centered ideal. And finally, that the appropriate Jewish ground for such an imperative is a Divine Voice that renders it a Divine Command, complexly human in its interpretation and execution but divine in its origin.[12]

Other moral philosophers and religious thinkers may have the problem of being sufficiently attentive to the concrete particularity of the Holocaust and its momentousness. Fackenheim has the problem of showing that obligations generated by such attentiveness are sufficiently rich to frame broad concerns about human dignity, justice, and so on. Indeed, Fackenheim's problem is even deeper. For he explicitly eschews, in his own thinking, any strategy of rational justification for such obligations. What we want to know of Fackenheim's obligations is how secure their grounding is, the grounds, that is, for the obligation to oppose this evil, the conditions that make such opposition possible, and the results that flow from it.

For our purposes, we begin where Fackenheim shows us that theological, philosophical thought—indeed, all thought—reaches an impasse—with a recognition of the depth of the evil, its particularity, and the resulting obligation to oppose that evil:

> A Jew at Auschwitz . . . was *singled out* by a demonic power which sought his death *absolutely*, i.e., as an end in itself. For a Jew today merely to affirm

> his Jewish existence is to accept his singled-out condition; it is to oppose the demons of Auschwitz: and it is to oppose them in the only way in which they can be opposed—with an *absolute* opposition. (81)

Fackenheim takes this to be the situation of religious and secular Jew alike. He focuses on the secular Jew who "knows that the devil, if not God, is alive," who "has relativized all former absolutes," but who "as a Jewish secularist . . . opposes the demons of Auschwitz absolutely by his mere commitment to Jewish survival" (82).[13] But alongside this relativistic sort of Jewish secularist, who is confounded by the contradiction of universality and particularity, of relativism and accepting an absolute obligation, there is another Jewish secularist, who tries, albeit unsuccessfully, to oppose "the demons of Auschwitz absolutely—but in behalf of 'free,' autonomous post-religious humanity" (82). Why unsuccessfully? Because, as Fackenheim argues, both "humanly created ideals" and "internalized absolutes"—those of Reason or Progress, for example, "either cannot single out or else cannot remain absolute" (83). In short, the Jewish secularist cannot respond to principles of either sort, for they cannot do justice to the evil, the victims, or the unconditionality of the opposition. Fackenheim concludes:

> Jewish opposition to Auschwitz cannot be grasped in terms of humanly created ideals but only as an imposed Commandment. And the Jewish secularist, no less than the believer, is absolutely singled out by a Voice as truly other than man-made ideals—an imperative as truly given—as was the Voice of Sinai. (83)

Today, the class of authentic Jews who affirm their Jewishness includes both secular and religious Jews, who "are united by a commanding Voice which speaks from Auschwitz" (84), and what it speaks is—interpreted as—the 614th Commandment, that of opposition to Hitler's purposes.

Fackenheim begins this line of thinking by identifying an imperative of opposition to Nazi purposes. We can ignore how he arrives at it.[14] But then, in the face of attempts to ground that imperative in rational principles or ideals, he argues that such theories fail for lack of particularity or absoluteness or both. Now this claim, made rather quickly, might be denied, but let us accept it, and follow Fackenheim a step further. If such ideals cannot ground the imperative, what can? Fackenheim infers that it must be "an imposed commandment," the singling-out revelation of a Divine Commanding Voice. Even if we ignore the problems that cloud the secularist's relation to such a Voice, there are other problems, more serious still, and it is these that Fackenheim himself comes to appreciate. What we seem to have here is a transcendental-style argument for the Divine Presence, an attempt to show that no such imposed commandment is possible without a Divine Commanding Voice. But how can either the believer or the skeptic, especially after Auschwitz, be inclined to accept such an argument? If Divine Command is the ground of the imperative, then in fact there *is* no ground—at least not yet. Perhaps Fackenheim is right that the imperative is received as *imposed*, but why as a command? And why as God's command? And if we hold the Divine out of it—at least until faith can be recovered more slowly and patiently—what makes the imperative *imposed*? And furthermore, what, without Divine Grace, makes it possible for us to perform it? What, finally, is its real ground—once the humanly created ideals are seen to be insufficient?

Fackenheim, in other words, reaches his conclusions too hastily, both that the imperative is imposed and that it is a commandment. Indeed, perhaps even the claim that opposition requires an imperative is already too hasty. Why not a reaction to threat? Or a repugnance to a storied ugliness or hatred? In part, Fackenheim's problem arises because he directs thought, once stopped in its tracks, to turn to subsequent Jewish life in order to seek guidance about a response. Such life is not clearly a response, nor is it based on more than defiance or revulsion or conformity, at least not consciously and intentionally. But in part the problem is deeper, for even once an imperative of opposition is identified, its *ground* is not so easily got. It may be clear that in order for it to pick out its subjects and in order not to be conditioned by human will it must be *imposed* from the outside and also enabled from the outside. But if faith is not yet assumed,[15] what grounds its status as imposed? What, in different terms, makes it both possible and necessary? What gives opposition its realism and its authority?

In subsequent essays and books Fackenheim makes it clear that for him moral principles and traditional ideas must be reinterpreted in the light of "epoch-making" events.[16] Nevertheless, he does not rule out the possibility that some idea or principle might emerge that would transcend history and achieve an objectivity and permanence as yet unrealized. But in terms of the Holocaust, as he sees it, all is called into question. This historicist outcome of the impact of the Holocaust can, for our purposes, be accepted. The central issue concerns not the *content* of post-Holocaust moral principles but rather their *ground*, i.e., the source of their possibility and their necessity. Does Fackenheim, deferring theological recovery to a future not-yet, nonetheless find a ground sufficiently deep, secure, and rich to support a mandate of opposition?

In *To Mend the World*[17] Fackenheim knows that this problem is *an aspect* of the "central question" facing him: how thought—Jewish, Christian, philosophical, and so on—"can both expose itself to the Holocaust and survive" (24). But what aspect is it? Here Fackenheim focuses on the question of possibility. His earlier treatment, couched in the terms of the 614th Commandment, was, he says, either Kantian or neoorthodox. That is, the possibility of response, of acknowledging and obeying the imperative, was rooted in the Kantian answer "that we *can* do what we *ought* to do," or the neoorthodox one "that a Grace that gives commandments also gives the freedom to obey them" (24).[18] His task, in *To Mend the World*, as he sees it, is to rectify the shallowness of these solutions, to show that obedience is only possible *now* because *during the event itself* resistance was actual.[19] That is, he will acknowledge the role of those who, in Auschwitz, "heard orders not of their making, and found the will and the strength to obey them" (26).[20] In short, Fackenheim seeks to ground both the orders, the imperative of opposition, and the possibility of obedience to them without inferring the latter from the former or using any glib notion of grace to account for that possibility, a human possibility given at the moment of imposition. For the victims of Nazism it is the very possibility of resistance that surprises, and Fackenheim wants to understand its ground. This, then, is his task as he sees it. Our question, not unconnected with it, is nonetheless different, for it concerns the ground of the imperative's *necessity* and not its possibility.[21]

First, Fackenheim argues that there *is* an imperative to live a post-Holocaust life, to recover from "the total rupture."[22] He calls such a life a *Tikkun* or mending of the rupture and says that it is mandatory: "A *Tikkun*, here and now, is mandatory for a *Tikkun*, then and there, was actual" (254). Such a *Tikkun*, he says, is both impossible and necessary. Impossible, for how could anyone, at any time, rectify or repair the murderous slaughter of millions, their souls, their bodies? Necessary, because. . . . That is our question: why is it necessary?

Fackenheim says this:

> Authentic thought was *actual during* the Holocaust among resisting victims; therefore such thought must be possible *for us after* the event: and, being possible, it is mandatory. Moreover, *their* resisting thought pointed to and helped make possible a *resisting life*; *our* post-Holocaust thought, however authentic in other respects, would still lapse into inauthenticity if it remained in an academically self-enclosed circle—if it failed to point to, and help make possible, a post-Holocaust life. (249)

He then calls this an "imperative," which must mean that the victims' recognition of the Nazi logic of destruction had given rise to an imperative to resist in life. Hence, both that recognition and that imperative are mandatory, necessary, binding upon us, "resistance in thought and resistance in life" (248).

The derivation of this conclusion includes two stages, one descriptive, the other analytical. First, Fackenheim describes, through memoir and report, different manifestations of resistance during the Holocaust and resistance's phenomenology, how the victims experienced and understood the "logic of destruction" employed against them, how they responded, and what they thought of their murderers, the system, and their own responsibility. Crucial to this descriptive account is the report of those who "confronted and grasped this whole-of-horror even while they were in it and trapped by it" and of their self-conscious opposition understood as a response to "orders" to live.[23] There were both believers and nonbelievers who sensed these "orders," although one but not the other testified to any awareness of their source (218–19).[24] Second, Fackenheim argues against explaining away or reducing these experiences by means of psychological or other historical categories. He seeks to show that these experiences, like the evil that engulfed them and gave rise to them, are "ultimate" and foundational experiences, incapable of analysis in general terms. We cannot explain away the "orders" as a mere psychological reaction, but rather the experience of them is sufficient reason to take them as presented. The victims' testimony should be accepted as truth-revealing. Nor can we explain away their testimony of the horror and its murderous logic. Our thought, Fackenheim shows, as it moves from agent to agent, can only grasp so much, as it tries to encompass both the details and then the whole-of-horror itself. In the end, the philosopher realizes this:

> On our part . . . we confront in the Holocaust world a *whole of horror*. We cannot comprehend it but only comprehend its incomprehensibility. We cannot transcend it but only be struck by the brutal truth that it cannot be transcended. . . .
>
> The philosopher may feel—he believes that nothing human is alien to him—that this whole is not unintelligible after all. He wants to understand Eichmann and Himmler, for he wants to understand Auschwitz. And he wants to understand Auschwitz, for he wants to understand Eichmann and Himmler. Thus his understanding gets *inside* them and their world, bold enough not to be stopped even by Eichmann's smirk and Himmler's gloves. To get inside them is to get inside the ideas behind the smirk and the gloves; and whereas this is not necessarily to accept these ideas it is in any case to obtain a kind of empathy. And thus it comes to pass, little by little, that a philosopher's *comprehension* of the Holocaust whole-of-horror turns into a *surrender*, for which the horror has vanished from the whole and the *Unwelt* has become a *Welt* like any other. In this way, one obtains a glimpse of the Ph.D.s among the murderers, and shudders.
>
> The truth disclosed in this shudder is that to grasp the Holocaust whole-of-horror is not to comprehend or transcend it, but rather *to say no to it, or resist it*. The Holocaust whole-of-horror *is* (for it *has been*); but it *ought not* to be (and *not* to have been). It ought *not* to be (and have been), but it *is* (for it has been). Thought would lapse into escapism if it held fast to the "ought not" alone; and it would lapse into paralyzed impotence if it confronted, nakedly, the devastating "is" alone. *Only by holding fast at once to the "is" and "ought not" can thought achieve an authentic survival. Thought, that is, must take the form of resistance.* (238–39)

But even this is not sufficient: "*resisting thought must point beyond the sphere of thought altogether, to a resistance which is not in 'mere' thought but rather in overt, flesh-and-blood action and life*" (239).

How does this happen, this "ecstatic" shift from resisting thought to a life of resistance? What takes the thinker from horrified amazement to an acknowledged mandate to oppose in life what thought could never comprehend? What makes this movement necessary? What makes it possible?

In order to answer these questions Fackenheim takes us on a tour of the whole-of-horror, from the torturers and murderers to Hoess, to Eichmann, Himmler, and finally Hitler. In each case, the intellect seeks satisfaction, understanding, only to resist, to doubt, to be bewildered, dismayed, until finally the thinker acknowledges how utterly impossible it is to place thought and the evil in the same space, as it were, except insofar as thought grasps the evil as a whole.[25] But the grasp, as Fackenheim cautions, is not a comprehension. That is, the grasp of the whole-of-horror includes both surprise at what it has surveyed and horror at it, so that acceptance cannot abide but must issue, beyond itself, in opposition. We have, in the end, a cognitive state that simply cannot remain passive and reflective but must become active, and its activity cannot merely be cognitive activity, for the object is too horrible, too repelling. It is an object that cannot merely be eliminated in thought; it must be—it demands to be—eliminated in reality.

> It is, rather, at once a *surprised acceptance and a horrified resistance.* It is a horrified surprise and, since the thought that is *in* this surprise is forced to accept what is yet in all eternity unacceptable, *thought is required to become "ecstatic," such as to point beyond resistance within its own native sphere, to a resistance that is beyond the sphere of thought altogether, and in the sphere of life.* . . . Resistance-in-thought to the Holocaust would degenerate into academic self-satisfaction unless it climaxed in calling for, praying for, working for, resistance in life. (247)

Furthermore, the ground of the possibility of the thinker's resisting thought and resistance in life is the thinking and living of the resisting victims themselves. "Resistance in that extremity was a way of being. For our thought now, it is an ontological category" (248).[26]

In a sense, then, resistance during the Holocaust both confirms the mandate to opposition, to a *Tikkun* or mending of life after the rupture, and makes it possible. If Fackenheim is right, then the resistance of the victims exhibits an irreducible courage and capability, without which post-Holocaust resistance would be impossible. The primary locus of the possibility of resistance, then, is the resisting victim. But what of its necessity? Where is the ground of the necessity of resistance for us now? Does it reside in thought itself as it tries to comprehend the evil only to end up in "horrified surprise"? Or does it reside in the victims' resisting thought that issues in a resisting life? In both? Or elsewhere?

The answer, I think, is that there is no single ground. The ground of the necessity to resist in life, to oppose the "demons of Auschwitz," differs for different agents. For victims of faith, the ground resides in Divine Command; for nonbelievers, in the "orders" to live, which have no acknowledged or identifiable source at all. For post-Holocaust philosophers and thinkers, the imperative arises out of their thought itself, and it is confirmed by that of the victims, for, Fackenheim argues, the thinking of the victims cannot be explained away psychologically, historically, or in any other way. In the end, to the thinker, the necessity of resistance in life arises out of the very particular encounter of his or her thought, pushed to its greatest capacities, with the Holocaust's special features—its murderous criminals, its horror, its dehumanized victims. The results of this encounter are two: a cognitive state that is both passive and active, both receptive and resisting, a "surprised acceptance" that is also a "horrified resistance"; and a thought-motivated "calling for, praying for, working for, resistance in life" (247) that is a response to an uncompromisable, unavoidable, and to all appearances permanent mandate.[27] That mandate or imperative is *imposed* by thinking itself in its unique effort to grasp the incomprehensible horrors of Auschwitz.

Such a thinker or philosopher, later, might add to this picture another feature, and then he might revise his understanding of the ground of the imperative's necessity, taking it to be a Divine Commanding Presence. But this addition is just that, a supplement or revision that is neither necessary nor predictable for acknowledging the mandate, its necessity and possibility. Such an addition is wholly contingent, in part on whether he is a Jewish thinker, in part on whether he is capable of recovering an openness to that Presence, in part on historical events. However it turns out, this project of recovery, which he begins with the event itself and a painstaking encounter with it, establishes and confirms a mandate to *Tikkun* or mending that arises out of his exposure to the event and the thought and life of its resisting victims. It is a contingent mandate, arising out of a particular encounter, but it is necessary too, for it arises *necessarily* out of a cognitive grasping that is neither comprehensive nor acquiescent. That thought and its ecstatic transformation from description to prescription to action are confirmed by a similar occurrence in the lives of victims, as they came to a resisting recognition that led to a life of resistance.

For Fackenheim, then, the Holocaust is a total rupture in history, and it chases all thought into historicism. But, at the same time, those who respond have substantial moral resources out of which to shape an imperative of opposition into a life of *Tikkun*, of mending after the rupture. These resources—resisting victims and thought confronting them—yield an unconditional, unavoidable, yet historically situated result, a mandate to oppose the demons of Auschwitz by recovery and repair of a shattered world.

Finally, then, our original irony is dissolved, if, that is, Fackenheim's enterprise succeeds. We have not asked whether it does. That would require a much fuller analysis than we have attempted. For now it is sufficient to have shown that the irony of historicism and evil can be disengaged by a post-Holocaust thought that is both historically serious and morally deep. If Fackenheim succeeds, then his thinking is both, fully exposed to the evils of Auschwitz and yet able to survive that exposure in the form of a deeply grounded mandate to opposition and recovery. We all along have hoped that a deep sensitivity to the impact of the Holocaust on thought would not have left thought impotent against that evil, and if Fackenheim is right, then our hopes have not been in vain.

NINE

# Philosophy, History, and the Jewish Thinker

## Jewish Thought and Philosophy in Emil Fackenheim's *To Mend the World*

This chapter is about philosophy, religious thought, and history in Emil Fackenheim's work. It is, therefore, about Athens and Jerusalem. Fackenheim's early thinking treats these two as symbols of philosophical and theological thought and makes philosophy a desideratum for serious religious thinking. But in recent years, and especially in *To Mend the World*, Fackenheim's understanding of the relationship has become historical, and even philosophy is shown to need Jewish life and Jewish thought. Surely this is a remarkable, perhaps shocking demand, and one wonders whether it can be sustained. Is it possible that philosophical thinking reaches limits that can only be overcome through the very particular resources of Jewish life? Can philosophy survive a particular event and its historically particular aftermath? Does the self-exposure of philosophical thought to the evils of Auschwitz result in the dependence of post-Holocaust philosophy on Judaism? Or does it result in the demise of philosophy altogether?

At a crucial juncture in *To Mend the World*, having retrieved the Kabbalistic concept of *Tikkun Olam* as a category for articulating the imperative of resistance in post-Holocaust life and thought, Emil Fackenheim summarizes a historical hermeneutical teaching that he largely—although not wholly—endorses.[1] In the course of that summary he notices a feature of understanding the past, including texts, which applies to reading his own work as well as distant classics:

> . . . the past itself has many-faceted meaning in its own right, and this "speaks" to the hermeneutical activity only if this latter is also a faithful, receptive "listening." This is true of the past and its texts. It is eminently true of *great* past texts. Of these it has well been said that, while the conscious purpose of their finite human authors was limited, their meaning is inexhaustible. Here all else may *seem* to be, yet on account of the gap be-

tween past and present *cannot ever quite be*, overwhelmed by the hermeneutical task of being "ministerial to the text."[2]

Later we shall return to the role of this hermeneutic in Fackenheim's thought and what justifies his acceptance of it. We quote it here for its methodological counsel, for if we want to understand the precise way in which Fackenheim, in *To Mend the World*, confronts themes and problems that already arise decades earlier in his thought, we must "listen" closely to what he says and "minister to the text," following attentively the "systematic impulse"[3] that has guided his work for over forty years.

The systematic nature of Fackenheim's thought expresses itself differently in different works. On the one hand, it is a philosophical attribute that involves a rigorous, often dialectical movement of thought, a mode of reasoning tooled at Hegel's forge and finished in existential analysis—that of Kierkegaard, Buber, Sartre, and Heidegger. But there is another dimension of the systematic, and it is this other dimension that I want to focus on here. Fackenheim puts it this way in the Acknowledgments to *Encounters Between Judaism and Modern Philosophy*:

> . . . I urge the reader not to overlook the systematic impulse which animates [this book]. That impulse, in a word, is to join together two disciplines—philosophy and Jewish thought—which, for a variety of reasons . . . I had found myself forced to hold apart for nearly three decades. Obeying that impulse I consider a demand at this hour in Jewish history.[4]

If *Encounters* is the setting for the intermingling of these two disciplines by means of a transcendent and dialectical movement of thought between Judaism and various expressions of modern philosophy, it is, however, not yet a genuine joining-together of the two.[5] This latter unity, if ever achieved, comes only in *To Mend the World* and ultimately in its fourth chapter. Whether this joining-together of philosophy and Jewish thought occurs, why it is a central issue in understanding Fackenheim's thought, how he conceives of the issue, and what its implications are—these are the subjects of this chapter.[6]

## PHILOSOPHY AND JEWISH THOUGHT

There are two aspects of the problem that arise early in Fackenheim's thought.[7] The first aspect concerns a traditional role of philosophy for theology. In a review of Buber's *Israel and Palestine* Fackenheim identifies a "logical circle" in Buber's strategy:

> That historical understanding and philosophical outlook must be intimately related is the basic underlying conception of Buber's present work. . . . On the one hand, the history is determined by the philosophy.

> Refusing to report indiscriminately the profound and the trite, the living and the dead, Buber tries to fix attention on the essential. And what is essential depends on the standards provided by the philosophy. Yet on the other hand, the philosophy is determined by the history. For, Jewishly speaking, it is the history alone which saves the philosophy from arbitrariness.[8]

The problem, Fackenheim elaborates, is a problem for "all Jewish thought save the orthodox."[9] It is one of finding a middle ground between subjecting Jewish experience to wholly independent philosophical criteria—e.g., Kantian ethics—and totally immersing oneself in the Jewish past and Jewish life—without being able to "distinguish between the essential and the inessential, the profound and the trite, the living and the dead."[10] The dilemma of Jewish thought is the "dilemma of either seeking truth and value *de novo*, apart from the Jewish historical tradition, or else, abandoning the search for truth and value, becoming mere narrators of a dead Jewish past."[11] Fackenheim's problem, then, is as much a problem for him as a Jewish thinker as it is for Buber. It is the problem of what genuine Jewish religious thought should be like, for it cannot be merely philosophical or merely historical, nor at the same time can it eschew philosophy and history. Fackenheim's solution is that genuine Jewish theology must be "existential." Unlike history and like philosophy, it must seek "truth and value," but unlike philosophy and like history, it must "not be abstract and universally-human" but rather concretely Jewish. "It must, in its search for present and future, encounter and recollect the past. And the past can be encountered or recollected only if it is still dormantly alive."[12] This formulation, then, defines Jewish thought by making three points: (1) Jewish thought needs the philosophical task—the search for truth and value—in order to avoid being parochial or trite; (2) Jewish thought carries out that search within a particular history—in order to avoid being abstract and irrelevant; and (3) that particular past is retrievable only because it is alive today. But what does "alive" mean? What does it mean to say that the "Jewish past . . . is a spiritual reality still living and present"?[13]

The "spiritual reality" that is at the core of the Jewish past and that must be "alive" if that past is to be recoverable is revelation—what Buber himself calls, among other things, "reality" or "concreteness." Fackenheim, in his review, shows why Buber's Zionist thinking is an instance of genuine Jewish thought. What he does not do here, however, is show that its fundamental assumption is acceptable. He does not show why we should agree that the Jewish past is alive, for he does not show that revelation, affirmed in the past, is still possible in the present.

In a review of Nahum Glatzer's *Franz Rosenzweig: His Life and Thought*, Fackenheim addresses just this question and with it the second aspect of the relation between philosophy and theology. Franz Rosenzweig's "new thinking" is thinking from the personal standpoint, which is not new in religion, Fackenheim says, but is new in philosophy. And the question he asks is whether this thinking in which the person of the philosopher is essential to his philosophy is "compatible with the objective which, in philosophy, is indispensable."[14] Is the "new thinking" genuine thinking? "Can the personal standpoint claim objective validity?"[15] This is Fackenheim's interpretation of Rosenzweig's problem: "Is this still science?"

Rosenzweig's answer is this: "The bridge from the most subjective to the most objective is built by the theological concept of revelation."[16] Fackenheim proceeds to interpret this solution by distinguishing between an actual revelation and the *general* concept of revelation. What makes the new thinking *thinking* is that it requires and incorporates a philosophical consideration of the possibility of revelation, and this consideration, which proceeds by "theory, argument, system," is a defense or justification of revelation in the face of modern critiques, from Feuerbach to Marx to Freud and beyond. Personal or "new" thinking, then, is not anti-intellectual or dogmatic; if genuine, it rises to universality only to return to concreteness, and in so doing engages in genuine philosophical analysis with objective results.[17]

Theology, then, needs philosophy in this deeper sense. The genuine religious existentialist cannot avoid defending the possibility of revelation in the modern world and the necessary conditions for that defense—the real distinction among man, God, and world, for example, and this defense is a philosophical task. Furthermore, what is true for Rosenzweig is also, at this stage, true for Fackenheim himself. Not only does Fackenheim argue the case for revelation in Buber's thought;[18] he also appropriates the gist of that defense and makes it the core of his own response to the nineteenth-century critique of religiosity and faith, what he calls "subjective reductionism."[19]

In a deep sense, then, what bridges the gap between religious thought in general and philosophy is that authentic, existential religious thought requires a philosophical justification of the modern possibility of revelation. This is what is necessary for the past reality to be alive today. But if this joining-together of philosophy and theology is satisfactory for the Fackenheim of the 1960s, is it still satisfactory today? In *To Mend the World*, how are the two related? Can it be merely in the same way? Or has too much changed?

## HISTORICISM AND THE IMPACT OF THE HOLOCAUST

Before we can raise these questions of *To Mend the World* we must understand the role of that work in Fackenheim's philosophical-theological development. He himself begins to identify that role by contrasting *To Mend the World* (1982) with *Encounters* (1973) and with Franz Rosen-

*zweig's The Star of Redemption.*[20] But for our purposes two other settings may be more helpful. On the one hand, we need to investigate what Fackenheim says about historicism and, more general still, the relation between thought and history. This theme arises early in his writings, and to understand properly the changes wrought on it we need to contrast *To Mend the World* with earlier discussions in *Metaphysics and Historicity* (1961) and in "The Transcendence and Historicity of Philosophical Truth" (1967).[21] On the other hand, we should try to understand the recent work as Fackenheim's most profound attempt to appreciate the role of the Holocaust for subsequent life and thought. Therefore, we must consider how it enriches a line of thinking initiated in works written in the late 1960s, especially in "Jewish Faith and the Holocaust" (1968) and in the third chapter of *God's Presence in History* (1970).[22]

In *Metaphysics and Historicity* the theme of history and thought, specifically metaphysical thought, emerges in an explicit and exciting way. The book asks and answers the following question: if the doctrine of historicity is true and human being is inherently historical, then is timeless metaphysical truth still possible? Its answer is that even though metaphysical thinking is an activity of a person characterized as a self-constitutive process in a situation, with finite and infinite components, that thinking can nonetheless attain universality and transcendence. That universality, however, is restricted to an ontological analysis of human being—the role of temporality, death, freedom, compulsion, and so on—and the prescription for authentic existence. In short, timeless truth is possible only because the self can rise to a philosophical understanding of itself, to self-recognition.

The exploration of *Metaphysics and Historicity* is wholly hypothetical. Fackenheim never explicitly endorses the doctrine of historicity and the account of the self as self-making-in-a-situation.[23] What he attempts to show is that even such historicism does not rule out philosophical transcendence. There is reason to believe that Fackenheim, in his Jewish writings, does accept a conception of the self as radically situated, but until *To Mend the World* the issue is not urgent. What is vital, in contrast, is his opposition to historicism, an opposition manifest both in *Metaphysics and Historicity* and in its sequel, the 1967 article critical of Heidegger's later historicism. In an important note[24] Fackenheim addresses the later Heidegger's radical historicism and attempts to dispense with it as self-refuting. But a letter from Leo Strauss[25] led Fackenheim to rethink and reformulate his critique in a way that does not use the notion of the self, and in "The Transcendence and Historicity of Philosophical Truth" he argues that the notion of a "history of Being" that incorporates both thinking and poetry cannot do without transcendent truths even though they are ultimately reinterpreted historically.

Later we shall ask whether Fackenheim in *To Mend the World* finally yields to Heidegger's radical historicism or stays with the latter's earlier commitment to transcendence. For now we can ignore Fackenheim's arguments and yet must appreciate their goal—to defend philosophical universality against the threat of historicism. There is every reason to think that Fackenheim's motives were both epistemological and moral and that his antihistoricism extended beyond philosophy to religious thought as well. As he put it in a letter to Reinhold Niebuhr (1956), "unless philosophical reason can transcend, at least in principle, the existential corruption of self-interest, it cannot avoid a self-refuting relativism." To be sure, his argument against historicism becomes increasingly more subtle than a mere appeal to its self-refuting character, but the sentiment and the anxiety remain the same.[26] It is a sentiment that finds its most succinct religious expression in the statement that "religious faith can be, and is, empirically verifiable; but nothing empirical can possibly refute it."[27] With this commitment, then, Fackenheim's thinking gives history its due without capitulating to it, and with such a relationship we return to the conviction of the review of Buber, that history and philosophy somehow need each other and that genuine religious thought must incorporate both.

*To Mend the World* requires that we ask once again how strong is Fackenheim's antihistoricism. In the Introduction to *Quest for Past and Future* (1968) he announces a great shift in his thinking, the recognition that the Midrashic framework—native Jewish thought—is open to historical modification. The same shift to the openness of Midrash to history is hailed once more in the Introduction to *To Mend the World* as the single greatest change in his thinking. But if this commitment about Jewish thought mitigates Fackenheim's antihistoricism with regard to Judaism, one can still ask whether the Holocaust—as epoch-making event and radical rupture—also transforms his commitment to philosophical transcendence. If there is an answer to this problem, it lies within the pages of *To Mend the World*.

The heart of *To Mend the World* is chapter 4, sections 8 and 9, and the heart of that heart are subsections c–e of section 9.[28] The task of these sections is the definition of resistance during the Holocaust as an ultimate reality, the justification of that ultimacy, and the philosophical analysis that moves from the impotence of thought to resistance as ontic reality and finally to resistance as ontological category. This line of thought can be understood as a dramatic enrichment of an earlier line of thinking, first announced in Fackenheim's contribution to a symposium on "Jewish Values in a Post-Holocaust Future" (March 1967) and later developed in the third of the Charles Deems Lectures (delivered in 1968 and published as chapter 3 of *God's Presence in History*, 1970).

We cannot—and need not—review this line of thinking in detail. Broadly, Fackenheim examines the unprecedented character of the Holocaust, exposes theological and philosophical thought to it, and finds no meaning in the event. He then turns to subsequent Jewish life, which he interprets as a response to the Holocaust, and deduces, as conditions of that response, first an obligation and finally a Divine Commanding Presence as its ground. The obligation, characterized as a 614th Commandment—not to give Hitler posthumous victories—is subjected to interpretive judgment that results in four fragmentary articulations of what that commandment means for Jews today.[29]

## *TO MEND THE WORLD* AND HISTORICISM

This line of thinking, while systematic and openly exposed to the Holocaust, is nonetheless fragmentary. The account of the Holocaust's unprecedented character is preliminary and insufficient. The result that thought—theological, historical, psychological, philosophical—cannot comprehend the event is inadequately developed and supported. The turn to subsequent Jewish life, as a result of the impotence of thought, is unjustified and ungrounded, as is the *deduction* of the obligation and of the Commanding Presence. Hence, both the possibility and the necessity of opposition and recovery need a more secure ground. And finally the interpretation of the obligation first as an imperative to oppose Nazi purposes and further as a fourfold articulation seems arbitrary, or nearly so. In view of these weaknesses, *To Mend the World* can be understood as an attempt at enriching this line of thinking or, alternatively, at replacing it with a subtle, more developed movement of thought that thoroughly exposes thought to the Holocaust in order ultimately to identify resistance and mending as fundamental categories for subsequent life and thought.[30]

How, in the course of this enterprise, are theology or religious thought and philosophy joined together? Although simply stated, this question—the object of our attention from the outset—finds no direct or easy answer.

First, what is the role of "being-toward-death" in the recent work? At one level, *To Mend the World* involves four confrontations with the Holocaust, in each of which a significant thinker is shown to suffer *aporia* as a result of the confrontation. Three of these encounters—with Spinoza, with Rosenzweig, and with Heidegger—address the role of death in human being. Spinoza, who deals not with death itself but rather our fear of it, rises above that fear by means of intellectual achievement; the more we know, the less we fear death.[31] Rosenzweig, who encounters death at the very outset of *The Star of Redemption* and registers it as the sign of our temporality, recognizes a dimension of history and historical life that enables the individual and indeed all human beings to transcend personal death. That dimension is eternity, an intimacy between God and man that comes with revelation and that is expressed as man's love for God. The central section of *The Star of Redemption*, the heart of the book, deals with revelation, with eternity in time, and its motto—taken from the *Song of Songs*—is "love is as strong as death." For Rosenzweig, then, the possibility of revelation and its role in history bring with them a love that enables man to confront death and transcend it, not by rejecting temporality but rather by overcoming it with a trans-historical intimation of redemption or eternity.

The Holocaust shows Spinoza and Rosenzweig to have avoided rather than confronted openly history and its realities—death and the fear of finitude. Heidegger, in contrast, confronts history with utter seriousness, and as a result he identifies being-toward-death as an essential feature of human being. Rather than try to transcend finitude or rise above the fear of it, Heidegger understands that human self-recognition includes being-toward-death as a universal feature of the human condition. But while Heidegger is honest about history and does justice to death and human mortality, he, too, cannot endure exposure to Auschwitz. For there, as Primo Levi brilliantly describes, the "Holocaust Kingdom" created a new form of life—the *Muselmänner*—whose life cannot be called life, and whose death cannot be called death. The living-dead, a *novum* in history, threatens the universality of Heidegger's account of *Dasein*'s ontological self-recognition.

In *Metaphysics and Historicity* it was just such self-recognition that brought with it philosophical transcendence. In *To Mend the World* the content of that self-recognition, or at least its universality, is called into question. We are left to ask whether any transcendence remains and whether the Heideggerian self as a self-constitutive process remains as well. We must ask, that is, how thoroughgoing is Fackenheim's historicism in *To Mend the World* and also what conception of the self informs that work.

The nature of human being is not an explicit theme of *To Mend the World*. Yet it would be startling if the work, convinced as it is that Rosenzweig's "new thinking" is an advance over Spinoza's "old" and that Heidegger's existential conception of *Dasein* is an advance over Hegel's rise to Absolute Spirit, suggests no particular conception of self-hood. The natural question is whether the account of human being as self-making-in-a-situation, developed in *Metaphysics and Historicity*, lurks in the shadows of the more recent book. In particular, does not the historical hermeneutic—even with the modification brought by the Holocaust as a radical rupture between past and present—incorporate such a conception?[32] It certainly seems to do so, and at least one answer to the question why is that this much of the Heideggerian analysis of *Dasein* survives after its exposure to Auschwitz. The universality of its existential analysis, of its notion of decisiveness and its conception of technicity—all these aspects of Heidegger's thought may be refuted by Auschwitz and by Heidegger's incapacity to decide against it. But no such refutation sets aside the existential notion of a radically situated self-making.[33]

If man is radically situated self-making and the hermeneutical situation characterizes life as well as thought, then the encounter with historical events and the recovery of the past both arise "from an always-already-existing 'pre-understanding' of the past, 'prejudiced' in that it is historically situated."[34] Such a pre-understanding or prejudice is inescapable—both for life and for thought. But what this means is that such prejudice operates in Fackenheim's enterprise not only at the "late" stage when the past is retrieved as a constituent of an act of *Tikkun* or mending; it also operates at the early stages, when thinkers such as Spinoza, Rosenzweig, Hegel, and then Heidegger, Buber, Isaac Deutscher, and Paul Celan are judged, broadly speaking, to be escapist.[35]

The hermeneutical requirement, that the assessments along the way, which move thought to a recognition of its own impotency and beyond, be "prejudiced," should lead us to underscore the "personal standpoint" of Fackenheim's "new thinking." As a result we might justifiably wonder—as Rosenzweig once did—whether such thinking can still be "science." Can it, we might ask, escape the bounds of arbitrariness and subjectivity and claim "objective validity"? This question may not seem so pressing when we focus our attention on the dialectical assessment of thinkers that results in Theodor Adorno's query, even if provisional: "must it be and remain the case that, when confronted with the 'real hell' of Auschwitz, 'the metaphysical capacity is paralyzed'?"[36] It is certainly pressing, however, when we realize that similar judgments are made in *To Mend the World*, throughout the central sections 8 and 9 of chapter 4 where thought first describes and defines resistance, then provides an ontological analysis of resistance as an ultimate category, and finally becomes "deontic" in the form of an imperative to resistance *in actu*. If the whole movement of thought is fraught with subjectivity, then so is this wholly remarkable effort.

To put the matter somewhat differently, after sections 8 and 9 the resisting-mending recovery of the past for the present has a ground—the Ontological Category of Resistance, a category that makes subsequent resistance possible and mandatory both in thought and in life.[37] When thought is thoroughly exposed to Auschwitz, it becomes ontological and then deontological, that is, ecstatic, and this movement validates and directs subsequent interpretation, both in life and in thought. But *earlier* there is no such validation, no such imperative, and no such guidance. Need there be?[38]

The discussion of the notion of the radically situated self, the hermeneutical self, has led us back to the question of Fackenheim's historicism, and it has done so in two ways. First, we might ask why—if he does—Fackenheim still adheres, after the radical rupture of the Holocaust, to this conception of the individual as a self-constituting process. Is it, as I suggested, because to a large degree it is a conception that recommends itself and that survives exposure to the event? And if so, is it nonetheless in principle refutable? This query we can set aside, at least for the moment, in favor of another. Does the movement of thought that first concludes "where the Holocaust is, *no* thought can be, and . . . where there is thought it is in flight from the event,"[39] then defines resistance during the event, and finally provides an ontological analysis that becomes deonotological, rise to universality? Does the definition and its defense constitute a metaphysical truth that is at least provisionally universal, objective and not subjective, and, though arising out of history, nonetheless in a sense "timeless"? Does the definition of resistance and the ontological analysis that follows constitute a kind of transcendence?

Why is this question a serious one? In *Metaphysics and Historicity* the doctrine of historicism is mitigated by a kind of Heideggerian ontological analysis in which self-recognition yields objective, universal results about *Dasein*'s being. In *To Mend the World* the Holocaust confronts this universality—the concept of decisiveness-as-such, of being-toward-death, of technicity, and so on—and refutes it with its stark particularity—its evil, its methods, its victims, its criminals. But does Fackenheim then capitulate? Does he accept the radical "openness" of philosophical thought—indeed of *all* thought—as he once accepted the "openness" of the Midrashic Framework?[40] Or does the philosophical analysis of chapter 4, sections 8 and 9, yield an objective, universal result, rising—as it does so—to a new transcendence?

It is not clear that Fackenheim tells us either what status should be assigned to the category of resistance and its justification or how radical is his acceptance of historicism. That he thinks the results of sections 8 and 9 are more than *merely* subjective and more than arbitrary, however, is evident. If, in Rosenzweig's *The Star of Redemption*, the concept of revelation is the bridge between subjectivity and objective validity, if it is what makes theology philosophical and requires that it be so, then one wonders whether in *To Mend the World* the philosophical description, definition, and defense of resistance as an ontological and deontological category does not function in a similar way for Fackenheim. In short, is the concept of resistance—a concept that emerges from the resistor's own thought about the very character of his or her life—what joins theology to philosophy—what makes Fackenheim's "new thinking" scientific? Or is it the philosopher's own movement of thought that finally confronts the whole-of-horror within its surprised grasp that does so?

In one sense, *To Mend the World* exhibits Fackenheim's traumatic allegiance to philosophy and his struggle to identify its responsiveness to history without witnessing its self-destruction. The question about the extent and depth of Fackenheim's historicism is in part a question about his fidelity to philosophical thought. Suppose we intercept him, for example, at the point at which his "new thinking"—thinking through Buber, Deutscher, and Celan—concludes that thought is paralyzed. What might he have done at this juncture? Earlier, in *God's Presence in History* and other contemporary pieces, he turns to survivors and descendants, interpreting their ongoing existence as responsive and ultimately oppositional. The move now seems groundless and somewhat arbitrary, a *metabasis eis allo genos*.[41] Alternatively, like Leo Strauss, Fackenheim might have returned to the classics, to the old thinking and its *philosophia perennis*. But such a return, at *this* point in his analysis, would have differed significantly from a return as recovery, performed under the auspices of resistance as *Tikkun* or mending. This latter is Fackenheim's understanding of what Strauss in fact did, an act of new thinking returning to the old. My point about the alternative that faces Fackenheim at this earlier stage is more extreme: that the radical nature of the Holocaust might have led to escapism, to a renewed affirmation of an old style of thinking that never really takes the "low" for what it is.[42]

Clearly, neither of these options is possible for Fackenheim, one because it is too arbitrary, the other because it is simply inauthentic. But the option he does take is, if not surprising, at least perplexing. He chooses to stay with the event, *to think it through*, first describing resistance within it and then justifying that resistance, as manifest in the resistor's own self-awareness, by means of a philosophical movement through the levels of criminality responsible for the event and the objects of that resistance. The result of this movement of thought is that while thought never "understands" or "comprehends" the evil, it can confront it—but only as a "whole-of-horror" and with a surprised horror.[43] And when it does so, as the final result of a dialectical movement, thought recognizes that there is no understanding of the evil more epistemologically ultimate than that of the resistors themselves.[44] Furthermore, since their recognition did not remain reflective but rather led to action, to resistance, so must ours. It is here that ontological analysis becomes deontological imperative. A mode of being becomes an ontological category, a ground of possibility, and finally a mandate.

Why is this development perplexing? It is perplexing because of its character as a way of thinking, not especially because of its results. It is perplexing because it is an example, a brilliant example, of dialectical and existential thinking, of descriptive phenomenology and ontological analysis, of moving from personal experience and self-understanding to philosophical reflection and back again. There are antecedents here—Kant, Hegel, Heidegger, Buber, Rosenzweig—and there are those whose conception of philosophical method is rejected—Aristotle, Spinoza, Maimonides. In rejecting one *type* of philosophical thinking, Fackenheim grasps another. And, one wonders, why?

There is an old but profound question lurking here, a question about language, thought, and silence. Fackenheim addresses the problem, in a sense, when he concludes his discussion of inauthentic thought and the impotency of thought with a brief comment on Celan.[45] This is wholly appropriate. Surely Celan, together with Aharon Appelfeld and others, raises most profoundly the question of the impotency of language and thought before the horror. Some might be inclined to side with Celan; language and thought are not merely paralyzed, they are totally shattered. There is no coherent response. But it is at this juncture that Fackenheim's fidelity to philosophy reveals itself most dramatically. To be sure, he turns to the victims and the survivors, to their lives and their reflections. But as he turns to them, his mode of thinking through their actions and their self-understanding is philosophical, and the results—definition and defense—are philosophical results. Against this background, we might ask if dialectical philosophical thinking is in principle refutable; can a mode of thinking be discredited—or destroyed? Fackenheim does not ask this question, but we can, and in so doing we raise again the spectre of the "curse of historicity."

## PHILOSOPHY AND JUDAISM IN *TO MEND THE WORLD*

We also raise, now finally, the question: how are philosophy and theology or religious thought—specifically Jewish thought—joined together in Fackenheim's most recent work? Earlier we put the question in a slightly different form: does the concept of resistance as an ontological category bridge the gap between radical subjectivity and objective validity? Does it make theology philosophical?

It is possible that the question is wrongly put, that the issue in *To Mend the World*—unlike that in Rosenzweig and the early Fackenheim—is precisely reversed. In *The Star of Redemption* and in Fackenheim's early essays, the relationship between theology and philosophy is founded on the need to make theology, from the personal standpoint, philosophical, i.e., objective. This formulation even suits *Metaphysics and Historicity*, where a religious dimension is introduced into the account of the radically situated self-constituting process but nonetheless needs philosophical defense.[46] But here, in *To Mend the World*, religious thought, in one sense, only comes on the scene in chapter 4, section 10 with the concept of *Tikkun Olam*, mending the world. With this concept, wrestled from the Kabbalistic tradition, the Midrash, and the Bible,[47] it is not theology that is made philosophical but rather philosophy that is enriched, completed by Jewish thought. Perhaps, on such a reading, it is not Rosenzweig's *The Star of Redemption* but rather Hermann Cohen's *Religion of Reason out of the Sources of Judaism* that is the proper predecessor and model for *To Mend the World*. Might it be that the real issue is not what makes religious thought philosophical but rather the militantly Jewish one—what makes philosophy Jewish? Could it be that Fackenheim's book is even more "fanatical" than Rosenzweig's classic?[48]

On this reading, the Jewish concept of *Tikkun* gives content to the philosophical imperative of resistance. Without that content the ontological and deontological category is no more effective than Heidegger's "decisiveness-as-such" or Kant's categorical imperative by itself. In *The Star of Redemption* Judaism—as well as Christianity—arises on philosophical foundations and gives content to a history that is, in direction if not yet in character, philosophically defined. In *To Mend the World* Judaism itself may enter only at the eleventh hour, to give content to a philosophically articulated and defended imperative; but this is only half the story. The entire enterprise—from the encounters with Spinoza and Rosenzweig to the refutation of Heidegger and beyond—is framed by Fackenheim's "preunderstanding," a preunderstanding constituted in significant part by a Jewish life and thought of a very rich kind. Judaism, in other words, does not enter the work only at its end or near to it; it is there from the beginning of Fackenheim's labor, for it—Midrash, Bible, Jewish thought—is there in the author and hence in his life and his thought. Or, to put it otherwise, *To Mend the World* is a philosophical book from its outset, but it is also a Jewish book through and through.[49]

Here, I think, we come to the final and most profound answer to our question. Philosophy and theology are not united in *To Mend the World*, but philosophy and Jewish thought *are* joined together, and the joining together in the book occurs because the two are already joined together in its author's life and thought. As he responds, at every level of analysis and all along the way, to the event with an "unknowing horror," Fackenheim infuses his assessments, his judgments, and his systematic thinking with his own standpoint, his own point of view as one thoroughly Jewish and yet thoroughly philosophical. And he recognizes this, I think, and by recognizing it he vitiates its apparent viciousness. In a discussion of the ontic-ontological circle in Heidegger, Fackenheim remarks:

> Heidegger, of course, is aware of . . . the circle. . . . Also, he quite rightly rejects an escape from the circle by means of a return, after all, to the "old" thinking. Instead, he proposes to leap into the circle, affirming that it loses all semblance of viciousness if only the leap is conscious, "basic and complete." And it is nonvicious because *Dasein* is *itself* circular, i.e., always in-advance-of-itself and cast-back-on-itself.[50]

Surely what is true of Heidegger is true of Fackenheim as well.

Saved from the viciousness of a hermeneutical circle, we are thrust back to a further hermeneutical insight about *To Mend the World* and its role in Fackenheim's thought. In addition to being an enrichment of the reasoning in the third chapter of *God's Presence in History*, the later book is also, one might argue, a preface to the earlier work's first chapter. In that chapter, among other things, Fackenheim gives a formal-substantive account of Midrashic thought and Midrashic life. He does this in order, then, to expose *that world* first to the challenges of secularity and then to the Holocaust. But even then one might have asked, what is the hermeneutical situation out of which that return to the Midrashic world is initiated? What authorizes such a return at all, and what accounts for its specific content as Fackenheim understands it? Why is it understood in terms of a modern, Buberian concept of revelation and retrievable only in terms of the viability of that concept? *To Mend the World* gives a partial answer to these questions—the philosophically profound dimension of the answer. But the other, more existential dimension is not available anywhere in full. It is given primarily and wholly in Emil Fackenheim's life—and partially—with intimations—in the few autobiographical reflections that appear among his published works.[51]

## CONCLUSION

We have woven together discussion of many themes that arise out of a reading of *To Mend the World*, a strategy not inappropriate, I hope, to our goal. For the question, what is the relationship between philosophy and Jewish thought in Fackenheim's work, has always been before us. In the end, the answer can be best understood in terms Fackenheim uses to comprehend Heidegger's appreciation of the hermeneutical situation of human existence. To paraphrase Fackenheim's own comments on Heidegger, he refuses to reject the hermeneutical circle by fleeing into a mode of the old thinking, nor will he allow himself to flee history and its horror. Instead, he leaps into the circle, neutralizing its viciousness by his conscious recognition of who he is, what he is doing, and the very nature of particular human living as a perpetual quest for its own past and its own future within its own historical moment—a moment filled with despair and joy, with horror and elation.

TEN

# Franz Rosenzweig, Objectivity, and the New Thinking

After clearing away the reductive errors of the "old thinking," of traditional metaphysical philosophy, in the first part of *The Star of Redemption*, Franz Rosenzweig introduces his new method of philosophical inquiry, the "new thinking," and proceeds to employ it to arrive at a new philosophical understanding of the human condition.[1] This is the project of the second part of *The Star*.[2] But, at a crucial juncture, Rosenzweig stops to acknowledge a fundamental problem about his new method. It is, as we indicated in chapter nine, a problem about history, subjectivity, and the threat of relativism, and it harbors the concern that existential thinking, whether in the service of religious thought or not, might be an utter failure. Let me try to spell out, in my own way, the gist of this problem and then show how Rosenzweig claims to solve it. I want to focus on this solution, for it is not at all clear what Rosenzweig means by it and how it is intended to accomplish its task.

The problem that Rosenzweig identifies is one that could not have arisen prior to Montaigne and Descartes, for it requires a certain conception of selfhood and the role of personal experience in philosophical inquiry. The problem is about the objectivity or transcendence of philosophical thought. As long as the philosopher engages in his inquiry from an impersonal or disengaged point of view, then his results can claim to be objectively true. They are not prejudiced or biased by the individual, even personal features of the philosopher's situation. The philosopher's arguments and proposals and conclusions are carried out by him in a general and nonparticular way. Like the scientist, the philosopher conducts himself *qua* rational inquirer, analyst, and so forth. And this conception of the objectivity of philosophical thinking is a feature of virtually all such thinking prior to the late sixteenth and early seventeenth centuries. For until there arises a rich notion of a deeply inward and reflexive self, it makes little sense to treat the experiences of such a self as constitutive of philosophical thought. In short, traditional philosophical thinking, from Plato and Aristotle to Aquinas, Maimonides, and on through

Hobbes, Locke, Leibniz, and further, is always an attempt to understand nature, God, man, and more from a detached, impersonal, and hence objective perspective. This is what Thomas Nagel has recently called the "view from nowhere."[3]

But with the rise of a new conception of the self and the centrality of the self's first-person perspective or point of view, there arises the possibility that philosophical thinking may not begin with this impersonal and objective perspective and hence may never attain universality and truth. That is, there is the risk that a philosophical thinking that began as the first-person experience of the philosopher *qua* particular individual might never transcend that limited, subjective, perspectival posture. It might never, that is, arrive at objectivity and general truth. Hence, it might not yield general results and need never be accepted by others, for they might treat its results as the limited outcomes of one person's thinking, and that is all.[4]

This problem is precisely the one that Rosenzweig acknowledges and seeks to confront. In other words, he registers his criticisms of the old thinking but admits its virtue, that its claim to be "scientific" and objective was convincing. If indeed its results were true, then they were universally and objectively true. His criticism is that they are reductionist and hence false. But when he proposes his new method, "speech thinking" or "absolute empiricism," he realizes that if its results are true, they may nonetheless not be objectively true but only, as it were, "idiosyncratically" true. If this were so, then the loss might be greater than the gain. In place of a few erroneous routes Rosenzweig would find himself with a virtually infinite number of true ones. Surely this is one sense of Rosenzweig's fear of the curse of historicity.[5]

Rosenzweig's way of putting this problem is this: "Is it possible, still, to call this new thinking science? Can the term science be applied to a method that surveys each thing by itself, in its countless relations and from its multiple perspectives? Shall a survey whose unity can at best reside within the surveyer—and how dubious is even that!—still be passed off as science?"[6] Rosenzweig is convinced that philosophy cannot return to its old ways; those ways lead to deep and pervasive difficulties. "[Philosophy] must cling to her new point of departure, to the subjective, extremely personal, unique self, absorbed in it itself and the standpoint of self, and still attain to the objectivity of science. Where is the bridge to connect extreme subjectivity, one might even say, deaf and blind subjectivity, with the luminous clearness of infinite objectivity?"[7]

Implicitly Rosenzweig refuses two alternatives. The philosopher cannot collapse the subjective into the objective or the objective into the subjective. To do the former is to lapse into the old thinking, already discredited; to do the latter is to sink into subjectivism, if not outright solipsism. The task is somehow to bridge the gap between the nonreducible first-person point of view that characterizes the philosopher's thinking and the completely general and compelling objectivity that his thinking aspires to achieve. How, indeed, can the very same thinking be both subjective and objective at once? This is Rosenzweig's problem, and it is indeed a central one, for if he fails to solve it, then the remainder of *The Star* becomes at best an attractive story, the account of one person's thinking and not a general account of the human condition in all its relational complexity.[8]

I have presented this problem of the objectivity of the new thinking as a general problem about how a certain method of philosophical inquiry, one that follows the thinking and experience of the engaged agent and accepts the outcomes of that process, can be both utterly subjective and yet objective. But Rosenzweig, as we shall see, titles this section "Philosophy and Theology" because he sees this problem as specially connected with religious belief, with the experience of God, and with theological reflection. Hence, it is not surprising that Emil Fackenheim, in a subtle examination of this text, focuses on how the problem arises in the encounter between philosophy and religious belief.[9]

Fackenheim recognizes that the problem of objectivity is an old one for religious belief, for the issue always arises how the experience of a single believer has universal validity. That is, philosophy has always confronted the particular religious believer with the challenge of objectivity, of showing why the results of a single, individual experience should be compelling and generally accepted. As Fackenheim puts it, philosophy and its objectivity confront the particularity of religious belief with two possibilities. Either objective philosophy seeks to reduce the religious experience and overwhelm it, trying to show that philosophy yields a higher truth or that the religious experience can be explained away by philosophical or social scientific explanations, or, alternatively, philosophy can acknowledge its own limitations, admit the genuineness of the religious experience, and itself make a leap of faith. According to this second option, as Fackenheim says, "objective thought looks at the personal standpoint of faith and decides that it is authentic and true," and this implies that God really speaks, that He can only be heard from the personal standpoint, and that objectivity is less and not more than this relation.[10]

This way of understanding Rosenzweig's problem, moreover, provides Fackenheim with his interpretation of Rosenzweig's solution. According to Rosenzweig, "the theological concept of revelation must provide the bridge from the most subjective to the most objective. Man, as the recipient of revelation, as one who experiences the content of faith, contains both within himself."[11] The philosopher or new thinker who can solve his problem must be a theologian, and "the theologian whom philosophy requires in order to become scientific is a theologian who requires philosophy for the sake of his own honesty."[12] Confronting the believer, that is, the philosopher admits the authenticity of religious experience, becomes a believer, and hence instantiates utter subjectivity; the believer, moreover, "requires philosophy" to defend and justify the presuppositions without which the divine-human relation is impossible and hence becomes at the same time objective. The key to Rosenzweig's solution, Fackenheim says, is that the bridge is not the event of revelation itself but rather the concept of revelation (*der Offenbarungsbegriff*), that is, the philosophical defense of the possibility of revelation against attempts to reduce it to mental projects or something less than a genuine encounter. The experience of the believer, from her personal standpoint, her first-person point of view, is objectively valid because that same believer has that experience only as a philosopher who has systematically and rationally defended the possibility of revelation. Rosenzweig says that the bridge is the "theological concept of revelation," but the central point, for Fackenheim, is that the defense of this concept is philosophically grounded in "theory, argument, system."

Fackenheim's interpretation may be correct as far as it goes, but it surely fails to explain why Rosenzweig believes that philosophy as the new thinking *requires* theology, that the new thinker must also be a believer-theologian. Are there not in nonreligious, secular experience the resources to overcome the gap? Is this unification of philosophy and religion a necessary step in the redemption and legitimation of philosophy itself? Fackenheim shows that this interrelation is one strategy for redeeming the new thinking as philosophy, but is it the only strategy? Indeed, does Rosenzweig think that it is the only one?

Before we return to Rosenzweig's text and make our own suggestions, we should notice other questions that ought to be answered. First, Rosenzweig makes it clear that what he is after is something that is needed not just for a philosophy that has accepted religious belief but indeed for philosophy *per se*. He calls it "a requirement of philosophy which it evidently cannot meet out of its own resources" and "support for its scientific status."[13] Hence, Fackenheim's interpretation by itself will not do, for it assumes and does not show why the new philosophy *must* turn to religious belief and experience.

Second, if Fackenheim is right, then it seems likely that his model for Rosenzweig's conjunction of "philosophy and theology" is Kierkegaard's conception of faith as an immediacy after reflection.[14] But Rosenzweig's own words suggest that both the objectivity and the subjectivity are somehow united in the very same experience: "Man, as the recipient of revelation, as one who experiences the content of faith, contains both within himself."[15] This person, because of the features of his experience that is both a religious believing and a philosophical thinking, is the only genuine "scientifically possible" philosopher. In his experience, philosophy and theology are somehow one.

Finally, Rosenzweig prefaces his solution with these words: "our answer necessarily anticipates and yet stops halfway, with a hint."[16] If

Fackenheim is right, then what the solution anticipates when it suggests that the bridge is the "concept of revelation" is a subsequent account of how revelation occurs only after a systematic philosophical defense of the possibility of revelation. But, we must ask, is that what Rosenzweig later provides? Does he show that revelation occurs as an immediate experience prepared by philosophical thought? In the very next section, "Theology and Philosophy," Rosenzweig indicates in a preliminary fashion that just as the new philosophy needs theology, so does the new theology need philosophy. Ultimately, he says, "the miracle of the personal experience of revelation" will be verified through redemption, i.e., by the relation between revelation and redemption and hence by the individual's response to revelation. But that experience also needs a philosophical ground; Rosenzweig calls this "building a bridge from creation to revelation," and he glosses this process as "supplying a demonstration of the preconditions on which it rests." But, and this is the crucial point, Rosenzweig says that the new theology takes its experience to be not content but event so that its preconditions are not "conceptual elements" but rather "immanent reality."[17] If Fackenheim is correct, then this "immanent reality" or what Rosenzweig calls "the concept of creation" is constituted by a philosophical argument for the possibility of revelation and its presuppositions, e.g., the real separation between God, man, and world.[18] But is this what Rosenzweig thinks? Is this what the "created contents" of philosophy amounts to? Indeed, can it be?

What, from Rosenzweig's point of view, would make the philosopher's turn to theology necessary? Let me suggest an analogous case. In his longest and most famous essay, *The Apology for Raymond Sebond*, Montaigne employs a battery of skeptical arguments and tropes in order to discredit the reliability of reason and the senses. One interpretation of Montaigne's conclusions is that he is persuaded by the skeptical outcome, that one should not trust any source of cognitive authority, from reason and the senses to tradition and institutions. Another interpretation, however, shows exactly how the essay is a *defense* of Sebond, whose fifteenth-century rational defense of Christianity Montaigne had translated. On this interpretation, Montaigne, a genuine member of the Counter-Reformation, sought to show the limits of human capabilities and the need for complete and unqualified submission to God and the Church. Only human pride could lead us to reject God and Christian faith, once we were aware of the puny character of our own abilities. On such a view, then, reason and philosophy, among other skills and methods, prove to be limited and threaten total skepticism; the only way to find certainty is to receive it from another source.

Could it be that Rosenzweig in his own way employs a similar strategy? Could it be that once philosophy recognizes that it must become perspectival and personal, the only way to avoid subjectivism and more is to accept certainty and objectivity as a gift?[19] It may be true that the new theology also needs philosophy for its own reasons, but the crucial fact is that the new philosopher is threatened at least with skepticism if he does not accept the truth of religious belief, the reality and presence of the Absolute as the ground of nature and history.

How exactly would this solution work? Suppose we carry out Rosenzweig's project in the domain of ethics. Traditional moral theory is conducted from a detached point of view; it seeks to understand moral thinking and conduct from an ideal or neutral perspective and does so by grounding our conceptions of the right and the good in God or in nature or in human rationality. Now suppose that we show how each of these strategies is mistaken or narrow or otherwise misguided, and we recognize that the method for arriving at our understanding of morality has been in error from the start, for what is left out always has something to do with the precise individual, his or her distinctive situation, set of beliefs and attitudes, past, community, and so on. So we begin again, this time following the individual moral agent, tracing her experiences and registering what counts as right and good for her in her situation. But we soon recognize the threat that this method poses. It leaves us with no ground for its results other than the experiences and judgments of the individual whose thinking we are following. We have left behind any appeal to common natural characteristics or to a conception of universal rationality. All has been particularized and historicized. Like Nietzsche and Foucault, we risk the outcome that morality is utterly relative and fundamentally a matter of power.

We could accept this. Or alternatively we could demand a ground for objectivity and certainty, recognizing that if there is such a ground it must lie outside ourselves and our world. But what is left? Only the possibility that the individual agent's experience will point beyond her world and herelf and she will become receptive to such a ground, freely received but graciously given. So this is what we do; we trace the experiencing moral agent as she interprets a world and her action in it in such a way that she becomes receptive to an agency that empowers her judgments and gives them a significance that she takes now to be unconditional. She does not know how that empowerment has come, nor why, but it has, and she accepts it. In so doing, her utterly personal experiences and thinking have yielded objective results.[20]

Ultimately, Rosenzweig claims, the transition from revelation to redemption will bring confirmation for his system. Others have discussed this feature of his thinking, and we can ignore it here.[21] Our concern is with the way in which theology in its own way justifies or legitimates philosophy.

In addition, of course, philosophy serves the new conception of faith as the personal experience of revelation. In the text we are discussing, Rosenzweig says that philosophy will serve the new theology, the commitment to the "pure presentness of experience" and the "personal experience of revelation," by exhibiting creation as the precondition of revelation, as the "immanent reality" which makes revelation as event possible.[22] What this means is that the thinking experience of the new philosopher must exhibit the world as a created world, as contingent, as grounded in the miraculous and permeable by miracle. Only in such a world is revelation possible. If the experience of the new philosopher showed us that the world is causally closed and necessary, if its results were akin to Spinoza's in the *Ethics*, then the new theologian, committed to personal religious experience as the core of faith, would be unable to affirm, receive, or experience revelation. His way would be blocked, for the precondition, the required state, in which revelation as divine-human encounter can take place, would not exist for him. However, the new philosopher can exhibit the world as created, and "[T]hereby revelation regains before our amazed eyes the character of authentic miracle—authentic because it becomes wholly and solely the fulfillment of the promise made in creation."[23] Moreover, this promise is, in fact, made by a new philosopher who experiences the world as contingent, a post-Humean and post-Kantian new philosopher who appreciates the limits of that with which experience provides us, and the limits beyond which experience cannot go. Although one cannot be absolutely certain about what Rosenzweig here has in mind, he seems to be calling on one of the central findings of "traditional" empiricism and one of its skeptical results, i.e., about our inability to experience causal connections and, hence, natural necessity, in order to ground the new philosopher's experience of the created world.

In both cases, then, when theology grounds the objectivity of the new philosophy and when the new thinking grounds the possibility of the new theology, there is no hint of the old thinking. This is one of the problems of Fackenheim's account; where he requires system, reason, and argument, Rosenzweig demands interpreted fact or what he calls "immanent reality." The reason for this shift, moreover, has to do, I think, with an implicit shift in the meaning of "objectivity." According to the old thinking, "objectivity" is associated with certainty, unconditionality, universality, and necessity. It is the proper correlate of an impersonal, detached, disengaged, and transcendent perspective. Hence, it would be odd, in a sense, to demand this kind of objectivity for the new thinking, and I do not believe that Rosenzweig made this mistake. For the new thinking, on the other hand, "objectivity" can only mean agreement, acceptance, commitment, and such notions. To ask "can the new thinking be scientific?" is to ask how it can yield such agreement and commitment. And here everything depends on *whose* agreement. If one is persuaded by Rosenzweig's refutation of the old thinking and by the need to avoid relativism and subjectivism, then the personal experience of revelation will persuade you too, like the believer, to accept the impact of the Other, and your agreement will constitute what objectivity there is for such claims as the new thinking makes. Thereby, what the new thinking yields about the world as a created, miracle-permeated venue will be accepted as objective and hence as the genuine establishment of the precondition necessary for the possibility of revelation. In this sense, philosophy, as Rosenzweig puts it, is the "authentic *auctoritas* suited to [the] new form" of religious faith.[24] There is a circle here, but it is not vicious.

The problem of objectivity that Rosenzweig acknowledged and attempted to solve in his own context and for his own purposes is a problem of tremendous importance in contemporary thinking.[25] Various recent developments in philosophy, literary criticism, history of science, historiography, anthropology, and art have led to a widespread conviction that our conceptual schemes or *Weltanschauungen* are interpretations through and through, that there is nothing that is secure and certain, and that all of our theories or points of view are grounded only in utility, acceptance, or power. In such an environment, there is a great need to find some principles or values that are secure and fixed.[26] Some deny the entire account as relativist and dangerous;[27] others admit that we are irreducibly hermeneutical in our understanding but that we nonetheless value certain things unconditionally.[28] Others succumb to the relativism and historicism of the age. This is not the time to discuss these matters. It is sufficient to appreciate that these problems were, in a sense, already present to Rosenzweig and his colleagues. Like us, they recognized the deficiencies of old modes of thinking and were aware of the dangers of the new.

ELEVEN

# Jewish Philosophy and Historical Self-Consciousness

I would like to propose that we consider various instances of modern Jewish thinking as episodes in a process of increasing self-consciousness or self-recognition. The kind of self-consciousness that I have in mind slowly emerges, with varying degrees of complexity and clarity, in the course of over three hundred years of thinking about Judaism in the modern world. It is a self-consciousness about the relationships between Judaism and history, a set of moments of self-recognition about the ways in which Judaism is related to and influenced by history.

To some, history is what has happened, events, occurrences; to others it is the written accounts of what has happened. But "history," as I use the term, refers not only to these, the events and the record of them, but also to a host of features that we associate with the temporal character of historical events and their records. These features include transiency, change, conditionality, finitude, supersession, pastness or remoteness, and relativity. Hence, when I speak about the relationships between Judaism and history, I mean the various ways in which Jewish life, beliefs, and conduct are seen to be related to the changeable, conditional, and finite character of the world in which they occur. I am interested in the relation between Judaism and time, change, and the past, and my suggestion is that modern Jewish thinking can be understood as a series of occasions when this relationship becomes the object of self-awareness and increasingly subtle reflection and revision.

In this chapter I shall focus on three episodes that I have touched upon in earlier discussions and that illustrate an increasing sophistication and subtlety in the self-consciousness of this relationship between Judaism and history. The first involves Mendelssohn's response to Spinoza concerning the authority of the ritual or ceremonial law. The second deals with Franz Rosenzweig's rethinking of the grounds and nature of Jewish history. The final case comes from post-Holocaust Jewish thought and involves showing how Emil Fackenheim's thinking powerfully raises the question of historical realism and transcendence for future Jewish thought.

In his *Tractatus Theologico-Politicus*, published anonymously in 1670, Spinoza formulates a famous interpretation of the meaning and authority of ceremonial law in Judaism. This account is embedded in a larger project, which includes the development of a method of biblical interpretation, its defense, and its application to the biblical text. For our purposes most of this innovative and important enterprise can be ignored, but not all of it, for the gist of Spinoza's treatment of the ceremonial laws of Judaism draws significantly on both the form and the content of Spinoza's hermeneutic.

Spinoza proposes that Scripture is a literary work like any other and ought to be understood as any other work or in fact as any other natural object would be understood, according to an examination of its history. The interpreter ought to treat the work or any of its parts as historically situated in a particular linguistic, cultural, and political setting, composed by authors with special skills, abilities, and interests for audiences with their own capabilities and customs. The Bible, that is, is a thoroughly historical document, and although Spinoza certainly has a very special idea of what natural-historical inquiry requires and consists of, still the important point about biblical interpretation is the general one, that it involves a careful reading of the text itself but always with a keen attentiveness to its historical context. It is Spinoza's contention, moreover, that the outcome of such a reading is a distinction between the pervasive, general biblical teaching that concerns moral probity, encouraging a life of justice and charity, and a variety of particular, contextually defined narratives. In short, the Bible contains both historical and ahistorical teachings.

Spinoza, in the course of his study of the Bible, examines some important, recurrent expressions and concepts. Among these are the expressions that concern divine help or aid, salvation, and the chosenness of the people of Israel. Generally Spinoza provides a natural translation of these expressions. God's help or salvation or redemption is nothing more than the means a people devises, by virtue of its own abilities and insight, to satisfy its economic, social, and political needs and thereby to promote its well-being and survival. Hence, divine help actually manifests itself as agricultural techniques or political institutions or policies that enable a people to live and live well. Therefore, if the chosenness of the people of Israel refers to a special case of divine aid, it simply refers to those special means, political and military, that this people devised that enabled it to survive in an especially hostile environment. In the end, then, chosenness occurs as the institutions of Jewish civil autonomy, during the first two commonwealths. After their destruction, the survival of the people is not a function of chosenness and hence of their own ingenuity but rather of the hatred of others and of the physical sign of circumcision.

For Spinoza, then, Jewish survival, distinctiveness, and independence are crucially historical, and their deepest historical roots are political. It is no surprise, therefore, that his account of the role and significance of ritual observance and ritual law is also crucially historical. What, he asks, is the purpose of ceremonial legislation and ritual action? Obedience is essential to political life, for the purpose of a polity is to protect rights through law, and law requires authority and the right to expect obedience. But obedience ultimately derives from the fact that the state's authority rests on the consent of the individual citizens who constitute it. Hence, in a democratic republic there is no problem of obedience, precisely because the citizens themselves are both makers of the law and bound to obey it; as Rousseau was later to announce with the greatest clarity, in such a state the individual gives up nothing insofar as he really in effect gives up everything only to himself. But, as Spinoza realizes, in a monarchy obedience does become an issue, since the monarch is at best a representative of the citizens' own will. In the ancient Jewish state, which was a monarchy, this was the case. Hence, there was a need to encourage obedience and stimulate allegiance to the state, and it was for these purposes that the ceremonial laws of Judaism were devised.[1]

According to Spinoza, then, the individual Jew's relation to the ceremonial law is mediated by the Jewish state, for the Jew is obligated to ceremonial or ritual observance only insofar as such conduct will encourage his sense of obedience to the laws of the Jewish state. The primary relationship is between the individual Jew and the Jewish state, and it is facilitated by ceremonial law. Hence, just as the state is a historical contingency and, in 1670, a remote historical phenomenon no longer extant, so the ceremonial law, as a set of authoritative prescriptions, is also contingent, historical, and in the end remote and distant. In short, the authority of ritual observance for Judaism and for Jews is not ahistorical and timeless; rather, it is subordinate to political authority and hence to the existence of the Jewish state. As long as the Jewish state exists, then the ceremonial law is binding; when it no longer exists, the law loses its function and its force. Hence the law's contingency, its temporary character, and, given the nature of the case in 1670, its remoteness. It is a law which, when appreciated historically and in its own precise historical, cultural, political setting, is detached from and inaccessible to the Jew of 1670. The final outcome of a historical interpretation of the ceremonial law is to make its appropriation as a living form of conduct both unnecessary and impossible.

These views, about the historical character of Spinoza's understanding of ritual obligation and its implications, are mine and not his, but I am inclined to think that he would have found them accurate. Indeed, I think that a century later, in 1783, when Moses Mendelssohn published his own *apologia* for religious tolerance and Jewish particularity, he both appreciated the force of Spinoza's account and sensed as well the threat of the historical as I have outlined it. To be sure, Mendelssohn did not clearly say that Spinoza's account would destroy Jewish distinctiveness by making the ceremonial law ineffective and inaccessible, a victim of history and historical inquiry, but his own attempt to save the authority of ritual observance suggests that he was aware of this challenge.

Mendelssohn wrote *Jerusalem* in 1783 as a response to those who challenged his claim that abolishing the traditional right to excommunication or *cherem* was compatible with continued Jewish life and commitment. At the same time, it was an opportunity to clarify his advocacy of religious toleration.[2] Our interest is the very precise one of focusing on how Mendelssohn responded to Spinoza's historical disposal of the ceremonial law and hence of one central dimension of Jewish particularity and Jewish tradition. There is reason to think that Mendelssohn's response is not a simple one and that it involves trying to confront the historical problem in two ways, both by transcending it and by meeting it head-on.

In the first part of *Jerusalem* Mendelssohn, drawing on Hobbes, Locke, and the tradition of ecclesiastical law, develops a social contract political theory, an argument for the separation of church and state, an account of the nature of civil and religious institutions, and a defense of tolerance. The centerpiece of this wholly philosophical effort is an attempt to delineate the authority of civil and religious institutions regarding belief or conviction, on the one hand, and action, on the other. The result is a Lockian argument for toleration that underscores Mendelssohn's opposition to the ecclesiastic right of excommunication.[3]

In the second part of the work Mendelssohn proceeds to an account of Judaism and especially a defense of Jewish distinctiveness in the face of the charge that without sanctions there is no remaining authority for the ceremonial law. A careful reading of Mendelssohn's thinking reveals a two-stage argument. The first defends the authority of ceremonial observance by subordinating it to the unconditional authority of moral principles. The second defends it by an appeal to a historical fact. Hence, while one stage of the argument encounters history by transcending it, the other does so by confronting it directly.

The first stage is well-known. All human beings are both equipped with rational capacities and rationally cognizant of the imperatives of morality, to seek happiness and aspire to a life of virtue. But, Mendelssohn points out, genuine moral aspiration requires knowledge of certain eternal truths, among which are the existence of God, His unity and uniqueness, and Divine Providence. In effect, Mendelssohn believes that genuine morality requires metaphysical knowledge. But, in the course of historical development, both the Jews and other peoples have come to forget these truths; hence, there is a need for a device to bring these truths back to mind and thereby to enable the process of moral perfection. Mendelssohn, in a long digression, tries to show why language is not the most effective device for stimulating such recollection. God ordained, instead of language, a variety of typical actions to perform this function, i.e., the ceremonial laws of Judaism. Their authority, then, derives from the unconditional, timeless authority of the moral law itself, for the means are as obligatory as the end, if the means can be shown to be the most effective way of arriving at the end in question. To be sure, as Mendelssohn points out, the original Jewish commonwealth, under God's rule, was a polity *sui generis*, but while the ceremonial laws then were legislated as part of a state that no longer exists, the crucial fact is that their authority both then and now is tied to the timeless authority of moral law. Spinoza's historical disposal of ritual requirement is overcome by a strategy of transcendence; ritual law is not remote and inaccessible, because it is essentially not historical at all.

But Mendelssohn buttresses this argument with another that appreciates more explicitly the historical threat posed by Spinoza's account. Alluding to a Hobbesian principle, that a sovereign's silence is a *de facto* endorsement, Mendelssohn argues that the ceremonial law is just as binding now as it was when the Jewish state existed. The reason is the obvious one, he claims, that the Divine Legislator who was responsible for its legality has not, in the interim, publicly revoked that law. Hence, Mendelssohn implies, the divine silence is tantamount to continued endorsement. In other terms, the historical fact of divine silence counts as evidence that the ceremonial law is not after all historically remote and inaccessible. Rather, it is still in force, and, he implies, will remain in force as long as God does not reveal a contrary will.[4]

Deep down, I think, these two arguments reflect a common theme, for they show how Mendelssohn confronts or is made to confront the problem of historical remoteness and traditional continuity in terms of an account of the sources of religious authority and religious obligation. In a sense, he struggles to answer the question, how is continuity with the Jewish tradition both necessary and possible? His intuitions move him to believe that such continuity is desirable; he therefore is inclined to treat historical, particular matters as less central than transcendent, universal ones. But at the same time he cannot abandon wholly the distinctiveness of the tradition in question in favor of objectivity and generality. The outcome is confusion, but instructive confusion. For what Mendelssohn exhibits is a hint of a realization that by treating Jewish law as historical one runs the risk of alienating it completely, a danger that he and not he alone will want to avoid.

One hundred years after Mendelssohn's death in Berlin, Franz Rosenzweig was born in Cassel, into a world that is significantly shaped by Mendelssohn, Enlightenment thought, and Mendelssohn's progeny.[5] In a sense, Rosenzweig attempts to respond to two alternative ways in which Judaism appeared to him: one is formalism, and the other is voluntarism. One, that is, involves a Judaism of mechanical and abstract practice, both moral and ritual; the other involves a Judaism reduced to human will and autonomy. These are not distinct modes of Jewish life as much as tendencies that seemed to him to pervade all the Jewish life with which he was acquainted in Germany and Western Europe. One tendency is ahistorical and without vitality and excitement; the other is wholly historical and voluntaristic but to the point where all continuity and essence are threatened. Hence, Rosenzweig offers his solution. Judaism is a communal enterprise organized around moments of revelation, of eternity. The continuity of the flesh-and-blood people is grounded in its utterly historical, indeed biological character. But the essence of that people lies not in its historicity but rather in its utterly ahistorical round of life and aspiration to eternity, to divine-human encounter that issues in interpersonal intimacy and community. Christianity, on the other hand, is a wholly historical institution, a "way" or path through history whose purpose is to make available to the uninitiated a vehicle for recognizing and working toward the final redemption, the eternity that Judaism signifies and anticipates. Christianity, then, is in and of history, a missionizing and political means to promote the realization of redemption. Judaism is wholly transcendent, *in* but not *of* history, a timeless milieu of ritual opportunities for bringing eternity into time, for creating moments of revelation that point toward a future oriented by the divine-human intimacy which they exemplify. Hence, Rosenzweig repeats the words of *The Song of Songs*, love is stronger than death, i.e., in Judaism revelation and eternity overshadow and subordinate history and temporality. All historical events, truths, and practices are only that, historical, partial, and temporary; real truth is ahistorical. It reveals itself momentarily and proleptically in history and only comes to full realization when history ends and yields to eternity. Hence, for the eternal people, there is no real, transient, flowing history; there is no real past, no real future. Nothing of real importance, as Rosenzweig says, happens between Creation and the End of Days.[6]

Rosenzweig, then, is tremendously sensitive to the subtle interplay between history and eternity, between the mundane and the deeply religious, and between historicity and transcendence. In a sense, his perspective on Judaism and its richness is dictated by his complex appreciation of these dichotomies. The result, moreover, can be summarized this way, that the historical influences Rosenzweig's thinking at three crucial points. First, history plays a vital role in Rosenzweig's account of revelation. Second, history is fundamental to his "new thinking" and the way in which it grounds the categories of human experience and hence the human condition. Finally, history is a basic feature of his account of Jewish and Christian existence. Let me say something about each of these three points.

First, Rosenzweig's conception of revelation, as an event in which the Divine and the human encounter each other in the world, both attracts and repels the historical, as it were. As Rosenzweig says, revelation is an event, a meeting, an occasion of eternity in time; the human conduct and accounts, narrative and otherwise, that are associated with it are, however, human interpretations. Whereas revelation itself is ahistorical, the preparation and receptivity that precede it and the actions and words that follow it are completely human and hence historical. The human and historical gain their meaning insofar as they are oriented in terms of an ahistorical encounter. The round of Jewish life, then, that is so oriented never changes in essence; it forever attempts to create occasions for revelation which point toward the final redemption. In a sense, while Rosenzweig's account of revelation seems to respect the distinct roles of eternity and time, of the event of revelation and its historical surroundings, in the end it reduces the historical character of time, the fact that it involves development, change, detachment, and anticipation. For the Church, to be sure, these features are retained, within limitations, but for the Synagogue they are diminished, so that, for example, the key features and episodes of Jewish life are *de facto* as timeless as the revelation which is their center.

Second, Rosenzweig's philosophical and systematic achievement involves a critique of the old thinking and an employment of the new to locate the genuine foundations of an account of the human situation and human history. Crucially, as we indicated, the new thinking involves a phenomenological description and interpretation from the subjective point of view. It involves, that is, a tracking of experience, as it were, through increasingly subtle relationships with the world, with God, and with other human beings. But, and this is a crucial point, Rosenzweig recognizes that in order to provide general foundations for religious thought, the new thinking as radical empiricism cannot remain the unique outcome of completely personal experience and thinking. It must, at some point and in some way, rise to the level of objectivity. It must, that is, leave the historical behind and gain philosophical or, as he puts it, "scientific" generality. Here I do not want to repeat my account of how Rosenzweig thinks that subjective thinking rises to the level of objectivity; it is sufficient to realize that he believes that it must.[7] In so doing, he acknowledges the role of historical experience from the subjective perspective only to rise above it and, in a sense, to leave it behind.[8] It is his conviction that as philosophy, the new thinking must begin with history but not stay with it; it must begin with the world and all of its objects as experienced by the agent only to rise above them to a perspective of objective detachment and understanding. Like Hegel in the *Phenomenology*, then, Rosenzweig realizes that in giving history its due, thought must nonetheless leave it behind and transcend it.

Finally, one outcome of Rosenzweig's new thinking and his new conception of revelation is his portrait of Judaism as an ahistorical, eternal people. To be sure, the character and continuity of this people is ultimately rooted in the biological fact that each generation is related by blood to its predecessors and its progeny. The Jewish people is a flesh-and-blood people whose existence cannot be voluntaristic but must be as necessary as nature can make it be, and with this natural necessity already comes an intimation of eternity. But here too a natural, historical foundation is transcended, for the meaning of Jewish existence and its continuity arises out of its unique association with redemption, the task of redemption, the hope of redemption, i.e., with eternity. The Jewish festivals and round of life are orchestrated to create an environment for opportunities of divine-human intimacy, when God and man draw near to each other, inspiring a hope in a future wholly shaped by such events. Judaism points toward this end; it is not *of* history. Its historical festivals, such as Hanukah and Purim, are associated, in Rosenzweig's mind, with Christianity. Its political interests must be minimized. Nothing essentially historical is part of the Jewish soul; ritual and repetition are central to it. Once again, Rosenzweig acknowledges the role of history, time, and experience, only to find the special virtues of Judaism in its atemporality, its desire to separate itself from the limitations and tasks and demands of the historical.

In the end, then, Rosenzweig's appreciation of the ways in which Judaism is and is not historical is far richer than Mendelssohn's. It is also more self-conscious. Rosenzweig, student of the famous historian Friedrich Meinecke and author of a masterly work on Hegel's political philosophy, could not but take history seriously. He realized how history was understood in the modern world. He also recognized, as Paul Mendes-Flohr has shown, the threats of historicism, its "curse," as he called it.[9] What is exciting about Rosenzweig, then, is that his subtle mind both acknowledged and constrained the role of history for an understanding of Judaism and Jewish life. The historical could not be peremptorily dismissed; nor could it be allowed to dominate and subsume, as so many historians are inclined it should. As we now turn to Jewish thought of more recent decades, especially as it seeks to locate itself within the parameters provided by utterly historical events, the Holocaust and the Jewish state, we shall see this delicate balance threatened. One way of understanding contemporary, post-Holocaust Jewish thought is precisely as an attempt to find a third way between Rosenzweig's subtle ahistoricism and the relativizing historicism of historians, social scientists, and politicians.

It was not easy for Jewish thinkers to confront the Nazi Holocaust and its horrors, but when they did they found that that dark event, in an extreme form, raised for Jewish self-understanding the problems of historical remoteness and continuity that we have discussed, as well as the problem of absolutism and historicism. In a radical way, the event seemed to demand that honest attempts to understand Judaism today be both historicist and antirealist; it seemed to require, that is, that the event be treated both as an abyss that could not be bridged and as a rupture that was and had to be traversed. How to admit and cope with these seemingly incommensurable requirements became one of the central tasks of post-Holocaust Jewish thought.

For our purposes, the deepest, most comprehensive and systematic account is provided by Emil Fackenheim, whose first important statements appeared in 1967 and 1968 and whose subsequent confrontation with the Holocaust, Israel, and contemporary Jewish experience includes dozens of articles and, at last count, six books.

Fackenheim often recalls that the crucial shift in his thinking occurred when he came to realize that nothing in Judaism is immune to historical alteration and even refutation. At one time he had spoken of God and faith as features of Jewish commitment that could be confirmed by history and experience but not falsified by them, as what he called the *existential a priori* of Jewish experience.[10] Then, in 1967, he came to speak of the Midrashic Framework as being open to historical modification and of Jewish faith as exposed to history, and especially to the extremities of human possibility. Only when this openness is admitted can the atrocities, the horror, the radical evil of the Nazi Holocaust be honestly and seriously confronted. It is this admission that makes genuine encounter possible between thought—historical, psychological, religious, philosophical—and the event. And once that encounter is possible, it can be conducted, and once conducted, one can and must wrestle with its outcome, an impasse that makes continued life and thought both questionable and necessary. At this point, then, Fackenheim *in principle* admits historicism only to argue that *in fact* Jewish continuity with the past is both necessary and possible.

When thought, confronting Auschwitz, cannot proceed, what does it then do? How does the thinker cope with such failure? with such paralysis? In a series of writings of 1967–68 Fackenheim gropes to a breakthrough: that thought must somehow go on and become responsive to the event, even without comprehension. This is the crucial step, to distinguish between a meaning or understanding that is impossible and a responsiveness that is necessary. To be sure, at that time Fackenheim took for granted that the thinker *could* go on and that the mandate for so doing could be derived from an understanding of how Jewish people, after the event, had themselves gone on. Once the event revealed itself to the thinker in all its particularity, unprecedented in so many ways, and hence when the limits of theory exposed themselves, there was still a way out, a path that led beyond immobilization to a new mode of post-Holocaust living—for Jews, Christians, Germans, philosophers, historians, and others as well. All of this is packed into the statement for which he became well-known, that the outcome of the serious encounter with Auschwitz is a Divine Command, a 614th Commandment, that one ought not give Hitler any posthumous victories. This celebrated slogan, hailed and assailed, does have its deficiencies, but they are not the ones so often cited. In it Fackenheim packed too much, unwarranted hopes and unjustified commitments.

The chief problems with the 614th Commandment concern both its form and its content. What is the origin or ground of its imperative force, its obligatoriness? What justifies its status as a command and hence as the outcome of a Divine Will? What grounds its possibility and the assumption that any such imperative could be followed? And what determines its specific content, a content that begins with resistance to Nazi purposes and develops in a host of religious and moral directions? During the years between the delivery of the lectures, *God's Presence in History* (1968), and the publication of *To Mend the World* (1982), Fackenheim, I think, came to appreciate these problems and their power. He also came to appreciate what needed to be done in order to confront them and solve them, to the degree that solution was possible.

In *To Mend the World* he attempts his solutions, working through a probing analysis of the experience of the victims of the death camps, the intentions and conduct of the Nazi perpetrators, and even the evil itself in order, in the end, to ground both the necessity and the possibility of resistance, of recovery, and of repair, *Tikkun Olam*, a mending of the world. Earlier, in *God's Presence in History*, the key problem was one of necessity; now it is one of *possibility*. Neither a neoorthodox grace nor a Kantian inference from ought to can will do. The real ground of the possibility of resistance is a brute fact properly understood, the actual resistance of the victims themselves; the real ground of our understanding of resistance is the understanding of the victims. And the turning point for the thinker comes when his thought, following the victim's own thought, can grasp the evil only with a thought that is both amazed and repelled, all at once. Such thinking, moreover, which achieves as much comprehension as is possible and does so only while being horrified and repelled as well, cannot, as Fackenheim argues, remain mere thinking and survive. It must become more than repelled thinking; it must become opposing action, and so active resistance arises not by dictate but by the necessity of thought's own nature and itinerary. Active resistance is what happens to thinking about Auschwitz when it thinks all that it can but must go on nonetheless.

The outcome, for Fackenheim, is a mandate for recovery that involves the appropriation of a Jewish category and a new evaluation and interpretation of the past—its texts, traditional practices, models, and so forth—to see what can be appropriated today, in a world after Auschwitz. This mandate is both necessary and possible for Jews, Christians, historians, Germans, and a host of others. Hence, for Fackenheim, the Holocaust is both radically separated from the past and yet an event out of which a reinterpretation and recovery of that past are made necessary and possible.

The special form that recovery or *teshuvah* takes, then, is a mending of a world that has been ruptured, shattered, and in many ways destroyed. But it is important to appreciate that it was indeed not one world but many, a Jewish world, a Christian world, a world of humanistic culture, and much else. In *God's Presence in History* Fackenheim developed a partial portrait of the Jewish world in terms of his notion of Midrash and the Midrashic Framework. What he recognized even then was that the thinker's encounter with Auschwitz is an encounter of someone whose life and thought are already shaped by a particular tradition, by particular concepts, ideas, beliefs, commitments, hopes, values, and purposes. In attempting to characterize the basic features and ideas of the Midrashic Framework or the world of the Midrash, Fackenheim was trying to define his own Jewish world and the Midrashic influence on it *prior* to his encounter with the Holocaust. Hermeneutically speaking, he was trying to identify the particular way in which the Jewish past, the Midrashic tradition, presented itself to him and shaped him. Then, in the final chapter of that work, he tried to show how that world and that framework failed to encompass, to comprehend and understand, the Holocaust and its unprecedented evil. In short, he wanted to show how the event was unassimilable into that framework and hence how inaccessible that framework now became for a genuine post-Holocaust Jewish life.

In a number of essays, many reprinted in *The Jewish Return into History*, and in *To Mend the World* Fackenheim elaborates the account of his pre-Holocaust philosophical and theological self. He tries, that is, to identify and discuss the most profound influences on his philosophical and theological understanding—from Spinoza and Rosenzweig to Buber, Hegel, and Heidegger. All along he tries to understand them on their own terms in order later to rethink them in confrontation with the horrors of the death camps. Then, after such confrontation, Fackenheim attempts to reinterpret his Jewish and philosophical past, to reappropriate it but now in a way distinctly filtered through the encounter with the victims of the death camps, their conduct, their thinking, and his own rethinking of their experience, thinking, and beyond. Simply put, Fackenheim recognizes the hermeneutical demands placed on him and any serious contemporary Jewish thinker—to return to the pre-Holocaust world and in the end to rethink that world in terms of our new situation.

Fackenheim recognizes the attractions and indeed the necessity of being both a historicist and an antirealist. He sees that who we are at any moment is influenced by our past, our tradition, and our history. But, at the same time, after the Holocaust everything has been changed and, in being changed, changes even the past, the tradition of which we are a part. Or, to put it otherwise, to take Auschwitz seriously and with unconditional honesty, one must respond to it as a person and thinker whose world is influenced by a millennial past, but for whom, at the same time, the event first makes that past remote and inaccessible and then requires and makes possible a recovery of it. Furthermore, if Fackenheim is right, then an honest encounter with Auschwitz by means of a return to the lives and the thinking of its victims places important constraints on that recovery of the past. Not any reappropriation of Jewish ideas, ritual, models, and history will be acceptable; there are limitations, directions, guidance, and conditions that are always submitted to us for evaluation and interpretation but that do make demands on us as well. These limitations, directions, and conditions arise for the thinker out of a serious and honest encounter with Auschwitz and with the testimony of its victims and survivors, an encounter that is itself shaped by the thinker's situation and also gives shape to the thinker's subsequent recovery of the past.

For Fackenheim, then, the past is remote in two ways: initially because it includes rituals, events, people, and writings that are historically remote and need to be retrieved in their own terms, and subsequently because it is a past that exists on *the other side* of the unprecedented evils of Auschwitz. Once the Holocaust is recognized as a radical rupture, then one can no longer simply assume that the concepts, beliefs, and attitudes that shaped the past and its traditions can be uncritically reappropriated in a post-Holocaust world. The Jewish thinker's hermeneutical task is to reenact both of these remote pasts, separated as they are by a serious encounter with Auschwitz, its victims, its perpetrators, and its evil. In this way, the thinker becomes both a historicist and an antirealist at once and yet not a relativist. Some values, directions, and imperatives are *now* unconditional, although they arise out of this confrontation of tradition with event. For Fackenheim, such values and directions include a manifold commitment to Judaism, the Jewish people, and human dignity.

Hence, in post-Holocaust Jewish thought Mendelssohn's problem of the remoteness of the past and Rosenzweig's appreciation of the problematic of historicity are incorporated into Jewish thought with greater self-consciousness and in new ways. The past is made remote by both historical thinking and history itself. Historicity becomes undeniable but not wholly destructive, for after Auschwitz there is available a type of philosophical and religious transcendence, although it is temporary and rooted in the historical experience of the victims of Nazism and a contemporary understanding of them.

In the course of the past three centuries a variety of Jewish intellectuals have reflected on Torah and its authority, on the role of freedom in Jewish life and thought, on Israel, and on revelation and faith. But, at the same time that they have concentrated on such a variety of substantive issues, they have also come to an increasingly keen awareness of the subtle ways in which history is related to Jewish life and Jewish thought. I have indicated how Spinoza, Mendelssohn, Rosenzweig, and Fackenheim do indeed reflect on important features of Judaism, from the ritual law to the nature of revelation and our understanding of evil, Jewish survival, and the imperatives of Jewish life. But at the same time I have tried to show that their thought exhibits an equally important development in historical self-consciousness. History and its associated notions, from change and temporality to finitude and conditionality, slowly come to pervade Jewish self-understanding. It has been my task to try to show how this has been so and thereby to argue that post-Holocaust Jewish thought marks an important stage in this process. Auschwitz may have been a radical rupture in the continuity of Jewish life and experience, but post-Holocaust Jewish thought is not. Rather, it is a crucial stage in the continuous development of modern Jewish self-understanding, a stage at which the problematics of historicity are deeply appreciated and confronted in an effort to provide foundations for the Jewish life and Jewish thought of the future.

TWELVE

# Contemporary Jewish Thought in America

Jewish theology or Jewish thought is one expression of Jewish self-understanding, probably the most academic and certainly the most didactic and discursive. At virtually all times and in all places, some Jews have felt the need or been compelled to articulate what Judaism and Jewish life mean to them and their community. Some of them have responded to that need by rewriting and restructuring ritual and liturgy, some by writing poems and songs, others by revising Jewish law. But others, usually responding to challenges of non-Jewish culture and intellectual life as well as to the special character of Jewish life in times of historical, social, and political change, have written essays and books of a more reflective and abstract kind, books of Jewish philosophy or Jewish theology. In this chapter, at least initially, when I speak about Jewish thought it is to these types of writings that I refer. But in the course of things, this fact about Jewish thought will change, and that change will play an important role in the story I am about to tell.

The history of Jewish thought in America since the end of World War II and the Holocaust can be told as a history of four stages. Such a narrative is a caricature, of course, to one degree or another; there are no such precise divisions in history itself, and the tendencies dominant in the four stages are only that, tendencies. There is a great deal of overlap and much more complexity than I shall be able to discuss. But it is helpful, I think, to view the course of recent American Jewish thought in this schematic way, if only to set before ourselves a picture that can eventually be revised and made more accurate.

The first stage, which takes up the 1950s, can be called the period of *religious revival*. Already during the war there were indications that Jewish theologians, mostly rabbis, were concerned about the religious character of American Jewish life. The tensions with secularism were already apparent, and questions about the role of God, covenant, chosenness, and faith in Judaism had already been raised. In this first stage of post-War Jewish thought, Jewish thinkers wrestled with these questions. Liberal theologians worried about the nature and possibility of revelation and faith, about the tension between human freedom and divine authority, about the role and character of the divine-human covenant, and about the nature of Jewish community and the notion of the people of Israel. More traditional thinkers, committed to the centrality of the Halachah, wrestled with the tensions between law and morality and between Halachah and human self-determination or autonomy. And both, the liberal advocates of a renewed Jewish faith and the adherents of traditional piety and Halachah, tried to meet the challenges of Jewish naturalism and secularism. To both, secularism and humanism threatened to relativize the absolute, to dispose of transcendence, and to make of Judaism merely one option among many.

One of the hallmarks of this stage is the retrieval of the writings and the thinking of Martin Buber and Franz Rosenzweig for the arsenal of both liberal and traditional Jewish theologians. Buber's notion of dialogue became a vehicle for understanding the experience of faith and the character of covenant, and Rosenzweig's understanding of revelation, justified by his refutation of the "old thinking" and his development of the "new thinking," came to underpin many attempts to defend the possibility and indeed priority of faith and hence of God in Jewish experience. Both, moreover, provided understandings of the divine-human encounter that enabled liberal thinkers to incorporate both authority and human freedom within the very event of revelation and certainly within the subsequent Jewish life that was taken to be both divinely commanded and humanly interpreted. To be sure, there are a variety of understandings of Buber and Rosenzweig and a plethora of appropriations of them. But it is their widespread influence in this period that is remarkable, as religious heroes whose attempt to confront a world of technological materialism and arid modernity in pre-War Europe could be appropriated to suit a similar American situation.

As one looks back on this period, so dominated by the debate over religiosity and faith, it is easy to see evidence of older and deeper tensions in American Jewish thought and hints of subsequent developments. It was a time, for example, when the established problematic of universalism and particularism was influential. Both the advocates of naturalism, the defenders of Mordecai Kaplan's Reconstructionism, and the classical Reformers, who emphasized the primacy of ethics, universality, and rationality, formed one kind of opposition to the defenders of the new fideism, if one can call it that. The American context had encouraged effacing distinctiveness, but some sought a vigorous return to Jewishness, and this meant a return to faith, to covenant, to chosenness, and ultimately to God and the special relationship between God and the people of Israel.

But if the dichotomy of universality and particularity cuts one way, that between authority and autonomy cuts another. Here too there was an indebtedness to European thought, but this time it was to the existentialist tradition, primarily represented by Sartre and Kierkegaard and, to a degree, Nietzsche, and to the Kantian tradition, through Hermann Cohen back to Kant himself. And if the lines of conflict concerning particularity separated classical Reform Jews and naturalists from both traditional and liberal fideists, the conflict over authority divided the traditional, Halachic thinkers from all others. And if one set of Jewish interests emphasized covenant and chosenness, the other focused on ethics and law. The very possibility of a genuine Halachah, of its authority, of the role of interpretation, and of the grounds for change and transformation—all this came under scrutiny by Jewish thinkers of all kinds.

The second stage of contemporary American Jewish thought was relatively brief and less innovative. Largely a phenomenon of the 1960s, it involved the Jewish intellectual involvement in the Civil Rights Movement and the Movement for Peace in Vietnam. Its central focus was on the "canonization" of the Jewish moral tradition of justice and equality and peace, and hence it encouraged the entrance into the venue of Jewish thought of social thinkers, historians, political theorists, and social commentators. At the same time, it encouraged Jewish thinkers, some traditionalists, some liberals, and classical Reform Jewish thinkers, to reinstall the "prophetic" tradition as the centerpiece of contemporary Jewish piety. Still, to be sure, the debate raged over the very nature of revelation and the possibility of Halachah, the tension between authority and freedom, but it raged below the surface. The surface was occupied by a largely homogenized ethical monotheism wholly in tune with the decade-long revolt over rights—first by blacks, then by other minorities, by those against the Vietnam War, and finally by women.

From one point of view, the third stage was ushered in abruptly in June 1967, when American Jews, indeed all Jews the world over, suffered the recognition of mortality that accompanied the Six Day War and the intense appropriation of the memory of the Nazi Holocaust. This transformation, which radically altered both Jewish communal life and Jewish consciousness, occurred at a time when the Civil Rights Movement had shifted from its universal to its more parochial and nationalist phase. Hence, during the several years following 1967, Jewish life too changed, moving slowly from a focus on social and political issues to a set of more provincial interests, in ritual, community, and education.

The change in Jewish thought was also dramatic, although its clear outline at one level hides a cluster of features that are more difficult to discern. The primacy of the Holocaust as a determinative challenge to Jewish faith and self-understanding was already announced in the early 1960s by Elie Wiesel and Richard Rubenstein, but it was only after 1967 that its force was really felt. The number of Jewish thinkers who tried to confront and respond seriously to Auschwitz has been few—Emil Fackenheim, Eliezer Berkovits, Irving Greenberg, Arthur Cohen, and Rubenstein. We have discussed some of them in earlier chapters and especially Fackenheim, who has written dozens of articles and six books that reflect a deeper and deeper understanding of what Jewish life and thought can and must be like in the "age of Auschwitz and a new Jerusalem." During the two and a half decades since 1967, the dominant voice in American Jewish thought has been theirs, the thinkers who try to rethink Jewish experience in terms of an event that has threatened continuity and survival. Some minimize the event's theological implications; others maximize them. But all of these thinkers take the Holocaust seriously and try to rebuild Judaism, by a retrieval of Midrashic or biblical models, of an enduring conception of human dignity and worth and of some notion of God, covenant, and more. To be sure, thinkers like Rubenstein advocate a secular Judaism of one kind or another, but generally all recognize the *mitzvah* of Jewish existence after Auschwitz.

Alongside the phenomenon of post-Holocaust Jewish thought, however, other Jewish thinking has arisen or continued. There has been traditional Jewish thought, for some clinging to the centrality of covenant and Halachah and focused on Israel, for others seeking a new association of religious existentialism and orthodoxy. But more important is the emergence of a vast array of nontheological and nonphilosophical versions of Jewish thought. Primary among those who have come to understand and articulate the nature of Jewish life are the historians, often academics and professors of Jewish studies. In one sense, this should not have been surprising, for the legacy of *Wissenschaft* and anti-*Wissenschaft* Jewish historiography—the name of Gershom Scholem prominent above all others—suggests an important modern role for Jewish historians in the project of Jewish self-understanding. But the special role of the Jewish historians in recent decades in America is founded on more than this tradition. It is associated with the need many have felt to flatten out Auschwitz, to understand it by placing it historically, in the context of recent Jewish and world history and in the context of Jewish history back to antiquity. At the same time, it thrives on the American propensity to think that identity is a matter of genetic inquiry, of exploring and recovering one's past. The paradox in all of this, of course, is that in the end authentic history can only tell you who you were and not who you are, for genuine history is remote and in a sense inaccessible.[1]

Less explicitly, however, this third stage, with its focus on historical events, the Holocaust and Israel, has raised powerfully what I shall call the question of historicism. This is the question whether the central and most profound features of Jewish belief and Jewish conduct are completely and utterly historical or whether there is a core, or more than a core, that transcends history, is immune to it, and is hence unchangeable. In a sense, this question has been around at least since the nineteenth century; it is a major question for Nachman Krochmal, for Rosenzweig, and for others. But the Holocaust raised it again, and the really important separation in post-Holocaust Jewish thought is between those who now take Judaism to be utterly historical and try to respond to that fact and those who deny or ignore the issue altogether.[2]

The Holocaust has also raised, in a powerful and dramatic way, the problem of continuity and discontinuity in Judaism. Once again, this is an old problem, especially when it is asked as a question about quantity, selectivity, and so forth. Indeed, it is one aspect of the older tension between authority and tradition on the one hand and freedom and autonomy on the other. But after Auschwitz, and the possibility of *complete rupture* and the necessity of recovery, the question of continuity and discontinuity becomes urgent. Directly and immediately, it is the question of how to do justice to the event and yet to overcome its momentousness, the chasm it creates. Indirectly, it raises the general question, together with the issue of historicism, of whether all Jewish self-understanding is not interpretive and hermeneutical in a deep sense, so that the real Jewish questions are always ones of self-interpretation, historical interpretation, and interpretive recovery.

The wholesale entrance of the historians into the arena of American Jewish thought, together with the prominence of the notion of interpretation and the fact that post-Holocaust thinking seems to have reached a plateau, has ushered in the fourth and current stage. It is hard to date its beginnings, and it is equally hard to say what its major characteristics are. But we can say this much. First, the major practitioners of recent Jewish thought in America are not rabbis or theologians or even philosophers. They are historians, social theorists, literary critics, and a wide variety of others. Second, their interests lie in interpretations of Jewish literature, Jewish life, and the Jewish past, with an eye to the imaginative, conceptual, and broadly intellectual models that Jews have used to understand their world and orient themselves within it. Third, there is no explicit, dominating, substantive agenda that has emerged from these writings, although there is a heavy literary dimension to the enterprise and the use of biblical, Midrashic, Kabbalistic, and Medieval philosophical texts is extensive.

This tendency in American Jewish thought today is not surprising. The influence of historical thinking and the historicizing impact of the Holocaust and Israel suit the almost idealist and antifoundationalist convictions of a broadly interpretive understanding of Jewish thought as the search for and use of literary and imaginative models for giving shape and direction to Jewish life. And this strategy, treating Judaism not as a set of theoretical and practical truths but rather as an interpretive framework for dealing with the world, is compatible with recent sociology of knowledge, with the work of Heidegger, Gadamer, Ricouer, Foucault, Geertz, and others. Hence, it has some academic respectability and suits the proclivities and skills of Jewish thinkers who are often Jewish academics. There is also the advantage that this approach enables the thinker to efface commitment and to present an account of biblical models or Midrashic themes or whatever as an interpretive possibility, without advocating it as particularly retrievable in the modern world or even desirable.

Moreover, it provides a particularly convenient vehicle for avoiding or at least setting aside the question of God in Judaism and the role of the divine-human relationship in one's understanding of Jewish experience. To be sure, the biblical or Midrashic or Kabbalistic authors assumed that God played a major role in their conceptual frameworks, but in the course of articulating, elaborating, and examining these frameworks the contemporary Jewish interpretive thinker need not commit to this role or indeed to the existence of anything defined without the framework. He or she may, of course, have a strong personal inclination, but that is not necessary for their work, which involves a literary or historical or quasi-historical attempt to understand an interpreted world and display it as an option for contemporary Jewish appropriation.

But this last and most recent stage of American Jewish thinking, the one in which we currently find ourselves, has other dimensions. There are philosophers seeking to return to premodern and early modern Jewish thinkers, from Maimonides to Hermann Cohen, Rosenzweig, and Emanuel Levinas; there are traditional Jewish theologians seeking an understanding of Halachah within the context of recent moral theory and philosophy of law; there are those sensitive to the crisis in contemporary moral and political thought who recognize in post-Holocaust theology an important beginning for a postmodern Jewish theology; and there are those who continue to struggle with the problems left unsolved by the recent decades of Jewish thinkers—the problems of authority and freedom, of God and covenant, of Halachah and revelation, and of much else.

One indication of the diversity of contemporary work is the publication of *Contemporary Jewish Religious Thought*, a monumental and massive volume that is advertised as a "dictionary" of contemporary Jewish "concepts, movements, and beliefs."[3] The articles, which range in length from two to twenty-two pages, are written by 105 contributors from a great variety of disciplines, backgrounds, and areas of study. Fifty-seven live and/or teach in Israel. A significant number are younger academics who have been busy establishing their scholarly credentials and have only recently begun to exhibit publicly their understanding of Jewish life and Judaism today. The articles cover virtually every concept of importance to contemporary Judaism and many that once had significance but do so no longer.

The article on history, for example, written by Paul Mendes-Flohr, is a richly detailed discussion of the Jewish involvement with temporality, eternity, history, the past, and the future. In the end, Mendes-Flohr articulates but does not really solve the central problem facing the Jew and history, the problem of historicism (383–84). How can one reconcile both the changing character of historical events and the remoteness of the past with the eternality and permanence of the Torah, of the divine truth? At one level, historicism is a problem about how to find a way between anachronism and utter abandonment of the past. Mendes-Flohr takes it to be such a problem of retrieval, and he refers to Gershom Scholem and Walter Benjamin for a way of understanding what such retrieval must be like. But at another level, historicism is a problem about the status of *any* understanding of Torah, past, present, or future. It is a claim *against* the universality and permanence of religious, indeed all truth. And as such it is not a problem that can be resolved by arguing for a retrieval that appropriates the past without cutting it off from the present. For if historicism is endorsed, then neither the past teaching nor the present retrieval acknowledges a truth that is eternal and immune to historical refutation. Rosenzweig, as Mendes-Flohr realizes, confronted just this problem, but for Judaism he ties history to eternity only by sacrificing the narrative character of the former. This is to overcome historicism by treating historical experiences as potential "parables" of eternity, which is less an acceptance than a denial of what makes history historical.

Interpretation within the Jewish tradition has a variety of objects, from texts to events, ritual acts to ceremonial items, but preeminent among them are language and gesture. Josef Stern's two articles on these subjects are, in my judgment, among the most novel, subtle, and provocative essays in the volume; certainly they are among the most sophisticated philosophically, and they show best of any how analytic philosophy can be employed to the benefit of Jewish self-understanding.

In "Gesture and Symbol" Stern appropriates the work of Nelson Goodman and Israel Scheffler on modes of symbolic and ritual reference to develop a taxonomy of Jewish ritual objects and acts.[4] He then examines several cases in which the objects or actions involve patterns or chains of reference. The results, especially the particular illustrations—the Passover shankbone (*zeroa*), the *lulav* (palmfrond) of Sukkot, the recital of the *Avodah* on Yom Kippur—are fascinating. Stern's use of traditional texts and teachings to illuminate symbolic reference not only impresses but also stimulates the thought that there is more here than exegetical sensitivity, philosophical analysis, and clever integration of the two.

A central problem for modern Jewish thought and a central feature of the confrontation between tradition and modernity concerns the authority of commandment (*mitzvah*). How to maintain the necessity of the Halachah in the face of doubts about divine authority and of the fragile character of autonomy, ethnic fidelity, and the like, this has been one of the persistent problems of post-Enlightenment Judaism. Stern's approach to understanding ritual suggests an interesting strategy for coping with the old problem. Following Goodman and Scheffler, Stern focuses on modes of symbolic reference, where reference is taken to be the structural relation that holds between a symbol and what is symbolized. The three modes of reference or symbolization that Stern appropriates from Goodman are representation or denotation, exemplification, and expression. But in experience and in gestural acts themselves, for the agent or for the detached analyst, reference is itself an act or at least a component of an act whereby the agent's or analyst's thoughts, as it were, track the relation from symbol to *relatum*. Reference, that is, has a psychological character and occurs only if the agent and/or analyst has access to the interpretation(s) whereby a gestural act is associated with its referent. In his essay, Stern, by looking at traditional texts and interpretations, identifies the referential connection and then examines the type of reference involved and how it works. But for the observing Jew the ritual act has no reference, psychologically speaking, unless he or she, properly educated and informed, performs the mental act of referring either before, during, or after performing the ritual act itself. Now there are at least two ways in which this understanding of the referential component of ritual, which can, as Stern has shown, be subtle and complex, registers an impact on the role of ritual in contemporary Jewish life.

At one level, the ritual act, enriched by its referential dimension, secures a sense of identification with past performances and those of other contemporaries, a sense of identification that is far richer and deeper than that which comes from the mere mechanical repetition of ritual acts. As Stern notes, the creation of "a community conscious of its own tradition in its present practices is a central aim of much ritual" (282). The very process of a community's self-constitution, integral to any commitment to continuity and survival, mandates some ritual, and, if Stern is right, such performance is enriched by understanding the referential fabric of symbolic acts.

At another level, the act confirms fidelity to properties, ideas, beliefs, and so forth that are found in traditional texts and teachings and that are represented, exemplified, and expressed in the same gestures by Jews of all times and all places. Insofar as these referents are bound by necessity, so are the acts that refer to them, to the degree that the ideas and beliefs can be objects of conviction only by means of some vehicle of reinforcement and communication. If the belief in divine might, for example, is binding, then so is the shankbone of the Passover Seder; if fidelity to Israel and joy in her successes have compelling significance, then so too the waving of the *lulav* on Sukkot.

Two observations about these suggestions concerning ritual and reference should be made. The first is that implicit in them, especially in the second, is the notion that obligation to the ritual commandments of Judaism might better be viewed individually rather than globally. That is, modern Jewish thinkers, sharing the assumption with their predecessors, have treated ritual obligation as requiring a general justification, usually involving divine command and Halachic authority. But Stern's approach encourages us to think that ritual obligation might best be treated in terms of the binding character of those ideas, beliefs, etc. that are referentially tied to individual acts. In short, each ritual might be required to defend itself in terms of its value, so to speak, rather than the Jewish thinker seeking a general justification for the authority of all commandments, taken as a totality.[5] The second point is that Stern's approach turns on a recovery of traditional texts and teachings that become the resources for analyzing (and enacting) symbolization and its modes in specific cases. But Stern's appropriation of these texts is without sufficient appreciation of the historical context for that textual interpretation. Hence, a sense of identification comes too easy for him, for in a way it is built into his interpretations from the outset.

Stern's second essay is on language. He begins by claiming that the divine language which God employs to facilitate creation and the language of Adam share a common presupposition: that words, especially proper and common names, express the essences or natures of things and kinds of things and are, as it were, abbreviations for the accounts of those essences, knowledge of which is at once knowledge of the essences of things and of the meanings of the words themselves. Hence, "language is primarily a source of knowledge about the world" (544).[6] Stern devotes himself to this essentialist view of language as it emerges in medieval Jewish philosophy, first in Halevi, who distinguishes between ideal essentialist language and the everyday, human language, and then in Maimonides. The tension between the two kinds of language reaches a climax in Maimonides' discussion of language and God in the first part of the *Guide*. How are we to understand the Torah's linguistic references to God, Maimonides asks. Stern discusses his program of philosophically informed interpretation of the biblical text's God-language and the conclusion to which Maimonides is driven, that in the end there is no way for man to refer in language to God.[7] When employed in the service of a philosophical reflection on human language about God, then, the essentialist view of language ultimately immobilizes language and prevents knowledge of the divine essence at the very point at which one wants most to have language serve human aspiration. The end of the essentialist view of language is its own self-destruction.

Stern's essay shows how helpful would be a systematic examination of the conceptions of language that emerge at different times, for different purposes, and with different outcomes in the course of rabbinic, mystical, and philosophical thinking. Such an account of course would have to extend itself into the twentieth century and deal with a modern Jewish thinking that is indebted to a conception of language, which Stern mentions but sets aside, in which philosophical thinking, time, and spoken language are intimately connected. This is the "new thinking" of Franz Rosenzweig, Martin Buber, and their followers. Such an account would, as a result, be pressed to discuss two problems that arise out of the challenges posed for Jewish thought by modern thinking and history itself. The first problem concerns the role of language in revelation and whether it is best conceived as a bridge, an obstacle, or a response to the encounter with God. The second concerns language and the horrors of Auschwitz, in a sense the antithesis to Stern's problem of language and the knowledge of God, and whether Paul Celan and others are right that a "language of silence" is alone appropriate to an authentic confrontation with that dark event.

These examples indicate how extensive and how rich is the variety of the current stage of Jewish thinking in America. But where that richness will lead and what it will produce, one can only guess.

Having briefly sketched these four stages of post-War American Jewish thought, it is tempting to make some observations and to identify themes or tendencies that only become apparent when the picture is before us. First, there is an appearance of increased commitment to Jewish particularity and distinctiveness, but this appearance should not be misunderstood. The recent intense interest in Jewish history and traditional Jewish texts, models, and so forth, couched in the language of interpretive recovery, is no obvious continuation of the attempted renewal of faith and covenant of the 1950s and 1960s. At a deeper level, it may be a masquerade in which the academic study of Judaism and its apparent commitment to Jewish particularity masks strong universalist, secular convictions. Second, a more precise picture of the developments during these four decades should be based on a careful study of the most central figures and their writings, for the continuity and alteration of their thinking will tell us much about what has happened. These central figures include Emil Fackenheim, Joseph Soloveitchik, Jakob Petuchowski, Eugene Borowitz, Eliezer Berkovits, Arthur Cohen, among others.

Finally, the dominant moment, as it were, in post-War American Jewish thought involves the issue of historicism and the historical character of Jewish beliefs, norms, and so forth. The impact of the Holocaust and Israel demand that the questions about Halachah, ethics, revelation, peoplehood, covenant, and much else now be rethought within the new problematic defined by the issues of continuity and discontinuity and of historicity and transcendence. Not all recent Jewish thinkers have realized this fact, of course, even when their thinking expresses it. But as we look back over the Jewish thinking of the past several decades, this reorientation shows itself vividly and powerfully as the most central turning point in recent American Jewish self-understanding.

# *Notes*

## Introduction

1. See Richard Rorty, *Contingency, Irony, and Solidarity* (Cambridge: Cambridge University Press, 1989); Hilary Putnam, *Reason, Truth and History* (Cambridge: Cambridge University Press, 1981); Charles Taylor, *Sources of the Self* (Cambridge, Mass.: Harvard University Press, 1989).

## 1. Overcoming the Remoteness of the Past

This chapter has been adapted from my article "Overcoming the Remoteness of the Past: Memory and Historiography in Modern Jewish Thought," which originally appeared in JUDAISM, 38,2 (1989), 160–73.

1. In this chapter I use "historiography" to refer to the analysis and writing that historians engage in; "history" then refers to the events of the past, i.e., to what has happened.

2. Yosef Yerushalmi, *Zakhor: Jewish History and Jewish Memory* (Seattle: University of Washington Press, 1982), xiii–xiv; see also 87–103.

3. In trying to say something about how group remembering differs from historiographical understanding I realize that I am treading on very thin ice. In particular I claim that there is a special kind of objectivity that plays a role in historiography and is impossible for either literal, first-person remembering or "metaphorical" reenactive group remembering. Some historians today would deny the possibility or desirability of the kind of objectivity I describe, but I try to defend it, as desirable and possible, and also as being the kind of notion that eighteenth- and nineteenth-century historians would have found congenial.

4. I think that this subjectivity of memory applies not only to remembering past experiences but also to remembering information. In some cases the subjective point of view is *vividly* part of the act of remembering; in some it is not. But it is always present. Philosophers of the seventeenth century, such as Hobbes, realized this when they understood memory as a kind of imagination and imagination as "nothing but *decaying sense*" (*Leviathan*, Ch. 2).

5. See John Locke, *Essay Concerning Human Understanding*, Book II, Ch. 27; John Perry, "Personal Identity, Memory, and the Problem of Circularity," in John Perry (ed.), *Personal Identity* (Berkeley: University of California Press, 1975).

6. See *Zakhor*, 44–45. Yerushalmi here discusses the process of identification through commemorative rituals, especially the Passover Seder. He seems to realize that we do not have literal memory here, for he says that "memory here is no longer recollection, which still preserves a sense of distance, but reactualization" (44). I am not sure what he has in mind by this last word, but without the connection to memory, such an activity will hardly serve as a vehicle for group identification *in terms of an orientation to the past*.

7. For example, the historian describes an incident as part of an economic recession or an episode as part of a revolution, when no participating agent could have known that the larger sequence of events constituted a recession or a revolution. See William Dray, " 'Explaining What' in History," in Patrick Gardiner (ed.), *Theories of History* (New York: Free Press, 1959), 402–408; W. H. Walsh, *Introduction to Philosophy of History* (London: Hutchinson University Library, 1951), 59–64.

8. See Michael Meyer's comments on Yerushalmi's *Zakhor* in *Association*

*for Jewish Studies Newsletter* 36 (Fall 1986), 14–16, for comments along these lines, specifically with regard to modern Jewish historians.

9. As Sam Westfall put it to me in conversation, historians themselves would want to distinguish making the past relevant emotionally from making it relevant cognitively, i.e., to our understanding.

10. To be sure, much historical writing is heavily ideological (which is Meyer's point; see note 8). But even in an ideologically determined piece of historiography, we can, for analytical purposes, distinguish the attempt to understand an event in its own context from the appropriative determination and use of that understanding. In the end propaganda and history may look the same, but history does not *aim for* a one-sided vantage point on an event or episode, whereas memory does and must.

11. See *Zakhor*, 93–101.

12. J. G. A. Pocock, *The Ancient Constitution and the Feudal Law* (Cambridge: Cambridge University Press, 1957, 1987), Ch. 1; see also David R. Kelley, *Foundations of Modern Historical Scholarship: Language, Law and History in the French Renaissance* (New York: Columbia University Press, 1970); Julian H. Franklin, *Jean Bodin and the 16th-Century Revolution in Law and History* (New York: Columbia University Press, 1963).

13. As Pocock argues later, in the course of discussing Brady, it was still a "threshold" in the seventeenth century, for even Brady was unable to integrate his new understanding of law and society and history with a narrative of men's deeds; see Pocock, *The Ancient Constitution*, 225–26.

14. *The Ancient Constitution*, 11: "In the name of a more accurate interpretation, a historical interpretation had been formulated; and in the name of historical interpretation, the relevance of the past to the present was apparently being denied."

15. See *ibid.*, 15.

16. *Ibid.*, 15–21.

17. *Leviathan*, Chs. 14–15, 26.

18. Lewis White Beck, *Early German Philosophy* (Cambridge, Mass.: Harvard University Press, 1969), 323; see also 319–39 and 352–60.

19. The best accounts I know of are to be found in Alexander Altmann, *Moses Mendelssohn* (Tuscaloosa: University of Alabama Press, 1973), and Michael A. Meyer, *The Origins of the Modern Jew* (Detroit: Wayne State University Press, 1967), Chs. 1–2. See also David Patterson, "Moses Mendelssohn's Concept of Tolerance," in *Between East and West: Essays Dedicated to the Memory of Bela Horovitz* (London, 1958), 149–63.

20. Moses Mendelssohn, *Jerusalem*, trans. Allan Arkush (Hanover, N.H.: University Press of New England, 1983), 35–37.

21. I discuss Spinoza's importance for Mendelssohn more fully in chapter two.

22. Yerushalmi acknowledges this about Spinoza.

23. Spinoza, as biblical interpreter, is in the tradition of Isaac La Peyrere and Richard Simon.

24. See, generally, *Tractatus Theologico-Politicus*, Chs. 5, 19.

25. It is interesting to compare Spinoza to the Levellers, because of his views on political freedom and on history; see *The Ancient Constitution*, 125–27; 318–20; Christopher Hill, *The World Turned Upside Down* (Harmondsworth: Penguin, 1984).

26. It is not surprising that Pocock characterizes Locke as responding to Filmer "on the plane of sacred, not national history" (*The Ancient Constitution*, 235–39; 245–50, and his discussion of how the past lost its relevance to the present in the eighteenth century); see Mendelssohn on Locke, *Jerusalem*, 37–40.

27. On this argument, see Alexander Altmann, *Moses Mendelssohn*, 547–50; *Jerusalem*, notes by A. Altmann, 235–37. Altmann (236) notices that the argument is implicitly aimed at Spinoza and calls attention to Shlomo Pines's argument that Spinoza may have derived his view, which can be found in Bodin, from Marrano sources. My own point is that Spinoza's historiographical account of the ritual law's remoteness and irrelevance, together with Mendelssohn' s response, fits nicely seventeenth- and eighteenth-century discourse, regardless of the earlier provenance of either Spinoza's views or Mendelssohn's argument against them. The prominence of that discourse provides the context for Mendelssohn's *use* of the argument, no matter how often it had already appeared in sources familiar to him.

28. The strategy is Hobbesian, in a sense, since it relies on sovereign command, even though the command is divine. See David Gauthier, *The Logic of Leviathan* (Oxford: Oxford University Press, 1969), Ch. 5.

29. See David Gauthier; "Why Ought One Obey God? Reflections on Hobbes and Locke," *Canadian Journal of Philosophy* 7, 3 (1977), 425–46.

30. One might compare Maimonides and Spinoza, in the *Tractatus Theologico-Politicus*, on God, nature, and secondary causation. Although Altmann notices correctly that Mendelssohn is responding to Spinoza, he does not develop how the response works; he fails to recognize that there is a metaphysical difference as well as a political one between the two.

31. *Leviathan*, Ch. 26. See also Jean Hampton, *Hobbes and the Social Contract Tradition* (Cambridge: Cambridge University Press, 1986), 108–10, especially 109: "the fact that the sovereign does not at any time after taking office revoke the customary law is enough, on Hobbes's view, to allow us to regard it as law." Mendelssohn uses the argument from silence not to justify custom but to justify the continued obligatory character of original, revealed Torah-law.

32. *Zakhor*, 94–101.

## 2. History and Modern Jewish Thought

This chapter has been adapted from my article "History and Modern Jewish Thought: Spinoza and Mendelssohn on the Ritual Law," which originally appeared in JUDAISM, 30,4 (1981), 467–78. Some passages have been adapted from my article "Mendelssohn's Defense of Reason in *Jerusalem*," which originally appeared in JUDAISM, 38,4 (1989), 449–59.

1. The standard edition of the *Tractatus* can be found in the third volume of the Heidelberg Academy edition of *Spinoza Opera* (1924–26), edited by Carl Gebhardt. The most convenient English translation is still R. H. M. Elwes (trans.), *Benedict de Spinoza: A Theologico-Political Treatise and a Political Treatise* (New York: Dover, 1951). This is a reprint of Elwes's 1883 translation, originally under the title *The Works of Spinoza*, Volume I.

2. See especially the Elwes translation (hereafter *Spinoza: TPT*), p. 56 (G. III, 57) and Chs. 4, 5, 14, and 15.

3. See *Spinoza: TPT*, Chs. 1–15.

4. For a particularly important example of such a struggle, see the controversy between Martin Buber and Franz Rosenzweig regarding the status and role of the *mitzvot*, in Franz Rosenzweig, *On Jewish Learning* (New York: Schocken, 1955), 72–92, 109–24. For a traditional response, see Eliezer Berkovits, *Major Themes in Modern Philosophies of Judaism* (New York: KTAV, 1974), Ch. 4.

5. See *Spinoza: TPT*, Ch. 5.

6. For a discussion of this "unfairness," see Leo Strauss's Preface to the English translation of his study of the *Tractatus Theologico-Politicus*, *Spinoza's*

*Critique of Religion* (Schocken: New York, 1965), esp. 15–28. See also Isaac Franck, "Spinoza's Onslaught on Judaism," *Judaism* 28, 2 (Spring 1979), 177–93.

7. Unquestionably, the outstanding study of Mendelssohn's life and thought is Alexander Altmann, *Moses Mendelssohn*. Also valuable is Michael A. Meyer, *The Origins of the Modern Jew*, Chs. 1 and 2. Of some value to a philosophical discussion of Mendelssohn's *Jerusalem* are: Julius Guttmann, "*Mendelssohns Jerusalem und Spinozas Theologisch-Politisches Traktat*," *Achtundvierzigster Bericht der Hochschule für die Wissenschaft des Judentums in Berlin* (1931), 33–67; Lewis White Beck, *Early German Philosophy* (Cambridge, Mass.: Harvard University Press, 1969), 324–339; David Patterson, "Moses Mendelssohn's Concept of Tolerance"; Simon Rawidowicz, *Studies in Jewish Thought* (Philadelphia: Jewish Publication Society, 1974), Ch. 10; Steven S. Schwarzschild, "Do Noachites Have to Believe in Revelation?" *Jewish Quarterly Review* 52 (1961–62), 297–308, and 53 (1962–63), 30–65.

8. Unless otherwise noted, references to *Jerusalem* in this chapter are to Alfred Jospe (trans. and ed.), *Jerusalem and Other Writings by Moses Mendelssohn* (New York: Schocken, 1969).

9. Far and away the most extensive treatment of that argument is in Altmann, *Moses Mendelssohn*, 514–522. Helpful discussions, especially of Part I of *Jerusalem*, can also be found in Patterson and in Nathan Rotenstreich, *Jewish Philosophy in Modern Times* (New York: Holt, Rinehart and Winston: 1968), Ch. 1.

10. See *Jerusalem* (Jospe), 56–99.

11. See *ibid.*, 148.

12. See *ibid.*, 104–05.

13. See Altmann, *Moses Mendelssohn*, 520.

14. Modern discussions include Thomas Nagel, *The Possibility of Altruism*; Stuart Hampshire, *Thought and Action* (New York: Viking Press, 1959); Anthony Kenny, *Action, Emotion, and Will* (London: Routledge and Kegan Paul, 1963 [Princeton: Princeton University Press: 1970]); G. E. M. Anscombe, *Intention* (Ithaca, N.Y.: Cornell University Press, 1966); Hector-Neri Castañeda, *Thinking and Doing* (Dordrecht: D. R. Reidel, 1975). For a recent account of these themes in Aristotle, see Anthony Kenny, *Aristotle's Theory of the Will* (New Haven: Yale University Press, 1979).

15. See *Jerusalem* (Jospe), 46.

16. See *Spinoza: TPT*, Ch. 5.

17. For example, on Kant and the early Hegel; Nathan Rotenstreich discusses the treatment of Judaism in these and other thinkers in *The Recurring Pattern* (New York: Horizon Press, 1964). The most profound treatment of Kant and Hegel on Judaism is in Emil Fackenheim, *Encounters Between Judaism and Modern Philosophy* (New York: Basic Books, 1973), Chs. 2 and 3.

18. See *Spinoza: TPT*, Ch. 5. The terms "Pristine Jew" and "Contemporary or Diaspora Jew" are mine. They refer to the Jew of the Second Commonwealth and the Jew thereafter, at least until the late eighteenth century.

19. Much of this conception of a religion of nature or a rational moral religion goes back to Spinoza. In the *Tractatus* (Ch. 14 especially), in Spinoza's account of the "universal faith of all mankind," one already finds both the imperative and the dogmas later endorsed by Mendelssohn.

20. *Jerusalem* (Jospe), 74; cf. 71.

21. *Ibid.*, 98–99; cf. 90–156. Also see Julius Guttmann, *Philosophies of Judaism* (New York: Holt, Rinehart, and Winston, 1964), 300–01.

22. *Jerusalem* (Jospe), 104–05, and 155.

23. *Ibid.*, 148.

24. Moses Mendelssohn, *Jerusalem, Or On Religious Power and Judaism,*

trans. Allan Arkush (Hanover, N.H.: University Press of New England, 1983), 104–25. Subsequent page references in this discussion are to this edition.

25. See Frederick C. Beiser, *The Fate of Reason: German Philosophy from Kant to Fichte* (Cambridge, Mass.: Harvard University Press, 1987), 130–41.

26. See Nelson Goodman, *The Languages of Art* (Indianapolis: Hackett Publishing Co., 1968; 2nd ed. 1976), for an analysis of this type of reference, which he calls exemplification.

27. I have discussed this particular strategy and the Hobbesian background of the argument based on the fact of the sovereign's silence in chapter one.

28. Altmann, *Moses Mendelssohn*, 547.

### 3. Liberalism in Mendelssohn's *Jerusalem*

This chapter has been adapted from my article "Liberalism and Mendelssohn's *Jerusalem*," which originally appeared in *History of Political Thought*, 10,2 (1989), 281–94.

1. Bernard Williams, *The Problems of the Self* (Cambridge: Cambridge University Press, 1973); *Moral Luck* (Cambridge: Cambridge University Press, 1981); *Ethics and the Limits of Philosophy* (Cambridge, Mass.: Harvard University Press, 1985); Thomas Nagel, *The Possibility of Altruism* (Princeton: Princeton University Press, 1970); *Mortal Questions* (Cambridge: Cambridge University Press, 1979); *The View from Nowhere* (Oxford: Oxford University Press, 1986); Derek Parfit, *Reasons and Persons* (Oxford: Oxford University Press, 1986); Charles Taylor, *Philosophical Papers*, Vols. I and II (Cambridge: Cambridge University Press, 1985) and *Sources of the Self*.

2. Michael J. Sandel, *Liberalism and the Limits of Justice* (Cambridge: Cambridge University Press, 1982).

3. Gregory V. Kavka, *Hobbesian Moral and Political Theory* (Princeton: Princeton University Press, 1986).

4. See C. B. Macpherson, *The Political Theory of Possessive Individualism* (Oxford: Oxford University Press, 1962); *Democratic Theory* (Oxford: Oxford University Press, 1973).

5. There is a good English translation of *Jerusalem* with an excellent introduction and commentary: Moses Mendelssohn, *Jerusalem, or On Religious Power and Judaism*, trans. Allan Arkush, intro. and comm. Alexander Altmann (Hanover, N.H.: University Press of New England, 1983). All references to *Jerusalem* in this chapter are to this translation.

6. Jean-Paul Sartre, *Anti-Semite and Jew* (New York: Grove Press, 1946).

7. Sartre's conception of the self and of the human condition is fundamental to his philosophy. Elsewhere he distinguishes between the two constituents of that condition, calling them "freedom" or "transcendence" and "situation" or "facticity."

8. In addition to Altmann's magisterial biography and the notes to the German edition of *Jerusalem*, now translated in Arkush, see the several papers reprinted in *Studies in Jewish Intellectual History* (Hanover, N.H.: University Press of New England, 1981) and in *Die trostvolle Aufklarung* (Stuttgart-Bad Cannstatt, 1982).

9. Mendelssohn's reading of Hobbes conforms with the traditional interpretation. See S. Mintz, *The Hunting of Leviathan* (Cambridge: Cambridge University Press, 1962); for an excellent modern version, see Quentin Skinner, "History and Ideology in the English Revolution," *Historical Journal* 8, 2 (1965), 151–78. There are those, however, who argue that Hobbes was a natural law and natural rights theorist.

10. In chapter two I do not elaborate the differences between Hobbes and Mendelssohn concerning the *primary* role of the state and hence its reason for coming into being. Mendelssohn may believe that the government must legislate and then enforce the law, but in *Jerusalem* the *primary* reason for its constitution is distributional.

11. See Altmann's comments on Mendelssohn's debts to Samuel von Pufendorf and Hugo Grotius in his appropriation of these distinctions; see also Richard Tuck, *Natural Rights Theories* (Cambridge: Cambridge University Press, 1979).

12. In a hierarchical society political beneficence yields honor and authority, but in principle this works differently in an egalitarian society. Hence, regularization of redistribution and "philanthropy" is needed. See the discussion of liturgies in classical Greece, Moses Finley, *Politics in the Ancient World* (Cambridge: Cambridge University Press, 1983), 36–37, 39–49 on patronage as a source of authority.

13. Mendelssohn's treatment is indebted to Locke's in *A Letter on Toleration* (but not in Locke's *Second Treatise*, which was not available to Mendelssohn). For an excellent discussion of Locke's *Letter*, with its sharp distinction between civil and religious institutions and its natural law defense of freedom of conscience, see Richard Ashcraft, *Revolutionary Politics and Locke's Two Treatises of Government* (Princeton: Princeton University Press, 1986), 467–520; see also James Tully's outstanding introduction to his edition of the *Letter* (Indianapolis: Hackett Publishing, 1983).

14. It is not clear whether, for Mendelssohn, in pristine Judaism these two components are interwoven in a unique, inseparable way or whether they are identical.

15. Hobbes, *Leviathan*, Ch. 37; Spinoza, *Tractatus Theologico-Politicus*, Ch. 6.

16. For the details of that argument and a critique of it, see chapter two. See also *Jerusalem*, 117–120.

17. It is possible that Mendelssohn's argument that the ceremonial laws continue to apply as long as their original divine legislator has not withdrawn them, on the face of it such an odd argument for Mendelssohn to offer, might best be understood as a version of the argument from antiquity; see J. G. A. Pocock, *The Machiavellian Moment* (Princeton: Princeton University Press, 1975), 13–16, 19, and, on the argument and its rejection in Thomas Paine, see Christopher Hill, "The Norman Yoke," in *Puritanism and Revolution*, especially 101–02. I have tried to develop this possibility in chapter one.

18. Michael J. Sandel, *Liberalism and the Limits of Justice*.

19. In a sense, radically situated selves are simply their situations viewed from a point of view or, alternatively, a continuous set of alterations of that situation. Conceived in the extreme, such selves simply are the world, in a sense. Sartre is a radical version of Hume; Leibniz is the most radical of all, a Berkeley without the self or mind as substratum.

20. Is this a Cartesian self? It seems possible and perhaps likely.

21. See J. G. A. Pocock, *The Machiavellian Moment*, 522, and the emergence of interest-groups in America.

22. For such a conception of the self as historically situated, see Alasdair MacIntyre, *After Virtue* (South Bend: Notre Dame University Press, 1981), and Stanley Hauerwas, *A Community of Character* (South Bend: Notre Dame University Press, 1981); also Charles Taylor, *Philosophical Papers* I and II.

23. As in Locke, for example. Mendelssohn differs from Locke but not concerning his conception of human nature. Mendelssohn shows that he is familiar with Locke's first *Letter on Toleration*. As I indicated above, he did not have the

*Two Treatises on Government*, with which he would doubtless have found much to agree.

24. See Spinoza, *Tractatus Theologico-Politicus* (Hamburg, 1670), trans. Elwes, Ch. 5.

25. Mendelssohn, *Jerusalem*, 138.

26. On some implications of this notion, see I. Jarvie, *The Revolution in Anthropology* (London: Routledge and Kegan Paul, 1964), 7–16, on Enlightenment egalitarianism and diversity.

27. See Pocock, *The Machiavellian Moment*, 483–84 on parties and factions in eighteenth-century England; also, see Clifford Geertz, *Local Knowledge* (New York: Oxford University Press, 1983), 175–81, on excommunication and communities that have rigid status classifications.

28. Charles E. Larmore, *Patterns of Moral Complexity* (Cambridge: Cambridge University Press, 1987), Chs. 3–5.

29. See especially Ch. 3, 97–98, 123–24. For a similar conception of the neutral state see Bruce A. Ackerman, *Social Justice in the Liberal State* (New Haven: Yale University Press, 1980).

30. Larmore, *Patterns of Moral Complexity*, 76; cf. xii–xiii, 130, 175n.77.

31. Mendelssohn, *Jerusalem* (Arkush), 40; cf. 70: "State and church have for their object the promotion, by means of public measures, of human felicity in this life and in the future life."

32. Another way of putting this problem is that Mendelssohn reflects the dilemma of modern society that Hegel comes to recognize, between an aspiration to homogeneity and absolute freedom, on the one hand, and a need for community identification, on the other. See Charles Taylor, *Hegel and Modern Society* (Cambridge: Cambridge University Press, 1979), 111–18; see 111–13 especially for Hegel's critique of the *modus vivendi* view.

## 4. The Curse of Historicity

This chapter has been adapted from my article "The Curse of Historicity: The Role of History in Leo Strauss's Jewish Thought," which originally appeared in *The Journal of Religion*, 61,4 (1981), 345–63.

1. Leo Strauss, "Preface to the English Translation," in *Spinoza's Critique of Religion* (New York: Schocken Books, 1965), reprinted in Judah Goldin, ed., *The Jewish Expression* (New York: Bantam Books, 1970), 344–86. All further references to this essay are to the reprinted version (hereafter cited as "Preface"). Strauss also discusses contemporary Jewish matters, though far less extensively, in "Jerusalem and Athens. Some Preliminary Reflections," The Frank Cohen Public Lecture in Judaic Affairs, published in *The City College Papers*, no. 6 (New York: City College Library, 1967), and in his book *Liberalism: Ancient and Modern* (New York: Basic Books, 1968) (see introduction and also final chapter, "Perspectives on the Good Society," 260–72).

2. At the end of the preface to *Liberalism* (ix), Strauss suggests that it is "particularly difficult for a nonorthodox Jew to adopt a critical posture toward liberalism" and that this state of affairs provokes the following question: "In what sense or to what extent is Judaism one of the roots of liberalism? Are Jews compelled by their heritage or their self-interest to be liberals? Is liberalism necessarily friendly to Jews and Judaism? Can the liberal state claim to have solved the Jewish problem? Can any state claim to have solved it?" In important ways, the "Preface" we shall be examining is devoted to these same questions.

3. Strauss, "Preface," 352.

4. This is already a conviction of orthodoxy, that historical problems can

ultimately only be solved by God. Hence, by returning to orthodoxy, the modern Jew comes to understand and accept his insoluble political problem. We discuss this later in our assessment of Strauss's attitude toward history.

5. In a letter of September or October 1665 to Henry Oldenberg (Letter 30, A. Wolf [trans. and ed.], *The Correspondence of Spinoza* [New York: L. MacVeagh, 1927], 205–06), Spinoza writes: "I am now writing a Treatise about my interpretation of Scripture. This I am driven to do by the following reasons: 1. The Prejudices of the Theologians . . . 2. The opinion which the common people have of me, who do not cease to accuse me falsely of atheism . . . 3. The freedom of philosophizing, and of saying what we think. . . . "

6. That is, vulgar religion ought to transform itself into scriptural religion, a universal morality of justice and benevolence based on certain rational dogmas ("the universal faith of all mankind") to be found in Scripture, and to make room for that genuine and highest form of freedom which Spinoza associated with philosophical religion (described in *Ethica*, part 5).

7. Strauss, "Preface," 344.

8. For a variety of recent views on this question in the light of contemporary Jewish experience in America, see the symposium "Liberalism and the Jews," *Commentary* 69, 1 (January 1980), 15–82.

9. Strauss, "Preface," 351.

10. *Ibid.*, 351–52.

11. To this a priori argument based on an analysis of the concept of the liberal state, Strauss adds an empirical argument: Jews are always a minority and hence always dependent on the majority and its interests.

12. Strauss, "Preface," 349–50.

13. *Ibid.*, 350.

14. The Hebrew word *teshuvah* means both "turning" and "repentance." It was widely used by Buber, Rosenzweig, and other modern Jewish thinkers.

15. See E. L. Fackenheim, *Quest for Past and Future* (Bloomington: Indiana University Press, 1968), 146–47.

16. On the need for and structure of a modern response to attacks on the traditional concept of revelation, see E. L. Fackenheim, "Martin Buber's Concept of Revelation," in Paul A. Schilpp and Maurice Friedman, eds., *The Philosophy of Martin Buber* (LaSalle, Ill.: Open Court Press, 1967), 273–96, and E. L. Fackenheim, "Franz Rosenzweig: His Life and Thought" (a review), *Judaism* 2, 4 (October 1953), 370. I discuss Fackenheim's interpretation of Rosenzweig in chapter ten.

17. Strauss, "Preface," 362.

18. It is a matter of great dispute whether such objectivity in interpretation is either possible or desirable. For a modern attempt to establish the "author's" meaning as the standard for interpreting literature, see E. D. Hirsch, Jr., *Validity in Interpretation* (New Haven: Yale University Press, 1967).

19. I.e., in the sense in which Plato speaks of dialectic in the *Meno* 75d2–7. A dialectical argument is one that uses only those premises which are acceptable to the answerer. See also Aristotle, *De Sophisticus Elenchus* 1.165b3–4.

20. For a modern version of this "moral antagonism," the conflict between logical empiricism and Buber's believing openness, see E. L. Fackenheim, "Elijah and the Empiricists," in *Encounters Between Judaism and Modern Philosophy*.

21. Strauss here seems to be using a rather narrow view of rationality. One might consult William James's famous essay "The Will to Believe" and also W. K. Clifford's "The Ethics of Belief," to which it was in part a response. James too seems to think of rationality in a narrow way, for he argues that in certain types of decision-making situations our choices are passional. For even though

we have no better evidence for the truth of A than we have for the truth of B, which is incompatible with A, we still may have good reasons for believing A rather than B.

22. See n. 21. Strauss's claims about Spinoza as well as about rationality are certainly controversial. My own view is that Spinoza, in the *Tractatus*, did not so obviously lapse into the moral opposition Strauss finds; at any rate he tried, I think, very hard to avoid it.

23. Strauss, "Preface," 383.

24. Might this have something to do with the fact that Strauss himself was not a practicing orthodox Jew? Professor Werner Dannhauser has reminded me of this fact and raised the question of how the theory of the "Preface" is related to the practice of Strauss's own life. Although this is a matter of importance, I do not pursue it here.

25. See Nahum Glatzer, *Franz Rosenzweig: His Life and Thought* (New York: Schocken Books, 1953), xxi. According to Glatzer, Rosenzweig first used this phrase in 1914, near the end of an essay entitled "Atheistic Theology"; see *Kleinere Schriften* (Berlin: Schocken Verlag, 1937), 289.

26. Strauss, "Preface," 350. The passage can also be found, almost verbatim, in Strauss's *What Is Political Philosophy?* (New York: Free Press, 1959), 13. There Strauss suggests that the justification for Leo Pinsker's "silent rejection of the thought expressed in the omitted words" can be found in Spinoza's *Tractatus*, in the third and sixteenth chapters.

27. Strauss, "Preface," 350.

28. *Ibid.*

29. *Ibid.*, quoted from the end of chap. 3 of Spinoza's *Tractatus*.

30. See also "Preface," 351: "Finite, relative problems can be solved; infinite, absolute problems cannot be solved. In other words, human beings will never create a society which is free of contradictions. From every point of view it looks as if the Jewish people were the chosen people in the sense, at least, that the Jewish problem is the most manifest symbol of the human problem as a social or political problem."

31. For a discussion of how the Holocaust and the rebirth of the state of Israel have altered the significance and meaning of traditional concepts and categories, particularly the concepts of religiosity and secularity, see E. L. Fackenheim, *Encounters*, 166–68, and *The Jewish Return into History* (New York: Schocken Books, 1978), esp. part 3. See also Harold Fisch, *The Zionist Revolution* (London: Weidenfeld and Nicholson, 1978).

32. Strauss, "Preface," 362.

33. There are numerous passages in Midrashic collections in which the rabbinic sages notice the permanence of the *yetzer ha-ra* (the evil impulse) in human nature and the purpose of Torah as a constraint upon it. For a modern discussion of the relation between morality and human nature in terms of man's capacity for harm and injustice, see Stuart Hampshire, "Morality and Pessimism," *New York Review of Books* (January 1973), 26–33.

## 5. Leo Strauss and the Possibility of Jewish Philosophy

This chapter has been adapted from a paper delivered at the Philosophy Workshop of the International Center for the University Teaching of Jewish Civilization, Jerusalem, Israel, 1988.

1. Allan Bloom, "Leo Strauss: September 20, 1899–October 18, 1973," *Political Theory* 2, 4 (November 1974), 379.

2. See Leo Strauss, "Progress or Return? The Contemporary Crisis in Western

Civilization," *Modern Judaism* 1, 1 (May 1981), 44–45; idem, "The Mutual Influence of Theology and Philosophy," *The Independent Journal of Philosophy* 3 (1979), 111.

3. Leo Strauss, *Philosophy and Law* (Philadelphia: Jewish Publication Society, 1987), 3.

4. "Introduction," 14.

5. *Ibid.*, 18.

6. Leo Strauss, "Preface" to *Spinoza's Critique of Religion*, in *The Jewish Expression*, 383.

7. *Ibid.*, 344.

8. *Ibid.*, 348–62.

9. *Ibid.*, 362–63.

10. Among other writings, see the introduction to *The City and Man* (Chicago: University of Chicago Press, 1964), 1–12; *Natural Right and History* (Chicago: University of Chicago Press, 1953), 1–80; "Political Philosophy and the Crisis of Our Time," in George J. Graham, Jr., and George W. Carey (eds.), *The Post-Behavioral Era* (New York: David McKay Co., 1972), 217–42, adapted from Howard Spaeth (ed.), *The Predicament of Modern Politics* (Detroit: University of Detroit Press, 1964); "The Three Waves of Modernity," in Hilail Gildin (ed.), *Political Philosophy: Six Essays by Leo Strauss* (Indianapolis: Bobbs-Merrill, 1975), 81–98; "Progress or Return? The Contemporary Crisis of Western Civilization," *Modern Judaism* 1, 1 (May 1981), 17–45; *What Is Political Philosophy?* Chs. 1 and 2.

11. See, for example, John Gunnell, "Political Theory and Politics: The Case of Leo Strauss," *Political Theory* 13, 3 (August 1985), 339–61; *Political Theory: Tradition and Interpretation* (Cambridge: Winthrop, 1979).

12. I have tried here to itemize the main features of the shift to modernity as Strauss sees it. There is much to disagree with. For example, Strauss sees a shift from obligation to rights, but his understanding fails to be nuanced and sensitive to premodern examples of the notion of rights. He never gives a deep enough account of the kinds of rights, the relation between rights and obligations, and the role of rights in antiquity.

13. In an important passage in the "Preface," in the course of describing the weakness of Weimar Germany, and hence of modern liberal democracy, and the "precarious situation of the Jews in Germany," Strauss refers to Goethe, Nietzsche, and Heidegger ("Preface," 347–48).

14. This thought makes one wonder seriously about the *desiderata* for a viable Zionism or a viable liberal Judaism today.

15. Nazi Germany was the only German regime, Strauss says, indeed the only regime ever anywhere, whose sole purpose was the murderous hatred of the Jews—which I take to mean, of a particular group. See the famous passage in the "Preface," 347.

16. "Progress or Return?" 29.

17. *Ibid.*, 27–33; cf. *Natural Right and History*, 9–34. Strauss also considers Communism as an epitome of another sort of possibility for the modern world; see *The City and Man*, 4–6; "Political Philosophy and the Crisis of Our Time," 220–21.

18. "Progress or Return?" 33.

19. "Political Philosophy and the Crisis of Our Time," 226, 229; *The City and Man*, 8–12.

20. *The City and Man*, 12; cf. "Political Philosophy and the Crisis of Our Time," 226, "an elaboration of the pre-scientific primary citizens' understanding of political things."

21. The central texts are Strauss's "Preface" to the English translation of the

Spinoza book, his paper "Jerusalem and Athens" (1967), and the three lectures given at the University of Chicago in the early 1950s, published as "Progress or Return?" and "The Mutual Influence of Theology and Philosophy."

22. "Introduction," 1–27, especially 18–23, in Leo Strauss, *Studies in Platonic Political Philosophy* (Chicago: University of Chicago Press, 1983), Introduction by Thomas L. Pangle.

23. *New York Review of Books.*

24. Charles E. Larmore, *Patterns of Moral Complexity*, Chs. 3–5.

25. The key figure in Strauss's account of the philosophical way of life is Socrates. He exemplifies the desire for knowledge, the interrogative and critical character of reason, and the intellectual openness of philosophy. The biblical view, on the other hand, is based on revelation and is hence closed by a body of fixed legislation, of a code of life. There is, of course, much to object to in this account of Athens and Jerusalem.

26. "Progress or Return?" 33.

27. *Ibid.*, 37.

28. *Ibid.*, 44–45; cf. "The Mutual Influence . . . ," 111.

29. "The Mutual Influence . . . ," 116.

30. *Ibid.*, 117.

31. *Ibid.*, 118.

## 6. Judaism and Peter Berger's Heretical Imperative

This chapter has been adapted from my article "Judaism and the Heretical Imperative," which originally appeared in *Religious Studies*, 17 (1981), 109–20, published by Cambridge University Press.

1. For a useful selection of articles by phenomenological sociologists, see Thomas Luckmann (ed.), *Phenomenology and Sociology* (New York: Penguin Books, 1978).

2. See, for example, Peter L. Berger and Thomas Luckmann, *The Social Construction of Reality: A Treatise in the Sociology of Knowledge* (Garden City, N.Y.: Doubleday, 1966); Peter L. Berger, *The Sacred Canopy: Elements of a Sociological Theory of Religion* (Garden City, N.Y.: Doubleday, 1967).

3. See Peter L. Berger, *A Rumor of Angels: Modern Society and the Rediscovery of the Supernatural* (Garden City, N.Y.: Doubleday, 1969); idem, *Pyramids of Sacrifice: Political Ethics and Social Change* (Garden City, N.Y.: Doubleday, 1976); Peter L. Berger, Brigitte Berger, and Hansfried Kellner, *The Homeless Mind: Modernization and Consciousness* (New York: Random House, 1973).

4. Peter L. Berger, *Facing Up to Modernity: Excursions in Society, Politics, and Religion* (New York: Basic Books, 1977).

5. Peter L. Berger, *The Heretical Imperative: Contemporary Possibilities of Religious Affirmation* (Garden City, N.Y.: Doubleday, 1979).

6. There is an extensive literature on autonomy and authority, the past and the present, and similar themes in the Jewish experience. See, for example, Jakob J. Petuchowski, "The Dialectics of Reason and Revelation," in Arnold Wolf (ed.), *Rediscovering Judaism* (Chicago: Quadrangle Books, 1965); Emil L. Fackenheim, *Quest for Past and Future*, Chs. 8, 13, and 14; Bernard Martin (ed.), *Contemporary Reform Jewish Thought* (Chicago: Quadrangle Books, 1968).

7. I realize that this is—or at least may seem to be—a controversial judgment. To be sure, much of Rosenzweig's thought might still today play an important role in Jewish thought, e.g., his concept of revelation. But Rosenzweig pays a tremendous intellectual price for his return to and recovery of Judaism, a price that historical events may no longer allow us to pay.

8. For a Jewish book very much like Berger's in theme and structure, see Eugene B. Borowitz, *A New Jewish Theology in the Making* (Philadelphia: Westminster Press, 1968). The same argument I use against the Jewish relevance of Berger's book applies, *mutatis mutandis*, to Borowitz's theological proposals.

9. As I argue throughout this book, the relation between history and Jewish self-understanding ought to be the central theme of contemporary Jewish thought. That is, it ought to be the central *formal* theme. The central substantive themes concern the Holocaust, Israel, Diaspora, Jewish life, and the imperatives of the contemporary Jewish experience. I use the word "imperatives" intentionally but with a certain amount of trepidation. See Emil L. Fackenheim, *God's Presence in History*, Ch. 3; *The Jewish Return into History*.

## 7. Jewish Ethics after the Holocaust

This chapter has been adapted from my article "Jewish Ethics after the Holocaust," which originally appeared in *The Journal of Religious Ethics*, 12,2 (fall 1984), 256–77.

1. Irving J. Rosenbaum, *The Holocaust and Halakhah* (New York: KTAV Publishing House, 1976), 35–40.

2. Emil L. Fackenheim, *God's Presence in History* (New York: New York University Press, 1970), 8–9.

3. It is one of the assumptions of this chapter that Jewish moral obligations are a subset of Jewish obligations in general and that though moral, these obligations are also *Jewish* in important ways.

4. For example, see Marvin Fox (ed.), *Modern Jewish Ethics* (Columbus: Ohio State University Press, 1975); "The Philosophical Foundations of Jewish Ethics: Some Initial Reflections," Feinberg Memorial Lecture, Judaic Studies Program, University of Cincinnati, March 27, 1979; Menachem M. Kellner (ed.), *Contemporary Jewish Ethics* (New York: Hebrew Publishing Co., 1978).

5. There are many recent examples of both relativist and absolutist moral theories. As an instance of an absolutist theory, one might look at Alan Donagan's natural law theory (*The Theory of Morality* [Chicago: University of Chicago Press, 1977]). On the side of relativism, there is J. L. Mackie's *Ethics: Inventing Right and Wrong* (Harmondsworth: Penguin Books, 1977). The theory of Jewish ethics outlined in this chapter claims that Jewish moral obligations are objective and unconditional in status but relative and conditional in content.

6. For discussion of the logic of such theories, see Philip L. Quinn, *Divine Commands and Moral Requirements* (Oxford: Oxford University Press, 1978).

7. For the basis of this theory of revelation, see Martin Buber, *I and Thou* (New York: Scribners, 1970); idem, *Moses* (New York: Harper and Row, 1958), 75–77; Franz Rosenzweig, *The Star of Redemption* (New York: Holt, Rinehart, and Winston, 1970), 156–204; Nahum N. Glatzer, *Franz Rosenzweig: His Life and Thought*, 208–09, 242–47, 285; Emil L. Fackenheim, *Quest for Past and Future*, 13–17; idem, "Martin Buber's Concept of Revelation"; idem, *God's Presence in History*, Chs. 1 and 2; idem, *To Mend the World*, Ch. 3; Joshua O. Haberman, "Franz Rosenzweig's Doctrine of Revelation," *Judaism* 18, 3 (Summer 1969), 320–36.

8. The role of language in the modern Jewish account of revelation has not been thoroughly discussed. Gershom Scholem has treated the linguistic character of the Kabbalistic theory of revelation in "The Name of God and the Linguistic Theory of the Kabbala," *Diogenes* 79 (Fall 1972), 59–80, and 80 (Winter 1972), 164–94.

9. The justification of a moral theory is an enormously complex matter. Such theories are normally assessed and criticized in a piecemeal fashion and then in

terms of their simplicity, consistency, utility, satisfaction of our moral intuitions, compatibility with our understanding of human nature and rationality, and so on. By far the most elaborate recent attempt to develop and justify a moral theory can be found in John Rawls, *A Theory of Justice* (Cambridge, Mass.: Harvard University Press, 1971).

10. This is a pragmatic alternative in the sense that the theory is being tested not against fully developed views on human nature etc., but rather against our conception of an ideal moral agent and his or her beliefs, intuitions, etc. on these matters. In the present case, the ideal agent will be characterized by a keen moral sensibility and shaped by the Jewish and non-Jewish worlds in which he or she lives.

11. The relation between Divine Power and human freedom is articulated within the theory of revelation on which the moral theory is based. Buber comments that the philosophical antinomy of necessity and freedom here finds its real nemesis in the "lived" paradox of "the reality of [a person's] standing before God" (*I and Thou*, 144; see also Fackenheim, *God's Presence in History*, 15–16).

12. See, on Judaism and the liberal democrat, Sartre, *Anti-Semite and Jew*, 55–58; Emil L. Fackenheim, *Encounters Between Judaism and Modern Philosophy*, 203–13; idem, *The Jewish Return into History*, Chs. 11,14.

13. Such a Judaism, then, would be quite different from the "eternal people" derived and described by Rosenzweig in *The Star of Redemption*, a people *in* but not *of* history.

14. See Fackenheim, "Martin Buber's Concept of Revelation," 17–20; *God's Presence in History*, Ch. 3.

15. See Jean Améry, *At the Mind's Limits* (Bloomington: Indiana University Press, 1980); Terrence Des Pres, *The Survivor* (Oxford: Oxford University Press, 1976).

16. Jewish thought that confronts the Holocaust as an event determinative for our time is often castigated as wholly negative. This discussion is an attempt to belie that criticism. To begin with, history is a philosophical necessity; the unavoidable evil of the event which constitutes that historical beginning need not corrupt the thinking that reflects on it or the life that follows it.

17. This claim must not be misunderstood, as I try to explain. Rather than the more accurate term "unprecedented," I use the term "unique" intentionally, in part so that my explanation may serve to place its extensive use in perspective. See Fackenheim, *The Jewish Return into History*, 244–51, 278–81; idem, *To Mend the World, passim*; Hannah Arendt, *The Origins of Totalitarianism* (New York: Harcourt, Brace, Jovanovich, 1951), 437–59.

18. The key to the Holocaust's uniqueness, then, is its historical location together with its character. Fackenheim, in the passages cited above (note 17), calls the Nazi Empire "a *novum* in human history" (*The Jewish Return into History*, 245). Time is of the essence.

19. Fackenheim, *God's Presence in History*, 69–84; idem, *Encounters between Judaism and Modern Philosophy*, 192–95; idem, *To Mend the World*, Chs. 1 and 4.

20. Philosophers of language distinguish between language and speech, and between the meaning of a word in a language and its meaning for a person in a particular situation. The distinction I am drawing in the text is akin to this one. For a celebrated discussion of the meaning of "meaning," see H. P. Grice, "Meaning," *Philosophical Review* 66 (1957), 337–88.

21. Examples are not difficult to give. John is fired because he is untidy, cantankerous, and always late for work. But he is also the union organizer in his shop. The press and his supporters take the firing to be an attack on the union.

22. Later we shall see that what finally authenticates the description and our interpretation of the meaning of the Holocaust for subsequent Jewish life and

thought is an exposure of our thinking to the event itself via the diaries, memoirs, and accounts of its victims and survivors.

23. Fackenheim, *Quest for Past and Future,* 19; idem, *Encounters Between Judaism and Modern Philosophy,* 166–67.

24. I.e., those who oppose Nazi purposes do not do so conditionally or on a whim (see Fackenheim, *God's Presence in History,* 83).

25. In fact, this is surely too bold and anticipatory a claim to make at this point. What one can legitimately say is that there is a need for *some unconditional* ground for the obligation. It is at this stage unwarranted to identify this ground as the Commanding God. Until one articulates an obligation to maintain continuity with Jewish tradition, to identify *this* Voice as the *same* Voice that spoke at Sinai is premature. Buber discusses the question "Who Speaks?" and this problem of reidentification of the Divine Presence, though without reference to this precise situation, in "Dialogue" (*Between Man and Man,* New York: Macmillan, 1965, 14–15).

26. For arguments against such "humanly created ideals," see Fackenheim, *God's Presence in History,* 83.

27. For this concept of revelation, see Fackenheim, "Martin Buber's Concept of Revelation," and other works cited above.

28. Fackenheim, *God's Presence in History,* 84–92.

29. Action in defense of Israel is an important exception; see Fackenheim, *The Jewish Return into History,* Chs. 13 and 17.

30. Yehuda Bauer, *The Jewish Emergence from Powerlessness* (Toronto: University of Toronto Press, 1979), 26–40; Des Pres, *The Survivor;* Eliezer Berkovits, *With God in Hell* (New York: Hebrew Publishing Co., 1979); Fackenheim, *Encounters Between Judaism and Modern Philosophy,* 166–68; idem, *The Jewish Return into History,* Ch. 13.

31. Quoted by Berkovits, *With God in Hell,* 99–100.

32. Berkovits, *With God in Hell,* 110–11.

33. See Rosenbaum, *The Holocaust and Halakhah;* Bauer, *The Jewish Emergence from Powerlessness;* Berkovits, *With God in Hell;* Des Pres, *The Survivor.*

34. On epoch-making events, see Fackenheim, *God's Presence in History,* 8–9; on reidentification of the Divine Voice, see Buber, *Between Man and Man,* 14–15.

35. This is not to say that R. Oshry himself took this principle as the commandment of a God present to him then. Rather, he is evidence for us as we seek to interpret what our obligations are. The identification of the Divine Presence is part of our response to the event and need not have been part of his.

36. Rosenbaum, *The Holocaust and Halakhah,* 65–68.

37. See also Rosenbaum, *The Holocaust and Halakhah,* 17–21, 24–31, 50–51, 64–65, and 92–95.

38. The effect of these decisions is to *qualify* the authority of Halachah in two ways: (1) it is binding *only because* it is *now* obligatory to appropriate it, and (2) it is binding *only as* interpreted in the new situation.

39. Fackenheim, *Quest for Past and Future,* 20; idem, *God's Presence in History,* 84–92.

40. R. Oshry and others doubtless sought relevant precedents that would enable them to comply with and obey explicit Halachic commandments rather than merely respect them and give what look like contrary judgments. The effect of the principle of opposition, when treated as itself a divine command, is that even these seemingly contrary judgments become authoritative—and not merely because an authorized decisor made them.

41. See Joel Feinberg (ed.), *The Problem of Abortion* (Belmont, Cal.: Wadsworth Publishing Company, 1973).

42. See David M. Feldman, *Birth Control and Jewish Law* (New York: New York University Press, 1968), Chs. 14–15; J. David Bleich, "Abortion in Halakhic

Literature," in J. David Bleich, *Contemporary Halakhic Problems* (New York: KTAV Publishing Company, 1968), 325–71.

43. See Fackenheim, *To Mend the World*, 216–17.

44. It is important to notice that the subsidiary principles derived from this one initial principle are nonhierarchical. This is unlike the application procedure for the principle of utility, say, where every application to a specific case (whether it be to an action or a practice) must result in an exclusive ordinal ranking of the possible alternatives. If avoidance of moral conflicts is an advantage to a moral theory, which I doubt, then it is an advantage that our theory does not have (see Bernard Williams, "Ethical Consistency," in *Problems of the Self*, 166–86; Thomas Nagel, "War and Massacre," in *Mortal Questions*, 53–74).

45. In *Fear and Trembling*, Kierkegaard maintained the distinction between moral and religious obligations and then, in his famous formulation, advocated the "teleological suspension of the ethical." Insofar as our theory treats moral obligations as a species of religious ones, the Kierkegaardian strategy is undercut.

46. See Buber, *I and Thou*, 144; Fackenheim, *God's Presence in History*, 89–93; idem, *The Jewish Return into History*, 252–72.

47. See Fackenheim, *Encounters Between Judaism and Modern Philosophy*, 166–67; idem, *The Jewish Return into History*, Chs. 13, 17; Irving Greenberg, "Cloud of Smoke, Pillar of Fire: Judaism, Christianity, and Modernity after the Holocaust," in Eva Fleischner (ed.), *Auschwitz: Beginning of a New Era?* (New York: KTAV Publishing Company, 1977), 45–52.

48. Fackenheim, *Encounters Between Judaism and Modern Philosophy*, Ch. 2.

49. The way in which opposition to Nazi purposes involves a fidelity to humanity has not been developed in this chapter. But that the principle of opposition should result in a vigorous defense of human rights and dignity follows naturally from any responsible assessment of the nature of the concentration camps. Hannah Arendt, for example, speaks of the camps as the central institutions of Nazi totalitarianism, laboratories for an assault on human nature. Améry sees the camps as destructive of human dignity and as institutionalized attempts to annihilate any sense of human trust and solidarity.

50. It is not necessary to belabor the details. The theory respects the Jewish past (historical and Halachic precedents) and present (the contemporary Jewish situation), Divine Command and human freedom, the needs of the Jewish people and the struggle for human dignity. It identifies a central obligation and requires interpretation of it by an exposure of our thinking to the Holocaust and the experiences of its victims and survivors.

51. Modern liberal Jewish thinkers, like Moses Mendelssohn and Hermann Cohen, take the moral principles of Judaism to be identical with rational ethical obligations and hence binding on all rational agents. Of ritual laws, only those included in the Noahide commandments could possibly be incumbent upon non-Jews. Like traditional thinkers, both Mendelssohn and Cohen treat the Torah as containing a set of timeless commandments. Where they differ between themselves is over the authority of ceremonial law, and where they differ with orthodox thinkers is over the reasons that might underlie this authority. For Cohen, the core of the biblical teaching is morality. For Mendelssohn, the ritual law is instrumentally tied to the moral law. To orthodoxy, the entire Torah is authoritative as the Divine Word (see above, chapter two).

## 8. Historicism, Evil, and Post-Holocaust Moral Thought

This chapter has been adapted from my article "Morality, History, and Post-Holocaust Jewish Thought," which originally appeared in *Remembering the Future:*

*The Impact of the Holocaust and Genocide on Jews and Christians*, edited by Yehuda Bauer et al. (Oxford: Pergamon Press, 1989), with permission of Pergamon Press PLC.

1. Eliezer Berkovits, *Faith after the Holocaust* (New York: KTAV Publishing House, 1973), 36; see also 18. Subsequent page references in the text are to this work.

2. *Ibid.*, Ch. 4.

3. *Ibid.*, 128: "As far as our faith in an absolutely just and merciful God is concerned, the suffering of a single innocent child poses no less a problem than the undeserved suffering of millions."

4. One should note that for all of its virtues Berkovits's book has a very uncomfortable tone. He is exceedingly chauvanistic; his writing is inflated and highly rhetorical. And his philosophical categories, which are all traditional (nature and morality, is and ought, fact and value, etc.), are simply appropriated without critical assessment.

5. Irving Greenberg, "Cloud of Smoke, Pillar of Fire: Judaism, Christianity, and Modernity after the Holocaust," in Eva Fleischner (ed.), *Auschwitz: Beginning of a New Era?* 7–55. Subsequent page references in the text are to this work.

6. Cf. "Cloud of Smoke," 24–26; the classic Jewish and Christian traditions will resist revision, but Greenberg argues that such resistance is incompatible with their concern for history and their fundamental historicity. Greenberg associates these revisions, these new "orienting experiences," with "new revelations." But he provides no grounds for so doing. See 24, 35, 41, where Greenberg speaks of Auschwitz as a revelatory event, but without justification.

7. "Cloud of Smoke," 22–27.

8. This principle alludes to the testimony of the Polish guard at Auschwitz regarding the burning alive of Jewish babies in order to minimize costs.

9. Emil L. Fackenheim, *Metaphysics and Historicity* (Milwaukee: Marquette University Press, 1961).

10. See the introductions to *To Mend the World* and to *Quest for Past and Future.*

11. Emil L. Fackenheim, *God's Presence in History*, Ch. 3 (subsequent page references in the text are to this work); see also Fackenheim's contribution to the symposium in *Judaism*, "Jewish Values in a Post-Holocaust Future," reprinted as Ch. 2 in *The Jewish Return into History*, and "Jewish Faith and the Holocaust," reprinted as Ch. 3 in *The Jewish Return into History*.

12. Fackenheim's argument for these conclusions is complex. See the two essays and the entire chapter referred to in the previous note; see also my introductions in *The Jewish Thought of Emil Fackenheim: A Reader*, edited with introductions by Michael L. Morgan (Detroit: Wayne State University Press, 1987); and see above, chapter seven.

13. Fackenheim goes on to point out the problematic for Jewish secularism in our time: "Thus a radical contradiction has appeared in Jewish secularist existence in our time. As secularist the Jewish secularist seeks Jewish normalcy; as Jewish secularist he fragments this normalcy by accepting his singled-out Jewish condition. As secularist he reduces all absolute to relative affirmations; as Jewish secularist he opposes absolutely the demons of death with his own Jewish life. Throughout the ages the religious Jew was a witness to God. After Auschwitz even the most secularist of Jews bears witness, by the mere affirmation of his Jewishness, against the devil" (82). An excellent portrait of such a Jewish secularist can be found in Jean Améry, *At the Mind's Limit* (Bloomington: Indiana University Press, 1980), 82–101.

14. Perhaps, we might think, the evil is not so extreme, the victims not so particular, the imperative not so absolute. And indeed what does absolute mean here? Unqualifiedly strong or permanent? What?

15. See *God's Presence in History,* 88–89.

16. Fackenheim shows how this would work for the ideas of martyrdom, messianism, antisemitism, and others. See *Encounters Between Judaism and Modern Philosophy,* Ch. 2; *The Jewish Return into History,* Chs. 14, 15, 16, 17; *To Mend the World, passim.*

17. Emil Fackenheim, *To Mend the World,* Ch. 4, sections 8–9, 201–50, the core of the book. Subsequent page references in the text are to this work.

18. Fackenheim himself has used this neoorthodox argument in *Quest for Past and Future,* Ch. 14, revised in Ch. 2, *Encounters.*

19. Cf. *To Mend the World,* 25: "*To hear and obey the commanding Voice of Auschwitz is an 'ontological' possibility, here and now, because the hearing and obeying was already an 'ontic' reality, then and there.*"

20. See Nietzsche's statement, "one takes and does not ask who gives" (*Ecce Homo,* quoted often by Buber).

21. At 25–26 Fackenheim calls it a "Commanding Voice of Auschwitz" and says that it is theologically neutral. He seems to have had in mind the Nietzsche quote (see previous note), often cited by Buber.

22. *To Mend the World,* 249–50, 250–55.

23. The crucial case is that of Pelagia Lewinska at Auschwitz, *To Mend the World,* 25, 217; cf. Lewinska, 41ff., 54; Terrence Des Pres, *The Survivor.*

24. *To Mend the World,* Ch. 4, section 8, 201–25.

25. *Ibid.,* 247.

26. See *ibid.,* 25.

27. The direction of the ecstasy of thought is given by the encounter itself and the character of its object. That is, in this case the ecstasy is resisting and oppositional, for the event is wholly unacceptable.

## 9. Philosophy, History, and the Jewish Thinker

This chapter has been adapted from my article "Philosophy, History, and the Jewish Thinker: Philosophy and Jewish Thought in Emil Fackenheim's *To Mend the World,*" which originally appeared in *Fackenheim: German Idealism and Jewish Thought,* edited by L. Greenspan and G. Nicholson (Toronto: University of Toronto Press, 1992).

1. Fackenheim endorses five of the six features of the historical hermeneutical teaching that he summarizes. The one feature that he rejects is the *continuity* between past and present, for it is the primary role of the preceding sections of *To Mend the World,* Ch. 4, to show that the Holocaust is a *rupture* for all life and thought, a radical *discontinuity* between past and present that tests and then redefines the character of life and thought subsequent to it.

2. *To Mend the World,* 258.

3. *Ibid.,* 19; *Encounters Between Judaism and Modern Philosophy,* vii (hereafter *Encounters*).

4. *Encounters,* vii.

5. See *To Mend the World,* 21–22.

6. In a sense, then, this chapter is a gloss on Fackenheim's comment about what his wife, Rose, "knew before anyone else: that the thinker, no more than the man, can remain neatly compartmentalized forever" (*Encounters,* viii).

7. In both cases the question concerns the need for theological thinking in general to become philosophical. That the theological thinking is Jewish in Fackenheim's early work is certainly true, but arguably it is also accidental. Even in *Encounters* this remains so, and one of the remarkable achievements of *To Mend the World* is that it gains in sternness and "fanaticism" by making Judaism essential to its task and no longer accidental. But in his early essays, where the

issue of the relation between philosophy and theology is addressed, the theology is modern theology in general, not any religious thought in particular. The proviso, however, is important, for there are times when the specifically Jewish character of Fackenheim's commitments is decisive, e.g., when he is concerned about messianism or about the divine-human separation.

8. Review of Martin Buber, *Israel and Palestine, The Jewish Quarterly Review* 45, 2 (October 1954), 170–71; reprinted in Michael L. Morgan (ed.), *The Jewish Thought of Emil Fackenheim*, 65–68.

9. Review of Buber, 171.

10. *Ibid.*, 172.

11. *Ibid.*

12. *Ibid.*

13. *Ibid.*

14. Review of N. N. Glatzer, *Franz Rosenzweig: His Life and Thought*, 367–372, see 369; reprinted in *The Jewish Thought of Emil Fackenheim*, 59–64.

15. Review of Glatzer, 370.

16. *Ibid.*

17. I examine this problem, Rosenzweig's solution, and Fackenheim's interpretation more fully in chapter ten.

18. See "Martin Buber's Concept of Revelation," reprinted in *The Jewish Thought of Emil Fackenheim*, 85–101.

19. See "On the Eclipse of Faith," in *Quest for Past and Future*, 229–43; reprinted in *The Jewish Thought of Emil Fackenheim*, 85–110; *Encounters*, Chs. 1 and 3; *To Mend the World*, Ch. 3.

20. *To Mend the World*, 21–22.

21. *Metaphysics and Historicity* (Milwaukee: Marquette University Press, 1961); "The Transcendence and Historicity of Philosophical Truth," in *Proceedings of the 7th Inter-American Congress of Philosophy*, Vol. I (1967), 77–92.

22. See *The Jewish Thought of Emil Fackenheim*, Part Three, Section II.

23. But see *Metaphysics and Historicity* (98–99), where Fackenheim does argue against alternative conceptions of the self.

24. *Metaphysics and Historicity*, 77–79, note 44.

25. Dated May 2, 1961.

26. For the anxiety, although muted, see the discussion of "ideological fanaticism" at the outset of *Metaphysics and Historicity*, 6–8; reprinted in *The Jewish Thought of Emil Fackenheim*, 40.

27. "On the Eclipse of God," in *Quest for Past and Future*, 231.

28. Fackenheim himself identifies these sections (233–250) as the core of the book; see *To Mend the World*, 199.

29. See "The 614th Commandment," Fackenheim's contribution to the *Judaism* Symposium of March 1967, in *The Jewish Return into History*; "Jewish Faith and the Holocaust," also in *The Jewish Return*; *God's Presence in History*, Ch. 3, 69–93; all reprinted in *The Jewish Thought of Emil Fackenheim*, Part Three, Section II.

30. See *To Mend the World*, 299–300.

31. See *Ethica* IVP39S and VP38.

32. *To Mend the World*, 257–59.

33. If—in the section entitled "Philosophy after the Holocaust"—the Holocaust requires a reappraisal of the Kantian idea of man, how is this reappraisal relevant to the view that man is a radically situated process of self-constitution?

34. *To Mend the World*, 257.

35. See especially Chs. 2, 3, and 4, sections 1–7; section 7 deals with Buber, Deutscher, and Celan.

36. *To Mend the World*, 200.

37. *Ibid.*, 249.

38. This is the question: why write a book on Jewish thought that takes the Holocaust seriously at all? And, why choose Spinoza, Rosenzweig, Hegel, Heidegger, et al. to expose to the event?

39. *To Mend the World,* 200.

40. See *ibid.,* 200, 249, and especially section 9.

41. For it cannot provide a sufficiently ultimate ground for either the possibility or the necessity of opposition and recovery.

42. See *To Mend the World,* 262–64.

43. *Ibid.,* 247.

44. *Ibid.,* 248.

45. See *ibid.,* 26–28.

46. *Metaphysics and Historicity,* 89–90.

47. *To Mend the World,* 250–55.

48. Fackenheim frequently refers to Rosenzweig's own assessment of *The Star of Redemption,* made in a letter to Ernst Simon, that his own book is the only truly fanatical Jewish book he knows of.

49. One is reminded of Leo Strauss's remark, from his "Preface" to the English translation of his book on Spinoza, that Maimonides' *Guide* is a book that claims to be a philosophical book but is in fact a thoroughly Jewish one, while Rosenzweig's *Star,* which claims to be a Jewish book, is in fact a thoroughly philosophical one.

50. *To Mend the World,* 164.

51. See, for example, "Return to Berlin," *Moment* 10, 4 (April 1985), 55–59; "Reflections on Aliyah," *Midstream* (August/September 1985), 25–28; "An Interview with Emil Fackenheim," *New Traditions* 3 (Summer 1986); all reprinted in *The Jewish Thought of Emil Fackenheim,* Part Five.

## 10. Franz Rosenzweig, Objectivity, and the New Thinking

This chapter has been adapted from my article "Franz Rosenzweig, Objective Truth and the Personal Standpoint," which originally appeared in JUDAISM, 40,4 (1991), 521–30.

1. Not all students of Rosenzweig's work appreciate that he employs the new thinking, subjective or speech thinking, only in the second part of *The Star.* In the first part, he uses the old philosophical method to indict itself. For the error of wondering how the new thinking can, in Part One, result in abstract outcomes, i.e., God, Man, and World, see Julius Guttmann, *Philosophies of Judaism* (New York: Holt, Rinehart, and Winston, 1964), 376–77.

2. References to *The Star of Redemption* will be to the German edition, Franz Rosenzweig, *Der Stern der Erloesung* (Suhrkamp Verlag, 1988), which is a reprint of the Martinus Nijhoff edition of 1976. The only current English translation is by William Hallo, published by Holt, Rinehart and Winston in 1970. Sections of *The Star* are available in Nahum Glatzer (ed.), *Franz Rosenzweig: His Life and Thought.*

3. Thomas Nagel, *The View from Nowhere* (Oxford: Oxford University Press, 1980).

4. Rosenzweig calls the new philosopher "the philosopher of the *Weltanschauung*" and indicates that the question whether his philosophy is still science is a question addressed by Nietzsche (*Der Stern,* 117; Hallo, 105).

5. The problem that Rosenzweig faces, then, is a problem for all philosophical thinking that proceeds by following the experience and understanding of the engaged, situated agent. Hence, it is the problem that Hegel succeeds in solving by showing how a plethora of perspectival accounts accumulates and culminates in an absolute standpoint, the philosophical standpoint. It is also a problem for

Schelling's positive philosophy, for Kierkegaard, and for later figures in the existential tradition.

6. *Der Stern*, 117; Hallo, 105–06.

7. The translations in this paragraph are Glatzer's, 208–209.

8. Rosenzweig's problem has many implications. It is, first of all, a problem for his system and for *The Star*; if he cannot solve it, then the results of Parts Two and Three are at best his own experience and interpretation; why should others accept them? Furthermore, it is a problem for all situated thinking or existentialist philosophy, as it were, or all hermeneutically sensitive thinking. Finally, as we shall see, Fackenheim takes it to be a classic expression of the conflict between philosophy and religious faith.

9. See Emil L. Fackenheim, "Review of *Franz Rosenzweig: His Life and Thought* by Nahum Glatzer," reprinted in Michael L. Morgan (ed.), *The Jewish Thought of Emil Fackenheim*, 59–64. See also Emil Fackenheim, *To Mend the World*, 58–91, especially 72–73.

10. Fackenheim, "Review," 61–62 (in Morgan).

11. *Der Stern*, 117–18; Hallo, 106; Glatzer trans., 209.

12. *Ibid.*

13. *Der Stern*, 117; Hallo, 105–06.

14. See Søren Kierkegaard, *Fear and Trembling* (Anchor, 1954), 79, 92; Robert Bretall (ed.), *A Kierkegaard Anthology* (Princeton: Princeton University Press, 1946), 210–26 (from *Concluding Unscientific Postscript*). For discussion of Kierkegaard's conception of faith, see James Collins, "Faith and Reflection in Kierkegaard," 141–55, in Howard A. Johnson and Niels Thulstrup (eds.), *A Kierkegaard Critique* (Chicago: Gateway, 1962).

15. *Der Stern*, 118; Hallo, 106, Glatzer trans., 209.

16. *Der Stern*, 117; Hallo, 106.

17. *Der Stern*, 119–20; Hallo, 107–08.

18. In his brilliant discussion of Rosenzweig in *To Mend the World*, Fackenheim, I think, realizes the deficiencies of his earlier account. The new thinking, Rosenzweig says, "narrates how and when the far God becomes near, and the near God far" (*Kleinere Schriften*, 384). The outcome is, first, a narration of the world as created, of how "the 'far' God forever moving toward 'nearness' *creates an independent world and affirms it in its otherness. And only in a world thus affirmed can revelation take place*" (*To Mend the World*, 75). Here the philosophical preparation for revelation is an understanding of the relation between God and the world as this is portrayed through a narrated experience of the world as created. But if so, then the philosophy that the new theology needs is not the old philosophy—argument, system, reasoning—but the new philosophy, which of course cannot without circularity provide the grounds for its own objectivity. I discuss this important point later.

19. My suggestion, in other words, is that the strategy of Montaigne, like that of Luther, is to recognize human limitation and relocate the foundation of certitude and objectivity in God rather than man. There is good reason to see this neoorthodox strategy as appealing to Rosenzweig.

20. In a famous passage from *Ecce Homo*, which both Martin Buber and Fackenheim are fond of quoting, Nietzsche says that there are times when one receives and does not ask who gives.

21. See Fackenheim, *To Mend the World*, 78–91. See also Reiner Wiehl, "Experience in Rosenzweig's New Thinking," in Paul Mendes-Flohr (ed.), *The Philosophy of Franz Rosenzweig* (Hanover, N.H.: University Press of New England, 1988), 42–68; Heinz-Juergen Goertz, "Die Wahrheit der Erfahrung in Franz Rosenzweigs 'Neuem Denken'," *Philosophisches Jahrbuch* 88 (1981), 389–406.

22. *Der Stern*, 119–20; Hallo, 107–08.
23. *Der Stern*, 120; Hallo, 108.
24. *Ibid.*
25. Among philosophers, see, for example, Richard Rorty, *Contingency, Irony, and Solidarity*; Charles Taylor, *Sources of the Self*; Donald Davidson, "On the Very Idea of a Conceptual Scheme," reprinted in *Inquiries into Truth and Interpretation* (Oxford: Oxford University Press, 1984), 183–98; Hilary Putnam, *Reason, Truth and History*; Martha C. Nussbaum, *The Fragility of Goodness* (Cambridge: Cambridge University Press, 1986).
26. In Rorty's terms, an ironist must still seek principles of solidarity; in a world in which everything is interpretation through and through, there are still practices, like torture, that are unconditionally wrong.
27. This is the position of Leo Strauss, among others. For a recent version of the Straussian attack, see Allan Bloom, *The Closing of the American Mind* (New York: Simon and Schuster, 1987).
28. Something like this is the view of Charles Taylor in *Sources of the Self* and elsewhere.

## 11. Jewish Philosophy and Historical Self-Consciousness

This chapter has been adapted from my article "Jewish Philosophy and Historical Self-Consciousness," which originally appeared in *The Journal of Religion*, 71,1 (1991), 36–49.

1. See especially Benedict de Spinoza, *A Theologico-Political Treatise* (trans. Elwes) (New York: Dover, 1951), Chs. 3 and 5.
2. The best account can be found in Alexander Altmann's magisterial biography, *Moses Mendelssohn*. Michael Meyer provides a briefer treatment in *The Origins of the Modern Jew*, Chs. 1 and 2. For an examination of Mendelssohn's arguments in *Jerusalem*, both his political philosophy and his argument for the ceremonial law, see above, chapters two and three.
3. See Moses Mendelssohn, *Jerusalem, or On Religious Power and Judaism*, translated by Allan Arkush; introduction and commentary by Alexander Altmann.
4. Mendelssohn, *Jerusalem*, 133–34.
5. Paul Mendes-Flohr notices the relationship in "Mendelssohn and Rosenzweig," *European Judaism* 20, 2 (Winter 1986), 4–9.
6. For an excellent account of Rosenzweig's argument in *The Star of Redemption*, see Emil L. Fackenheim, *To Mend the World*, Ch. 2.
7. An account of how Rosenzweig thinks that this task can be accomplished can be found in Emil Fackenheim's review of Nahum Glatzer (ed.), *Franz Rosenzweig: His Life and Thought*, reprinted in Michael L. Morgan (ed.), *The Jewish Thought of Emil Fackenheim*, Ch. 5. I have discussed Rosenzweig's argument and Fackenheim's interpretation above, in chapter ten.
8. If Fackenheim is right, Buber does the same thing. See Emil Fackenheim, "Martin Buber's Concept of Revelation," reprinted in Morgan (ed.), *The Jewish Thought of Emil Fackenheim*, Ch. 8. For a recent discussion that is relevant to this whole matter and is conducted within the tradition of analytic philosophy, see Thomas Nagel, *The View from Nowhere*.
9. See Paul Mendes-Flohr, "Franz Rosenzweig and the Crisis of Historicism," in Paul Mendes-Flohr (ed.), *The Philosophy of Franz Rosenzweig* (Hanover, N.H.: University Press of New England, 1988), 138–61. The threat of historicism, understood in a variety of ways, is a dominant theme in twentieth-century philosophy. See Popper, Heidegger, Foucault, et al.

10. Fackenheim, "On the Eclipse of God," *Quest for Past and Future*, Ch. 17, reprinted in Morgan, *The Jewish Thought of Emil Fackenheim*, Ch. 19.

### 12. Contemporary Jewish Thought in America

This chapter has been adapted from an essay that originally appeared in French in *Les nouveaux cahiers*, 94 (1988), 47–51. Some passages have been adapted from my article "Jewish Thought Today," which originally appeared in *The Journal of Religion*, 68,3 (1988), 575–80.

1. I addressed this theme in chapter one.
2. This is one of the themes that I discussed in chapter eleven.
3. Arthur A. Cohen and Paul Mendes-Flohr (eds.), *Contemporary Jewish Religious Thought* (New York: Charles Scribner's Sons, 1987).
4. Nelson Goodman, *Languages of Art*; idem, "Routes of Reference," *Critical Inquiry* (Autumn 1981), 121–32; Israel Scheffler, "Ritual and Reference," *Synthese* (March 1981), 421–37. For an expanded version of the present essay, see J. Stern, "Modes of Reference in the Rituals of Judaism," *Religious Studies* (forthcoming).
5. One might argue in a similar fashion concerning the generality of political and legal obligation. For an attack on such a general obligation and a defense of an individualized approach to obedience, see A. John Simmons, *Moral Principles and Political Obligation* (Princeton: Princeton University Press, 1979).
6. I.e., the essentialist view is the realist position of Cratylus, in Plato's dialogue of that name, coupled with something like Aristotelian essentialism.
7. Stern does note that Maimonides leaves open the possibility of a nonlinguistic reference to God: "As an alternative to verbal prayer, Maimonides advocates silence as the only true praise of God. Here silence means, however, not an attitude emptied of all content but intellectual apprehension, which the individual simply restrains himself from verbalizing in spoken language (*Guide* I, 59)" (551).

# Index

MICHAEL L. MORGAN is Professor of Philosophy and Jewish Studies at Indiana University. His publications include *The Jewish Thought of Emil Fackenheim*, *Platonic Piety: Philosophy and Ritual in Fourth-Century Athens*, and *Classics of Moral and Political Theory*.

www.ingramcontent.com/pod-product-compliance
Lightning Source LLC
LaVergne TN
LVHW040157080826
844660LV00001B/11

* 9 7 8 0 2 5 3 3 3 8 7 8 5 *